The Social History
of Skepticism

The Johns Hopkins University Studies in
Historical and Political Science

— — — — — — — — — —

117th Series (1999)

1. Richard K. Marshall, *The Local Merchants of Prato: Small Entrepreneurs in the Late Medieval Economy*

2. Brendan Dooley, *The Social History of Skepticism: Experience and Doubt in Early Modern Culture*

3. Tommaso Astarita, *Village Justice: Community, Family, and Popular Culture in Early Modern Italy*

The Social History
of Skepticism

Experience and Doubt in
Early Modern Culture

Brendan Dooley

The Johns Hopkins University Press

Baltimore and London

© 1999 The Johns Hopkins University Press
All rights reserved. Published 1999
Printed in the United States of America on acid-free paper
2   4   6   8   9   7   5   3   1

The Johns Hopkins University Press
2715 North Charles Street
Baltimore, Maryland 21218-4363
www.press.jhu.edu

Library of Congress Cataloging-in-Publication Data will be found
at the end of this book.
A catalog record for this book is available from the British Library.

ISBN 0-8018-6142-X

FRONTISPIECE: Satirical print depicting a vendor of news. Giovanni Maria Mitelli,
"Compra chi vuole" (Buy as you will), Bologna, 1684 [Milan, Castillo Sforziaco,
Raccolta delli Stampe].

Contents

Acknowledgments

The information underground of early modern Europe these pages bring to life owes its discovery to archives in and around Rome. While researching a related topic in the superbly organized Vatican collections, I first came across my rogues' gallery of protagonists in the early art of communicating politics. There I found what now must be counted as the largest known single store of manuscript and printed news sheets in Europe—some four hundred thick bundles, organized by year and by place, produced in every major center from London to Prague to Messina to Constantinople, all directed to or procured in one way or another by the cardinal secretaries of state of every papacy between the mid-sixteenth and the mid-eighteenth centuries, and by other state officials as well—a veritable treasure trove for the hunter after the origins of events or, at least, of the narration of them and an unparalleled source for discovering the genesis of the trade in political information. They are the core of a study that in its final form ranges as far beyond Rome as my familiarity with other contexts would allow.

Aided by a grant from the National Endowment for the Humanities administered through the American Academy in Rome, I shifted my research across the Tiber to the Roman State Archives, where the newly catalogued penal records afford the possibility of identifying printers and purveyors of news. The vagabond pursuit of my quarry has taken me to collections throughout Italy, from the Marciana in Venice to the National Library in Naples, from the Biblioteca Estense in Modena to the Biblioteca dell'Archiginnasio in Bologna, from the Biblioteca Civica in Mantua to the Biblioteca Nazionale Centrale in Florence, including the state archives in all these cities, and many other places where newsletters, newspapers, and current histories are kept. And I concluded my peregrinations in the Houghton Library at Harvard, where a rare copy of the first verifiable Venetian newspaper now rests, side by side with the main products of seventeenth-century historians from all over Europe.

Acknowledgments

The ultimate presentation of results draws upon work I completed for other projects at other times while engaged in examining the significance of a marketplace in the history of ideas, and the debts I have accumulated are too numerous to list in any satisfactory way. It is a pleasure to acknowledge the support and encouragement I have received from Peter Burke, Ed Muir, Sam Cohn, Ted Rabb, Jim Hankins, Patrice Higonnet, Keith Baker, John Elliott, Burr Litchfield, Jules Kirshner, Joe Levine, and Mario Infelise, as well as Michele De Sivo, Augusto Pompeo, Riccardo Bassani, Sally Scully, David McNeill, Laurie Nussdorfer, and many others who have given generously of their time and expertise.

Portions, at various stages of revision, have been presented for discussion at Harvard University, the American Academy in Rome, the Institute for Advanced Study in Princeton, the Society for the History of Authorship, Reading, and Publishing, the Maison Rhône-Alpes des Sciences de l'Homme, and the North American Conference on British Studies, and published in other virtually unrecognizable forms in the *Annales: Histoire, sciences sociales* (chap. 1), the *Journal of European Economic History*, the *Memoirs of the American Academy in Rome* (chap. 2), and the *Journal of the History of Ideas* (chap. 4).

The Social History
of Skepticism

Introduction

"Truth has a history," Paul Veyne said in a recent study of the ancient Greeks and their myths.[1] So, indeed, has belief. And just as there can be a history of belief, there can be a history of skepticism. In fact, the modern history of skepticism is more than the history of a few disembodied minds engaging with the texts of Sextus Empiricus or Diogenes Laertius. It is more than the history of natural historians discovering that Pliny's descriptions do not always correspond to objects in nature. It is more than the history of the disappointments experienced by pious believers upon discovering that there might be more than one legitimate religion in the world or that the texts of the Holy Scriptures themselves, as well as the various interpretations of them, have a history. Such influences contributed powerfully to the so-called crisis of conscience that Paul Hazard long ago observed in European cultures in the last half of the seventeenth century.[2] And for the most abundant evidence of such influences the principal archaeological dig is still the *Opera omnia* of Pierre Bayle. This book tries to examine the social significance of a variety of skepticism closely related to but not included among the purely intellectual trends traced, from very different points of view, by Richard Popkin, Alan Charles Kors, and Barbara Shapiro. The skepticism in question concerned the veracity of certain kinds of historical and political information; and it had serious cultural consequences.[3]

The truths that animated early modern culture were situated in other areas of experience than philosophy and religion. They were also situated in the realm of politics, ranging from mythological stories about the foundation of particular cities to truths about the legitimacy of the ruler's

dynasty and what the ruler or anyone else was doing at any particular time. In the seventeenth century, these truths, like those of philosophy and religion, came under attack. And they came under attack for many reasons besides epistemological speculation. Epistemological speculation eroded the foundations of many unexamined truths, but its effect was heightened by a quite independent and specifically directed doubt about what people were being told in the political realm—a doubt that emerged when, for reasons that this book attempts to make clear, the means of communicating political information were taken over by entrepreneurs and converted to the purposes of particular polities by powerful elites.

To make a long story short, the transformation of information about present and past politics into a salable product, whether in the form of hired histories or in the form of journalism, turned writers into speculators, information into opinion, and readers into critics. The result was a powerful current of skepticism with extraordinary consequences. Combined with late-seventeenth-century developments in other areas of thought and writing, it produced skepticism about the possibility of gaining any historical knowledge at all. It was not necessary to be a Cartesian to feel the bite of this type of skepticism, although that could help. Nor was it necessary to be an atheist. Indeed, Jesuit scholars were some of the most skeptical of all, casting into doubt the broad course of classical antiquity in order to lead troubled souls back down the narrow path of faith. Whatever other forms of disbelief the century may have offered, the historical skepticism of the late seventeenth century threatened the very bonds of trust upon which early modern government was based, provoking a response at the level of practice as well as of theory.

Nowhere, in fact, were these trends better evidenced than in Italy. Here, after all, the accomplishments of the Galilean revolution in natural science seemed to offer the greatest hope for achieving true knowledge by human effort. Here the combined influence of religion and politics threatened these accomplishments almost from the outset. Here again, communities seemed closest to reaping the rich harvest of Renaissance state building, only to be cast down by plague, economic disaster, and political contention from within and without. In the midst of these miseries, the number of information entrepreneurs eager to offer their services to any of the dozens of small states on the peninsula, or to the transalpine arbiters of European affairs, seemed greater than anywhere else. Their works, churned out of the presses in more than 160 printing centers, spread far and wide to those who could read and even some who could not.

Meanwhile, the high tide of skepticism produced its converts to Cartesianism, here as everywhere else. Their names—Tommaso Cornelio, Gregorio Caloprese, Gian Vincenzo Gravina—are familiar to anyone who has read the Bergin and Fisch edition of Giambattista Vico's *Autobiography*. Skepticism about Descartes inspired not only fideists like Lorenzo Magalotti but also, arguably, Vico himself, who not only solved the problem of skepticism with characteristic originality but also incorporated the cycles of secrecy and publicity in his theory of historical sociology. And here, finally, Ludovico Antonio Muratori, in an effort to drive the last stake into the heart of skepticism, undertook the most ambitious project in modern times for editing and publishing the historical documents upon which these truths were based. Let not the reader be too surprised, therefore, to find Italy at the center of a story that reaches to the rest of Europe nor to find its contexts developed in fuller detail than all the rest.

This book thus combines three areas of inquiry that have hitherto remained discrete, without pretending to provide a comprehensive account of any of them. In the first place, to the history of skepticism it joins the history of journalism, or what passed for journalism in early modern Europe—namely, newsletters and news books and their heirs, the newspapers. Journalism was the soft underbelly of early modern truth; it was the medium of communication in which the difference between fact and rumor seemed the most difficult to identify, controls on the value of assertions seemed the most difficult to impose, and the imaginations of writers seemed to have the freest rein. Indeed, the history of journalism has until very recently been analyzed primarily from the point of view of the history of publishing, with an occasional thrust to the emergence of modern political practice. Current scholarship on newspapers by Joad Raymond and C. John Sommerville offers tantalizing glimpses into the newswriter's craft, and current work on the circulation of information and commentary by Arlette Farge, Craig Harline, and Jeffrey K. Sawyer shows the effects of information on opinion, often referring to the paradigm of Jürgen Habermas. What these contributions seem to imply about the length and breadth of the culture of information and its political and social consequences could well be at least as interesting as what they actually state.[4] The time has come to tell this story in all its compelling detail.

Finally, the social history of skepticism joins the history of journalism to the history of historiography. To be sure, Tommaso Campanella was more provocative than helpful when he gave the name of history indiscriminately to any sort of narrative. But even for Francesco Patrizi, his-

torical theorist par excellence, the history of the present was just as important as the history of the past. The connection between the two was far more evident to early modern readers than it is to modern ones. Let us enter into this forgotten world with renewed curiosity.

So far, recent historians of historiography, following Arnaldo Momigliano in pursuit of the origins of the modern methodological distinction between original and derivative sources, have occupied the same ground as scholars following Orest Ranum in pursuit of the social world of the historians: they have considered only the texts and their writers. What remains to be shown is how the ragged edge of time, whether relative or absolute, according to the categories suggested by Donald Wilcox, was perceived by the seventeenth-century people for whom the writers wrote.[5] Did they believe their historians? The answer is, as with the ancient Greeks and their myths, yes and no. The social history of skepticism attempts to find out when and why. It therefore examines some of those who got the information first: the newsletter purveyors of Rome and Venice. It then examines the gazette writers who bought their own information or received it from on high. It examines historians, both those of independent means and those employed by governments. It examines the episodes, political, social, and cultural, that caused them to write. It examines the readers who knew better than what they read, as well as those who had yet to find out. And it examines the cultural critics who bemoaned the politicization of truth.

The first chapter shows how information first became a commodity—not in printed form, as might be expected, but in the form of the manuscript newsletters produced and distributed throughout Europe from the late sixteenth century. Original sources of information like firsthand battle reports and letters sent by eyewitnesses to government officials leaked out of the circuits of power by way of bribery, thievery, or mere indiscretion. Newsletter writers added their own blend of rumor, invention, commentary, and invective. They then reproduced their sheets in multiple copies and distributed them to persons on a subscription list. Resold, recopied, modified, and excerpted, the original newsletters then formed the basis of yet other newsletters that provided a source of income for street vendors. Government officials sought to control what they regarded as a dangerous breach of secrecy and threat to reputation. But the patron-client relation established between the better-connected customers and the newsletter writers protected the network from too much interference.

Moreover, high rewards, general curiosity, and lack of available jobs of other kinds for literate immigrants into the major cities made the newsletters a thriving industry well into the eighteenth century.

The second chapter shows how printing and the search for new markets for information further transformed the commodity and deepened its effects. The convulsive course of seventeenth-century European politics and its local repercussions were followed with eager interest by persons well down in the middling ranks of society, if not below. Even those who remained untouched by the haphazard system of seventeenth-century literacy education received at least some of their political information by recitation from the medium of print. When interest in public affairs boiled over into rebellion against established authority, as it did in Naples in 1647, print was there to provide models of actions performed elsewhere—in Holland, England, and Sicily—as well as commentaries on what was being done from day to day. By the end of the seventeenth century, the first revolutionary newspaper was born in Messina. Printed news, of course, was subject to the same errors and modifications as the manuscripts on which it was often based. When government officials began to recognize the usefulness of print for state purposes, their interference added still another remove from the original sources of information and a further cause for dismay among those who worried about the elusiveness of truth and the bad faith of rulers.

Chapter 3 shows how the urgent quest for versions of contemporary events, flattering to the ruler and edifying to the subjects, blurred the distinction between fact and fiction in seventeenth-century historiography. Hard-pressed by disastrous wars and lured by the prospects of enhanced reputation, governments offered money and favors to whoever could place their actions in the most favorable light. Writers offered their services to the highest bidder, sometimes to several at once, promising to bring to bear on their accounts all the persuasiveness they could muster by seductive rhetoric and astute political observation. They sought to give the illusion of scholarly scrupulousness by punctuating their accounts with copies of what they claimed to be original documents and eyewitness reports on events, actually drawn from the maelstrom of unconfirmed and unverifiable texts circulating in the world of manuscript pamphlets, newsletters, and newspapers; and in so doing they produced an entirely new genre that was often as fantastic in its narrations and imaginative in its conclusions as were the novels for which many of these

writers were also justly famous. Whenever the new genre appeared, it submerged any other sort of modern historiography then in circulation— at least at first.

Chapter 4 shows how the dissemination of falsehood and fraud, by the end of the seventeenth century, produced skepticism about the very possibility of understanding the contemporary world or the recent past— not, of course, among all who read, nor even among most, but among enough thoughtful and intelligent readers to make a real difference for the history of modern culture. In fact, this result was particularly disappointing considering the epistemological breakthroughs of nearly a century before. Intellectuals nourished on the accomplishments of the new empirical science had high hopes for the application of these methods to other areas of knowledge. A few of them imagined that even historiography could be reduced to scientific laws guaranteed to produce verifiable results.

As the century wore on, however, they found this confidence harder and harder to sustain. The political stuff of history seemed more and more impervious to investigation as governments appeared to spin ever more complex webs of deception. Works that purported to elucidate the present and the past appeared more and more defective as their easy availability allowed comparisons between widely diverging accounts and their writers admitted less and less capacity to tell the truth. At the same time, in the realm of philosophy, strict empiricism began to lose ground in favor of a rationalist approach. Many intellectuals adopted—when they did not independently arrive at—the skepticism of Descartes about any experiential knowledge as uncertain as history. Only toward the end of the century did a few historians seek to reform historical method by joining the hitherto discrete fields of historiography and erudite antiquities. With the early-eighteenth-century emergence of modern historiography, the crisis of belief began to subside; but it would never really go away again.

Paul Hazard, in his now-classic work, analyzed the late seventeenth-century "crisis of consciousness" in the light of what he observed as its early-twentieth-century counterpart.[6] In both periods, an age of belief was followed by an age of skepticism—in the later case, skepticism about the progress of civilization, about the spread of democracy and prosperity, about the beneficence of science. The transition from late-seventeenth-century skepticism to the eighteenth-century Enlightenment, from dissatisfaction with received traditions to the formulation of positive programs

for social, political, and cultural renewal, was made possible, he observed, by a continuous undercurrent of belief in the efficacy of reason and the power of the sentiments that emerged with ever greater vigor once the crisis had passed. He hoped the same irrepressible traits of Western civilization would deliver his own time from the malaise of disillusionment. And so do we.

1

News Unfit to Print

In the early modern period political information became a commodity. Not in the modern sense, of course. Communications of knowledge or intelligence about political affairs did not crackle through the air, even figuratively. Few and contradictory were the assumptions about what might be a reasonable dosage of consciousness about the political environment, and what statements were made on the subject, usually by critics, lawyers, or consultants to the various emerging state governments, took account of the deep social stratifications and differences in education that marked this age. What you knew about affairs within the corridors of power depended upon who you were. A lawyer or a doctor was likely to be better informed than a butcher or a baker.

What you knew also depended on where you were; and not all cities were alike. Paris was better served by information than was Strasbourg. And the strands of urban Europe reached thinly from center to center across vast stretches of landscape, where the political environment seemed far less crucial than the natural environment to the daily practices of existence. And although the passage of troops from one battle to the next, as well as the movement of prices between boom and bust, could intrude profoundly into an otherwise self-contained and autarchic village culture, political knowledge and intelligence extended unevenly and with great difficulty beyond the great demographic concentrations.

Nevertheless, in this period, political information came to be bought and sold in appreciable quantities for the first time. The distribution of such knowledge and intelligence became a definite trade, although the mechanisms for this distribution evolved slowly. The results of this com-

merce now appear to have been as far removed from easy assumptions about the role of information in society as the structures for its production were from later and more familiar ones. How was the world of information lived and experienced three centuries ago? The archives in a few well-selected areas offer unusually rich material for our conjectures.

What our sources show is that the most daring peddlers of news about military, dynastic, and administrative affairs, at least at first, were not large printing houses or journalism tycoons but writers and distributors of the so-called *avvisi*, or handwritten newsletters, serving customers all over Europe.[1] These writers and distributors included respectable officials in government and ecclesiastical bureaucracies as well as a motley crew of lawyers, notaries, scribes, literary hacks, spies, unemployed intellectuals, and even murderers and extortionists. Forging the new genre from a hybrid of diplomatic and commercial correspondence, they began to circulate their newsletters on a weekly or semiweekly basis by the latter half of the sixteenth century. In spite of almost continuous persecution, they eventually provided, along with plain information and misinformation, the most mordant and incisive running commentary on and criticism of contemporary governments available anywhere.[2] They made up the seventeenth-century information underground described in the following pages. Threatened by almost continuous persecution and, eventually, by competition from the closely related and also newly emerging genre of printed newspapers, they would still not go away. And their persistence until well into the eighteenth century can be explained only by measuring the powerful yearnings they satisfied and tracing the powerful social and political structures from which they sprang.

At the heart of the newsletter story were the emerging state structures. Thus, at least part of what follows has already been told elsewhere. Political information of the kind with which we are concerned here was a by-product of a political leadership struggling to achieve some measure of central control. Writers and distributors were often connected in one way or another, either as employees or as clients, with the mechanisms being used by rulers in the struggle, from diplomatic corps to postal bureaus to notarial and judicial colleges.[3] Moreover, the episodes connected with the building of the new state structures—wars, rebellions, changes of rule, and the day-to-day exercise of authority—often formed the substance of communications. Without those structures a chief raison d'être, and probably the newsletters themselves, would have ceased to exist. However, viewing the newsletters as mere government departments

would be a serious mistake. They had lives of their own and affected the exercise of power in unique ways.

Economic structures, too, played their role. Political information was no less useful in business than in government. And by the time newsletters emerged in the late sixteenth century, correspondence within the largest commercial firms—the Fugger, the Strozzi—had carried political news almost as long as had diplomatic correspondence between governments and their representatives.[4] Commercial considerations were at least as important as political ones in the creation of the first public mail routes in this period by a fruitful collaboration between private firms and the governments of Europe. These routes were essential to the efforts of the people we are about to meet, who turned newsletter writing into a profession. No sooner did newsletters begin to proliferate than they became objects of commercial exchange themselves. And as objects of commercial exchange, they responded to market conditions. Thus, newsletters were at least as much children of capitalism as of the early modern state.

To be sure, the world of the newsletters, conceived as widely as possible, shaded off into the world of espionage and involved many different kinds of manuscript communication. At one end of the spectrum were carefully planted espionage sheets not intended for public distribution, secret manuscript pamphlets, including diplomatic reports as well as the so-called conclaves listing party alignments among the cardinals in Rome and occasionally attacking the institution of the papacy itself; next came semiprivate libels like the German *Schandbriefe,* which were intended mainly to offend the party in question.[5] At the opposite end of the spectrum stood more or less public pasquinades, some resembling the English ballads, and reports prepared by one or another of the parties in specific episodes—the Genoa civil war, the revolt of Naples, the revolt of Palermo, the revolt of Messina—and satirical works with titles like "Vomit of the Gods," "Consultation with the Grand Turk," and "Dialogue between St. Peter and the Lantern of Diogenes."[6] None of these writings, whether secret or public, could be entirely prevented from circulating, and action against them was sporadic.

Regular weekly or semiweekly newsletters were a separate genre, as anyone knows who has sifted through the records of a sixteenth- or seventeenth-century diplomatic archive. They were distinguished by their nearly invariable form across two centuries. Supplied with place name and date at the top instead of a standard salutation, they were as difficult

to confuse with simple private letters as with the printed *avisos* and other ephemeral prenewspaper printed works that were produced in every country on the continent. They were what passed for journalism in early modern Europe before printed newspapers arrived.[7] Although they succeeded in producing considerable incredulity among their readers and preoccupation among government officials along the way, they helped bring about important changes in social thought and political behavior. And they are our chief objects here.

The newsletters were also distinguished by their writers' almost exclusive concern with information about politics, as defined by seventeenth-century conventions. Like the historians who followed the classical and Renaissance definition of the object of history in focusing exclusively on affairs of state, the newsletter writers invariably wrote about the behavior of those wielding power. Occasionally they might carry stories concerning the punishment of a criminal or violence against the local Jews. But they covered such events for the same reasons they covered the marriages of dukes and princes—namely, because power was being exercised or because convictions about the nature of power were being expressed. Let us see how the social and economic mechanisms behind the newsletters are revealed in the motives and ambitions of the writers, in what went on inside their studios, and most of all, in their writings.

The Information Underground

We soon discover that the way a newsletter writer wrote depended to a considerable extent on the interests in play. Very often, a careful reading of the document reveals a definite partisanship for one or the other of the many sides to the power struggles of the age. Indeed, we should scarcely be surprised to find that Alessandro Botticelli, writing in 1630s Genoa, a city divided between the pro-French merchants and the pro-Spanish old nobility, tailored his accounts for customers among the latter. Nor should we be surprised that Theodore Ameyden, writing his newsletters from Rome in the 1640s for officials in the Spanish government, let his love and loyalty for Spain show through in every line.[8] He, after all, was expressing his own heartfelt convictions; whether the same might be said about Benedetto Giuliani, who wrote newsletters from Venice as a French spy, with obvious consequences for his interpretations, is another matter.[9] Most certainly in the case of Giovanni Quorli, also in Venice, interpretations depended on whether, at a specific moment, he happened to

be writing for the duke of Brunswick, the elector of Cologne, the duke of Mirandola, or any of his many other foreign customers. At least when it came to writing about the War of Candia, capitalizing on the suspicion and envy that the Venetians often excited among their neighbors, he consistently reported events in the most sinister light—to the joy of his correspondents but to the chagrin of the Venetian ambassador in Florence, in whose view they were "truly malevolent, and . . . represent the affairs of the Most Serene Republic as being in the most languishing condition."[10]

What a newsletter writer wrote sometimes depended on what he was told to write or on subtle hints dropped by this or that government seeking advantageous news. The temptation to taint the news was so irresistible that French officials gave in to it almost as soon as Spain secured the Valtelline passes in 1637, at least according to the Venetian ambassador. They planted stories in the newsletters to the effect that France, poised to retaliate for the affront, had received a hefty loan from the Genoese bankers.[11] Even a relatively minor player like the duke of Mantua took the opportunity to settle old accounts with Spain, when the latter was under severe duress during the War of Messina, by spreading word that he had decided to sell his duchy of Montferrat to his French allies.[12] And what went on at the level of interstate politics was repeated at the level of intrastate politics, where enemies of Cardinal Fabio Spada in 1670s Rome succeeded in planting a story that he had become the dependent of the rival Baglione family.[13] Wherever there was newswriting, the exercise of power and influence was never far away.

However, newswriting was a business, and for the week-to-week raw material of their sheets, newsletter writers depended most of all upon what they could glean from a wide variety of sources more or less close to political events. For the more recondite information they had to rely on stealth—their own or that of others. Fortunately, ambassadorial staffs were notoriously ill paid and susceptible to bribery, making the security of reserved information nearly impossible to protect. In vain, therefore, the Venetian ambassador in Naples complained that a spy, who had been planted in his retinue by the Spanish viceroy on the eve of the Spanish conspiracy against Venice, copied his papers and paid another employee to do the same.[14] After all, in Venice in the same period, a nobleman named Francesco Falier claimed that he could receive whatever letters and papers he wanted from the Spanish ambassador's boatman. Not all of these informants could expect what was being offered in Rome by

governments seeking particular items wherever political documents were to be found in the city—namely, several hundred *scudi* and a new house.[15] But any of them could potentially find themselves in the position of a certain Francesco Marchi, a newsletter writer in the court of the Venetian ambassador in Rome, who was able to report—with impunity, the ambassador complained—"everything he heard from my casual conversations, from the actions of this house, from the observation of who comes to see me, from the information that usually arrives in the courts of ambassadors."[16] And any of them might potentially become a newsletter writer.

Next in importance as a source for information was the mail system. Although postal routes in the early modern period were nominally controlled by governments, they were actually administered by powerful guilds or individuals who had purchased the privilege to deliver the mail. Governments could do little to protect security. In fact, the postmasters themselves made extra cash by preparing periodic reports and sending them along the main mail routes, noting the arrival and departure of public officials and their entourages by the public roads.[17] And even if they wished to do so, postmasters could do little more than the governments to enforce law and order. Robbery of diplomatic correspondence out of the public mailbag for purposes of espionage or for sale to anyone interested was a frequent and nearly irrepressible highway crime.[18] For divulging what was in the mailbags that passed through their systems, postmasters were frequent subjects of bribery and extortion.[19] The most unscrupulous, such as Pier Francesco Marini, master of the post of Genoa, customarily delivered such information to newsletter writers as well as to foreign nationals, in this case, the Ludovisi and the Barberini families in Rome.[20]

Information in the seventeenth century was nobody's property; and by one means or another newsletter writers were able to procure documents of the most extraordinary types. No amount of secrecy and reserve sufficed to keep even highly sensitive information from falling into their hands. Entirely typical was the manuscript "Letter from the Duke of Savoy to the King of France," circulated by a Roman scribe named Paolo Marri, which warned of an impending assassination attempt, along with the king's reply to the duke thanking him for his trouble. Whether he had actually obtained the letter from newsletter writer Bartolomeo Dardano, as he told the authorities in Rome, we may never know; nor can we discover where Dardano might have gotten it. All we know is that he sold

copies of it to a certain Count Alessandro in Parma and to an agent of the duke of Lerma.[21] Newsletter writers were no more anyone's property than were the things they wrote.

Far more than upon accredited sources, newsletter writers depended for their information upon rumor and hearsay. When they began a story with the customary diction, "It is said that," and variations thereof, this was exactly what they meant. Writers who were neither spies nor snitches found salable political rumors in the palaces of the great as often as in important streets and squares. Even conversations overheard while teaching elementary reading to young nobles at home could serve as newsletter material, according to Ottavio Carnevale, a scribe in Venice with a shop at Rialto, who then sold the sheets to the Spanish.[22] His companions lurked under the porticoes of the Ducal Palace, and their counterparts in Rome milled around the piazza before St. Peter's, as we know from a suspect who defended himself by accusing "those others who go to St. Peters and to other places to find out the news."[23] Little of what any of them reported is verifiable by reference to other sources. This is hardly surprising, because much of it may be false—although there is seldom any way of finding out which portion.

Newsletter writers were as much a part of the world of oral culture as of written culture. Like the composers of songs, polemical poetry, and political slogans ("Old Pope Urban, whose beard's a beauty, after Jubilee is going to raise the duty"),[24] they intended their works to be conveyed as much by word of mouth as by the actual written page. They composed stories to be remembered, not studied; and they expected them to become part of the vague and general world of common consciousness rather than the clearly determined and finite world of written text. They regarded the general thrust of a communication as more important than specific data. If they kept any notes at all about what to write, such notes more often included lists of topics than lists of important details—exactly the opposite of modern practice. After all, in a pinch, details could be invented.[25] They expected their sheets to be discarded after use or, as often happened, recycled; preservation in an archive they would regard as a peculiar trick of fate.

Nowhere in seventeenth-century cultural life was the concept of authorship as appropriation more accurate for describing how texts were generated than in the case of the newsletters. For newsletter texts were not like many other writings that circulated in this period. They were copied differently, and thus they had a distinctive look. They were seldom at-

tributed exclusively to a given writer, so we are rarely tempted to fall back upon Romantic conceptions of authorship that poststructuralist French literary criticism has taught us to view with a jaundiced eye. And without advancing to the next step of literary deconstruction by regarding the subject as an effect of language, or of text, or of power, we may well agree in demoting authorship in the traditional sense, at least in the case of newsletters, to the role of a sort of reprocessing of words.

Important newsletters directed to the most excellent purchasers were subsequently leased, borrowed, or stolen and copied either word for word or in combination with information from still other newsletters or documents and then distributed to still other customers. As soon as a newsletter left the desk of its composer it became fair game for legions of copyists and hacks with no more imagination or daring than that required to live off the labors of others. Writers were careful to draw the distinction between composing and copying, particularly as composing seemed to be a more serious crime. That, at least, is how Paolo Marri defended himself when apprehended, noting that "writing and making are two different things; and I never made the newsletters, although I did write them."[26] His business was no different from that of Giuseppe Molella, a fellow scribe who claimed he got his newsletters from a friend in a notary's office and simply wrote them up, or Giovan Geronimo Favella in Naples, who received one of the Roman newsletters and recopied it, adding his own commentaries and, reputedly, inventions.[27] When the Venetian newsletter writer Domenico Marchesati was accused of espionage based on what he wrote in his newsletter, he successfully defended himself by pointing out that he had received all his information from one of his counterparts in Rome.[28]

Quite apart from the interests involved, writers almost always disagreed about which of an entire week's doings were worth cramming into a single four-page 150-word newsletter and which were not. Consider the episodes singled out on March 17, 1631, by Alfonso Lucci, one of twenty or more newsletter writers in Rome at that time. He reported the Spanish ambassador's interview with the pope concerning the Spanish cardinals' residency requirements, the Savoy ambassador's efforts to gain ceremonial precedence for himself and his duke, the jailing of the duke of Parma's agents in Naples, the quarrels between the families Severini and Caetani, the return of Cardinal Colonna to Rome, and the concession of a rich benefice in Capua to Cardinal Brancaccio. On the same day, another Roman newsletter writer, one Bartolomeo Tadino, included only

the residency question from this list; in addition, he talked about infantry recruitment by the Spanish in Naples, the departure of Monsignor Balaguer for his residence in Malta, an examination of new bishops, the acquisition of a canonry by a Piedmontese candidate, the arrival of the prince of Piombino, incognito, from Naples to get a loan to pay for his new title from the emperor, and the arrest of persons in Naples for robbing the mail.[29] Newswriters not only wrote news; they made it.

Although newsletters became news of a sort as soon as they began to circulate, and as such provide a rich mine of material for understanding the seventeenth century, paradoxically, they are less rich as a source for information about actual events—in spite of their regular citation for this purpose by nearly everyone who has written about the period.[30] Ministers relying solely on the newsletters for information were liable to utter the most amazing nonsense. Fortunately for the Genoese ambassador in Venice, when he confidently reported to his government that the English revolutionaries had set fire to the city of London in 1649 after beheading the king, there was no one there to gainsay him.[31] At least for a time, people could be easily misled. And so they were in 1653, according to the Este ambassador to Venice, when he wrote, "Just so you can see how far mistaken the newsletter writers are, they think our Most Serene Duke is currently in Venice, and two ministers came to me to see about this." He concluded, "This shows that one has only to invent something and it will be taken for infallible truth."[32] Trying to rank the newsletters in order of reliability, therefore, was no easy matter, as the duke of Modena's representative in Venice found out when he reported, "The ones by Padre Sciro, which everyone likes, are mostly full of lies."[33] Of course, whatever the newsletters reported, their perils to the writer were always the same. "The folly of the newsletter writers is really remarkable," noted Pier Giovanni Capriata, the historian, "for they bring true disaster on themselves just to please others by the publication of falsehood."[34]

Newsletter writing qualities other than truthfulness were therefore customarily praised, qualities such as vivacity, intelligence, and analytic power. Getting one's money's worth involved complicated calculations, evident in the following remarks by a Venetian writer comparing two newsletters: "For twenty-five *giulii* a month I used to get, during the recent conflict, the same [newsletter] received by the Venetian ambassador in Rome—well-analyzed material, good and political, and not idiocies and concepts fit for dogs, that aren't worth anything and ought rather to be called satires than newsletters."[35] Needless to say, he dropped his sub-

scription to those corresponding to the latter description. Recipients sooner or later admitted that they were forced to choose between bad and worse. "I have chosen the oldest and most experienced newsletter writer in town. . . , and I found that he is an oracle compared with the twaddle of the others."[36]

Writers and Readers

If the newsletters had been merely private letters circulated between two correspondents, the quality of their communications would have been as indifferent a concern for the historian of the mechanisms of political information as their overall effects on readers. Instead, they were a budding protoindustry, and they reached more readers than even their writers and distributors themselves could trace. Their effects and diffusion are therefore of intense concern for us, to the extent that any conclusions about these questions can be drawn on the basis of the scanty evidence we have. Let us now consider what role the information underground might have played in early modern Europe.

One thing is certain: in spite of the newsletters' defects, readers who were passionate about politics greedily consumed even the most mediocre examples. Our source for the moment is Gaudenzio Paganini, the Rome-based polymath and teacher of ancient Greek at Sapienza University, who devoted an entire diary to his analyses of what he read on January 7, 1640. He read, "The prince of Sans was taken from Rome by the Spanish ambassador; the pope knows nothing."[37] Paganini remarked, "Everyone is amazed at how little like a ruler the pope is being treated, when the French ambassador dares to remove from custody someone sent to jail, and that of Spain presumes to remove, from the city where the pope resides, a prince awaiting judgment."[38] This provoked a reflection on the difficulty the pope had in getting information about what was going on in his own city. "The reason for this and so many other problems is that the nephews do not let things reach the pope's ears that might annoy him, which will eventually have many unfavorable effects."[39] Another piece of news seemed to raise the questions of "why the adjustment between Madama [Cristina, duchess of Savoy] and the princes [Tommaso and Maurizio] of Savoy is rendered difficult" and "why the Spanish wish to occupy Casale." Paganini replied that any resolution of the civil war in Piedmont was difficult because Spain, supposedly the supporter of the insurrection headed by the princes, wished to arrange affairs to increase its

own influence; and Spain wished to occupy Casale, a fortress in Savoy territory, in order to be able to back up their wish by a show of force.[40] Newsletters apparently provoked reflection as much by what they said as by what they seemed to imply.

Nor did the newsletters' inaccuracy prevent them from causing serious diplomatic consequences on occasion. Wrong or right, information was information; how a hostile power might react to it was anyone's guess. No one was better aware of this than the Venetian ambassador in Paris, who complained that "publication" of news about military maneuvers near Malta reaching the Grand Turk might "greatly influence things, to the prejudice of the common interests."[41] He was right. Not only did the Grand Turk use news of this kind as a pretext for attacking Candia: later, Giovanni Francesco Capponi complained that the sinister news reported by a Roman newsletter about his behavior in the War of Candia was ruining his reputation as general of the Venetian forces.[42] His experience was minor compared with that of the papacy during the first War of Castro in the 1640s, when the French ministers got wind of the pope's war preparations by reading the newsletters, as Marquis Salviati observed.[43] And if newsletters could cause events, they could also prevent them, as when a story planted by the duke of Mantua about his imminent deal to sell Montferrat to France caused the French to call the whole thing off.

To be sure, the actual rate of diffusion of the newsletters must not be exaggerated. They were designed for communication between elites, and very probably their chief circulation was indeed among these elites. Gaudenzio Paganini was entirely typical from this point of view. So were the diplomats, military advisers, and counselors who acquired the newsletters either in order to send them along with their regular reports or to digest them, incorporating the information with other information they may have gleaned, for the benefit of their employers.

Information in the newsletters was often relatively recondite, aimed at the level of knowledge that could be expected of court habitués in the writer's vicinity or in the rest of Europe. Few readers not initiated into the upper echelons of the Roman cultural scene, for instance, were likely to find much use for references to such contemporary phenomena as the Accademia degli Umoristi, a group of free-thinking aristocrats and their protegés, including the papal nephew Antonio Barberini, Prince Ludovisi of Venosa, and Giambattista Marino, the prince of Baroque poetry. Few were likely to care much about the new edition of the Florentine Crusca Academy's famous and exceedingly expensive vocabulary or the doctoral

ceremony of Prospero Caffarelli, scion of a famous family.[44] Few again were likely to appreciate the fine rhetorical flourishes of other examples that drew upon classical sources to liven up the information they wished to convey, such as the following: "The Marquis of Astorga, Spanish ambassador, is delaying his departure from Rome, perhaps thinking he has to bring along a whole crowd of Spanish ladies who hang around his palace, and fearing that because of the cold winter season, he will end up planting their bones along the wayside, which might grow up into not armed men but so many horrible harpies."[45]

However, the habit of relying upon the written word for communication of every sort in Italy guaranteed a potential audience at every social level from artisans on up, if only the newsletters could be made widely available. In fact, a fairly considerable diffusion of literacy among the trades was assumed even by regular government practice. Shopkeepers were required to post notices about the regulations regarding their trades in plain sight on the walls of their places of business. And infractions regarding the written word ran rampant. In a culture where honor and reputation were, besides money, what set noblemen off from shopkeepers and shopkeepers from servants, one of the most common complaints to the magistrates concerned written handbills attached to the doors of houses or shops and denouncing the morals of those within.[46] Sometimes illiterate libelers hired professional scribes or literate neighbors to produce these handbills. But more often, libelers did their own writing; and persons of every category can be found undergoing elementary graphological analysis, from carpenters, tailors, grocers, priests, and scholars to the scribes themselves.[47] Even soldiers were able to proffer credible alibis for misdeeds with the excuse that they had been reading a book at the time.[48]

Libel and political commentary intersected in the practice of posting anonymous muckraking handbills about this or that government official—on the statues of Pasquino and Marforio in Rome or on the Gobbo di Rialto in Venice, by tradition designated for this purpose (and hence the local epithet "speaking statues" and our term, *pasquinade*), as well as anywhere in town.[49] One day on a corner of the building of the Old Mint in Rome there appeared a handwritten anonymous proclamation, attached with chewed bread by Domenico Bassani, a notary, accusing a judge in the office of the papal vicar of "simony, larceny, and public blackmail," such that whenever he passed by, he "smelled so badly that everyone cried, 'make way, make way,'" and claiming that the only rea-

son the pope was unaware of this business was that "secret newsletters do not arrive at the ears of the Holy Mind of His Beatitude." The proclamation was clearly written in haste. A bystander, one Narciso Poliziani, described the scene thus: "I saw a group of people gathered there at the corner of the said Mint, going toward the Church of Santa Lucia." But when he got there to find out what was up, "there were so many people that I was able to read only the first line."[50] Efforts to be informed often met with frustration.

Indeed, what else could be expected in the cities of Italy and elsewhere, those vast *tableaux vivants* of the social and political culture of the time. Denizens and visitors wandering through the streets expected to be informed. Communications were imparted by the mute facades of the buildings, the carefully fashioned choreography of a ceremonial entrance or religio-political celebration, and the hierarchically ordered tailoring of everyday costume. Even reading was not altogether a private act. And the public performance of reading had by now joined the common repertoire of urban gesture that repeated, commented upon, and modified everyday experience.

The number of people who saw or heard the newsletters may have been considerable, although subscription lists are known only for well-heeled buyers.[51] Individuals who gave their profession, at least to their local priest, as "newsletter writer" were sprinkled throughout Rome. And a typical newsletter writer's shop kept "many youths" busy as copyists.[52] After the newsletters left the desk or shop of the original writer (or, in many cases, inventor) of the news, they acquired lives of their own, recopied many times over as they passed from copyist to copyist. It was a labor-intensive industry, and the production end alone gave many opportunities for diffusion of the contents. Then there were the legions of delivery boys who took the newsletters from one palazzo to another or to the main mail pickup point in Piazza Pasquino, around the corner from Piazza Navona. A street market is even attested by a late-sixteenth-century engraving, perhaps by Ambrogio Brambilla, and printed by van Aels. It depicts a peg-legged man hawking newsletters in a Roman square, probably Piazza Navona, where booksellers set up stands to sell printed books and handwritten manuscripts.[53] This was where they might be read aloud and reach the hoi polloi.

But the actual number of people who read the newsletters and the truths or falsehoods contained in them is far less important for our argument than the impression made on authorities. Before opinion polls and

Nielsen ratings, there was no telling how many people, and of what sort, might be interested in an event. And where nothing existed resembling democratic political practice, there was no way to gauge how an event might affect impressions of a regime. Riots and revolts were the methods par excellence for the expression of dissent; but there were many stages of popular alarm before a city came to that. And the sorts of views that circulated in newsletters seemed well suited to provoking contrary opinions likely one day to sour into protest.

A good example is from Rome in 1599, where the impression made by the surprisingly freewheeling antigovernment bias of some reporting on the clamorous Cenci case was profound indeed. The case opened up the lifestyles of the rich and famous to the amazed scrutiny of Romans. Francesco Cenci, a Roman aristocrat and the father of twelve children, managed, because of crimes committed against a horde of real and imagined enemies and because of his unconventional romantic attachments, to lose a good part of the family's huge fortune in fines and compositions. Eventually he made the members of his own family the objects of his maniacal fears of robbery and persecution and locked up his daughter Beatrice, along with another daughter and his second wife, in a castle outside L'Aquila. These tribulations, and perhaps some physical violence as well, finally drove Beatrice to desperate measures. She escaped and, with her stepmother and brother, masterminded a scheme to have Francesco murdered.

The evidence against Beatrice and her collaborators was circumstantial or based on the statements of a witness who died soon after initial testimony. At the urging of Pope Clement VIII, the governor resorted to the unusual step of using torture to wring confessions out of the suspects, which was almost never done in cases regarding the nobility. The newsletters at once raised doubts about the pope's motives in the case, suggesting that he wished to take advantage of the Cenci's misfortunes to confiscate their wealth. "In Rome the case is said to be very well advanced," said one, "and the [Cenci] women are said by some to have confessed to having ordered [Francesco's] fall [to his death], but others say this is not true and that nonetheless the [Apostolic] Chamber wants to steal something [from the family fortune] no matter what."[54] After the guilty verdict had been delivered, Beatrice petitioned for clemency and began an appeal. But in yet another unusual step, the pope refused to hear the opinions of her lawyers. This again was interpreted in a sinister sense. "The lawyers [responded] with humility," the newsletter pointed

out, "that they came only to defend justice and make sure no injustice was done."[55]

The circulation of news about the Cenci case among the Roman audience raised the political temperature by several degrees. With opinions already formed about what was going on and a strong suspicion about possible papal misbehavior in the air, the conclusion of the trial put the whole city on edge. "All Rome was moved to compassion by the girl, who was less than eighteen and had a dowry of more than forty thousand scudi," said the Este ambassador.[56] So many turned out to see the execution of Beatrice, her brother, and her stepmother that several bystanders were crushed under the crowd. And the execution transported the story from the realm of the everyday to that of legend. Caravaggio may well have been inspired to record the parricide as an innocent act of desperation in his painting, "Judith Killing Holofernes." Meanwhile, numerous manuscript accounts of the whole affair began to circulate along the same distribution network as the newsletters. To prevent the criticism from getting any further out of hand, the pope ordered searches of the shops of all the known newsletter sellers, copyists, printers, and booksellers.[57]

The Politics of Information

However limited the circulation of the newsletters may have been, at least in comparison with printed works, the information and commentary they provided stood in open defiance of key political and legal concepts of the time. And the political and legal concepts that informed the mental patterns of political practitioners were preeminently expressed in the most influential serious works of political theory. In the last decade of the sixteenth century, the accepted view among political theorists of northern and central Italy, including those loosely identifiable as Aristotelians, depicted political control as standing perpetually on the edge of dissolution. To avoid ruin, the prince had to remember that political stability in general, and his position in particular, depended far more on reputation than on any single policy—reputation that was to be nurtured and defended by a careful display of power, dignity, and social superiority. Reputation depended at least to some degree on dissembling; and a considerable literature on this topic began to emerge throughout Europe in the course of the century, summarized by Justus Lipsius in his *Politicorum*.[58] And according to Giovanni Botero, the Piedmontese writer whose widely read work translated the language of state theory into

terms acceptable to the anti-Machiavellian climate of the time, dissembling was possible only through the control of information.[59]

Reputation, Botero argued in his discussion of the best means for preserving any state, consisted in a sufficiently widespread opinion regarding all the prince's virtues. Far from being a mere asset, reputation was an essential element in the studious effort required to maintain stability in all states that had achieved greatness. Any prince could garner the affections of a people by opportune handouts and appropriate entertainment. To galvanize their support, however, he had to appeal to their minds. That meant showing superior virtue in princely attainments such as justice, political acumen, military ability, and reason of state, a special category embodying the type of wisdom proper to a prince. "For gaining the love of his subjects, [the prince] needs but a mediocre virtue; for gaining reputation on the other hand he must have excellence. Indeed, when the goodness and perfection of [the prince] exceed the ordinary and arrive at a certain eminent level, his excellence is overwhelming, whether or not he has a lovable nature."[60]

But the prince's superior attainments were clearly useless unless he managed to keep, over the long term, the reputation he gained by them. A fatal inclination to unseemly behavior or unworthy companionship, in a world where appearances counted and notions of decorum were becoming even more elaborate than those discussed famously in Castiglione's *The Courtier* of a hundred years before, could easily cost him the reputation once gained. The same might result from excessive candor concerning the actions and purposes of everyday politics, especially where reason of state collided with conventional ethics. Actions and purposes could, of course, be revealed against the prince's will, and hence he ought to observe a policy of the strictest secrecy, not only with regard to other princes, who might gain an advantage from inside information, but also from the subjects. The subjects, after all, said Botero, echoing Machiavelli, make hasty judgments of character; and if they suspect the prince is a scoundrel, he is finished. "Let [the prince] not be on familiar terms with just every sort of persons, with talkative sorts and chatterers, because these will divulge what must be kept secret and discredit [the prince] among the people."[61] Therefore, along with a careful policy regarding information and secrecy, the prince ought to cultivate the approval of those capable of the highest political acumen—that is, "the religious, the literary figures, and the virtuosi"—whose influence might keep the people's judgments safely on track.

Botero's ideas about reputation were developed into a full-blown theory of political competence in the work of other thinkers across the turn of the century—thinkers like Girolamo Frachetta. A Friulian adventurer who established himself in Rome as a political counselor to the Spanish ambassador, Frachetta wrote a political tract in 1597, evidently to improve his salary expectations. In spite of the respect for popular impressions he shared with Botero, he believed the subjects' political awareness should be limited to approval of the prince's prudence. He never considered that the subjects might have views of their own. Drawing (loosely) upon book 1 of Aristotle's *Politics,* he pointed out that the political realm was superior to the domestic realm of private persons, just as, in philosophy, general concepts were more excellent than particular ones. And because the prince was by definition the most virtuous and must be virtuous in the most excellent things, his political virtuosity must therefore be superior to the subject's. Thus, the subject should never be put in a position to judge politics.[62]

The most extreme account of the levels of political competence was presented by Federico Bonaventura, an Urbino aristocrat also writing around the turn of the century. He started out by examining St. Thomas Aquinas's famous analogy between the political world and the world of the household, and he found this simple analogy to be utterly false and misleading. If the political world in some way resembled the world of the household, as Thomas supposed, then the householder could be construed as being somewhat analogous to the politician and even compete with the politician in ability and competence. After all, one common definition justified the position of the prince on the basis of his superiority; and if this superiority lay in the same kinds of virtue as those cultivated by the householder, presumably a superior sort of householder could demand parity with the prince—a patent absurdity.

Fortunately, this could never be the case, said Bonaventura, pointing to the rather vague discussion of the problem in Aristotle's book 7. Householders require no great degree of prudence, and the virtues they cultivate have nothing to do with those of rulership. For Bonaventura, prince and subject belong to entirely different types. Indeed, the two types were characterized by particular kinds of mental activity. The typical mental activity of the prince involved not so much facts as the best way to think and act in certain circumstances—in other words, use of what he called the consultative faculty. The consultative faculty permitted the formation of hypotheses and the exploration of theories corre-

sponding to the necessities of rule embodied in the concept of reason of state. And hypotheses and theories could be useful bases for quick action even when they went against common knowledge, common canons of behavior, and laws. Violating a truce, lying to an enemy, assassinating a rival—all these could be prudent actions from the standpoint of reason of state, and only the prince's consultative faculty could decide. The sort of mental activity typical of the subject, on the other hand, involved belief—an inferior sort, indeed. While attending humbly to his trade, the subject required little deep knowledge of any kind and had little time to raise doubts about the practical objects of his necessities. He should never have occasion to question the expediency of obeying a law, any more than he should have to waste time wondering whether sovereignty reposes in one or in many.

The social consequence of these differences was a division of tasks. "The proper job of the prudent and of reason is to command," Bonaventura suggested, "and the proper job of belief is to allow oneself to be commanded."[63] Thus, he agreed with all the other writers that the subjects should keep clear of political affairs because they were unable to appreciate the higher political motives of what might appear to be criminal acts—such as confiscating huge fortunes on a slender pretext. For him, as for all the others, political affairs were not the subjects' province, and nasty things would happen if subjects found out about them.

The newsletters were obviously a significant threat to views like these; and in response to their proliferation, jurists rushed to incorporate them into their discussions of crime and punishment. Prospero Farinacci in Rome was among the most influential; and his comments, included in his manual on criminal law, were based on firsthand experience as the Cenci family's defense lawyer in the recent trial. His observations began with a definition of the concept of *laesa maiestas*, the worst crime in the political realm, as just about any act by a member of a political community that could endanger the community in some way. Because the revelation of state secrets in the newsletters could endanger the community by injuring the reputation of the prince, newsletter writers were subject to the same cruel torments and capital punishment reserved for anyone else guilty of laesa maiestas. Writers were also punishable as promulgators of a particularly noxious form of libel (because, as Farinacci said, "scripta manent"), punishments for which varied in intensity depending on the seriousness of the crimes imputed by the libeler to his victim. Indeed, Farinacci pointed out, the first decree against the newsletters, published by

Pius V in 1572, had linked the newsletters to the issues of libel, laesa maiestas, and the proper role of the subject.[64]

In response to the Cenci case, the Roman government reinforced the old rules against newsletters and added some new ones. By 1602 it specifically targeted the newsletters as an offensive category of writing and prohibited their circulation, whatever they contained. The statute decreed: "No one, of any state, condition, or preeminence, may dare or presume to write letters or newsletters or other sorts of writings, or cause such to be written, to any persons of any grade or condition under any pretext whatsoever, without the written permission of His Reverend Highness [the papal-appointed governor of Rome]."[65] The newsletters having become public writings just like printed works, they were now subject to an analogous censorship mechanism, with the difference that the material to be sent to the censor was already by definition prohibited. The paradox inherent in a decree that practically called for voluntary admission of crime, like having to pay taxes on illegally acquired profits, apparently did not bother anyone, because a similar decree was passed in Genoa in 1634.[66] The only problem was that both proved entirely impossible to enforce.

In spite of the new decree, the newsletters soon began circulating information about the next major papal embarrassment—the so-called Interdict controversy between Rome and Venice in 1606—with an antigovernment bias even more pronounced than during the Cenci case. Briefly put, the controversy involved Pope Paul V's opposition to the trying of two clerics in Venetian civil courts and to the enactment of certain laws limiting the accumulation of church property in Venetian territories. When Venice refused to back down, the pope interdicted the performance of the sacraments in Venice, and the Venetian government turned to its counselor in matters ecclesiastical, Servite friar Paolo Sarpi (now best known for his history of the Council of Trent), to defend it in print against Roberto Bellarmino, apologist for Rome. An anonymous Roman newsletter noted, "In this affair almost all the princes favor the Venetians because they have the same or similar business with the church."[67] Another, more concerned with Roman fears of war as the pope cast about for more violent ways of coercing the Venetians, suggested that the arrival of Venetian ambassador Leonardo Donà, a man of proven probity and later a doge, was awaited in Rome "as the Jews await the Messiah."[68] The pope was urged to submit the matter to the consideration of a congregation of cardinals, "where the latter might more freely speak

and show their reasonings, which they otherwise do not do out of reverence for His Holiness."[69] But the pope refused, and the general discontent with the silencing of other voices about what should be done was duly observed. Needless to say, the picture of papal government in disarray in the midst of a major military threat did little to reflect the majesty of the Roman prince.

In Venice, by contrast, there circulated a series of sheets predicting an eventual victory by the pope. "The reasons that are usually adduced on the side of the Venetian signori to corroborate and give just title to their decree against (as it is said) ecclesiastical liberty are all founded on reason of state, and they have some apparent plausibility; but they are refuted by those who judge things without passion."[70] In addition, the sheets provided handy resumés of the Venetians' arguments, giving those who would not take the trouble to follow the pamphlet battle plenty of opportunity to draw their own conclusions. They replied to the Venetian claim that freedom to bequeath as much land to the church as anyone wished would eventually leave no land in private hands. Any restrictions on this freedom, they stated, would finish by expropriating the church. To the Venetian claim that the church should pay taxes, they replied that the prayers of ecclesiastics should suffice for the good of the state, and in any case the church had always made some sort of monetary contribution. To the Venetians' claim that the increase in ecclesiastical establishments would leave no secular persons left to go to war, they replied that ecclesiastics often contributed to a war effort by supplying money, by protecting ecclesiastical property under attack, and, again, by prayer.

However, as the assault on papal authority all over Europe became powerfully armed with jurisdictional polemics originating from Catholic countries, the newsletter writers continued to show Rome to be a battleground for French and Spanish factionalism. Such was the inference of a newsletter of 1612, which sought signs of secret partisanship in the vacation plans of visiting Spanish dignitaries and saw particular significance in the efforts of Cardinal Anton Maria Gallo to entertain them, although he was reputedly on the French payroll. It speculated that the overtures made by the Spanish toward Cardinal Andrea Baroni Peretti might have been occasioned by the latter's complaints that he had been given the cold shoulder by the previous ambassador, suggesting that Cardinal Bonifacio Bevilacqua's absence from the scene might have been the result of his desire to appear his own man in spite of the rumors about his connection to the French.[71] At least according to a later series of newsletters, the French

party was on the decline by the 1620s, when the Spanish dumped the Colonna in order to devote their efforts full time to Cardinal Gaspare Borgia, although Cardinal Alessandro Orsini was still torn between the two competing sides.[72] Occasionally, the newsletters themselves openly supported one side or the other, referring to Spanish power, for instance, as "fearsome and hateful" and thus taking active part in the veritable party politics that was now beginning to affect even modes of dress in Rome (plain black for the "French").[73]

Both foreign and domestic policies and officials were duly excoriated in the other sorts of clandestine material that the copyists and distributors often included with newsletters. The Roman police took a beating in a lampoon circulated by the newsletter copier and distributor Paolo Marri, which began, "Cries of whores are being heard in the court." The Roman nobility were the object of a satirical dialogue cunningly pasted together from familiar Latin Vulgate quotations and circulated by the same copyist; and so were the Spanish, at that moment battling the rebellious Portuguese ("Castile: Quid ad nos? Portugal: Crucifigite, crucifigite").[74] The conclave that elected Paul V, the pro-Spanish party in the Curia, and particular prelates like Sforza Pallavicino, noted for his suspiciously rapid rise to fame and fortune, received equally unfavorable treatment in lampoons circulated by the newsletter copier and distributor Giovanni Amadeo and his collaborator Giuseppe Persico.[75] Papal foreign policy in the War of Mantua and Montferrat as well as the merits and demerits of various candidates for the next papacy were the objects of a series of manuscripts distributed by Cesare Tubiolo Ventone, a scribe who also did work for the newsletter writers.[76] Policies of all sorts were castigated in certain pasquinades that circulated for a brief time in Rome and reached larger audiences by way of descriptions or excerpts in the newsletters. Polemics that had begun in the world of the drawn image, by way of the many prints that circulated on behalf of one or another party or cause, were brought by the newsletters into the world of the written word.[77]

The pope's very existence was threatened by another category of works, among the most dangerous of all material distributed by the newsletters network—namely, judicial astrology. In seventeenth-century Italy, as in England, such interests were far more than mere popular superstitions fit for inclusion in almanacs and the butt of ridicule from the likes of Francis Bacon and Galileo; and they were a regular part of journalistic discourse long after they had been banned from serious discus-

sions in the Italian and French academies.[78] In Rome, astrology was particularly widespread. "Almost everyone practices astrology," said one observer. "Whoever can, tells fortunes; and there is no cardinal or prelate or prince who has not commissioned discourses concerning his own horoscope, with predictions of good fortune in contingent things—since everything finally depends upon God."[79] For whatever reason, whether because of the radical changes in regime from pope to pope or because of the exceptionally high stakes for understanding the appropriate moment to seize an opportunity for advancement, protection and patronage at the highest levels of Roman society guaranteed the survival of even the most flagrant practitioners. And among the most prodigious of the practitioners in Rome was Orazio Morandi, a member of the Vallombrosa order born in 1570, who learned his techniques in Florence. As procurator and one-time general of the order and abbot of the monastery of Santa Prassede, he became an important figure on the Roman cultural scene, entertaining cardinals now and then and Galileo Galilei in 1630.[80] The starry canopy he had painted on the inside of the apse of the monastery chapel to reflect his interests and those of most of his fellow monks is still visible today.

For Morandi, who openly curried favor with the supporters of the French monarchy as the least intrusive possible arbiter of otherwise chaotic Italian politics, astrology could even be an instrument of destruction. An outspoken critic of Urban VIII's apparent turn toward Spain in the 1620s, he authored numerous pasquinades, among them this apocalyptic one: "They will become bees," referring to the Barberini pope's coat of arms, "and they will make honey only in the corpse of Christendom."[81] In a manuscript newsletter falsely dated Lyon, February 21, 1630, he claimed that the pope's stars presaged death. The sun's auspicious ascendancy in the pope's geniture, he explained, was not affected, as might appear to the novice, by the right quartile with Mars and the Moon's position nearly partile. But in the sixty-second year, that is, the current one, a right quartile of Saturn to the sun would arrive at the center of the horoscope some time after the month of June. This sign of death was unequivocal.[82] When he read the letter to many on the monastery's extensive intellectual circuit and distributed it to others, his conclusion was disputed only by Raffaello Visconti, a Dominican mathematician who worked with Nicolo Ridolfi, Master of the Sacred Palace, in reviewing books for the Holy Office; and Visconti insisted that the sun in the pope's horoscope was so overwhelmed by the quartile with Mars

that it could no longer be called ascendant at all.[83] Others not only found Morandi's discussion persuasive but came up with similar analyses on their own. Whether Morandi believed he was right or not, he may well have hoped that the balefulness of the prophecy might make it self-fulfilling. And it almost was.

Morandi's conclusions, reinforced by his friends' investigations and his audiences' goodwill, quickly hit home. They naturally appeared in one form or another in newsletters authored by others—not necessarily with the greatest accuracy. For instance, Galileo happened to be in town seeking permission to print his *Dialogue concerning the Two Chief World Systems,* and he had nothing to do with astrology other than having done a few horoscopes for the Medici family. Nor was he connected in any way with the Roman astrologers except for having attended a few of their dinner parties. But he became the unwitting spokesman for all of them, at least according to one newsletter. "Galileo Galilei is here, the famous mathematician and astrologer; he is trying to publish a work against the Jesuits," Antonio Badelli reported, with mediocre comprehension. "He has said that Donna Anna [Colonna, wife of Taddeo Barberini, the pope's nephew] will have a male heir, that there will peace in Italy at the end of June, and that soon after this Don Taddeo will die and so will the pope."[84] Such reports were taken very seriously. True, it was not in response to Morandi's public predictions but to other similar ones by private dabblers two years before that Urban VIII had resorted to the rituals of the celebrated natural philosopher and astrologer Tommaso Campanella. Campanella's elaborate ceremony, involving flaming torches and odoriferous emanations to counter the fatal astral influences, apparently worked, because the pope lived on until 1644. More directly in response to Morandi, the Spanish cardinals dropped what they were doing in Spain and came to Rome for what they and many others thought would be the next conclave—all of which amounted to yet another major embarrassment for the papacy.[85]

The availability of clandestine material of all sorts, including newsletters, appears to have reached a climax in the late 1620s, when Morandi opened a veritable public lending library for the whole area around his monastery. Borrowers included local dignitaries, like the Venetian ambassador Angelo Contarini, as well as cultural figures, like Giovanni Battista Doni, an associate of the French libertine Gabriel Naudé. Cassiano Dal Pozzo, philanthropist and collector, might be found along with Theodore Ameyden, the famous jurist, and an astronomer, Andrea Ar-

goli. Less established artists like Pietro Mulier, Ludovico Stella, and Giuliano Finelli could borrow the same books as more established ones like Pietro Bernini and his son Gian Lorenzo. And copyists like Giovanni Battista Bertollo could compare notes with the newsletter writers Orazio Falerio, Giovanni Poli, and Matteo Vincenteschi.[86] Apart from astrological works, borrowers could check out the classics of condemned literature, ranging from Erasmus's *Praise of Folly* to Copernicus's *De revolutionibus* to Machiavelli's *The Prince*. They could enjoy Johannes Trithemius's *Steganographia* on automatic writing, a prohibited classic that had provided significant inspiration for the sixteenth-century chemical philosopher Paracelsus, whose works were also on the Index of Forbidden Books. And they could also borrow recent works critical of the current regime, including Jacques-Auguste de Thou's history of his own time. In that work they could read a favorable account of the gallican theses of the Parliament of Paris that had provoked a propapal refutation by Giovan Battista Gallo, also known as Jean de Machault. They could borrow John Barclay's recently condemned satire on the Jesuits, as well as manuscripts of Venetian Ambassador Renier Zeno's 1623 report on Rome, manuscripts of recent and future conclaves, and, last but not least, back copies of newsletters.[87]

Out on the streets, a main effect of the persecution of the clandestine spreaders of news appears to have been to create an ever more potent weapon in private quarrels. That newsmongers could be arrested for what they had on hand was a welcome revelation, especially among those casting about for ways of getting their neighbors into trouble. Accordingly, fellow workers vented their jealousy of Vincenzo Canatella, a copyist in the copy shop of Giovanni Landi near the Sapienza University, by falsely accusing him of being a newsletter writer. That, they apparently hoped, would stop Landi from giving him all the best commissions on the basis of his supposed superior maturity and experience.[88] More serious still was the case of Francesco Maria Vertena, a barber secretly denounced by his disgruntled former employees. By now, there was no doubt about the sort of things that might catch the attention of the authorities. And one thing that might catch their attention, Vertena's enemies could be sure, was to accuse him of claiming that "the pope buggered Machiavelli"—not, of course, Niccolò Machiavelli, long dead, but Francesco Maria, later cardinal.[89] They claimed he had written a sonnet to Pope Urban VIII ending with the line, "O blessed and holy arse, fit to be buggered by a holy cock," and had circulated rumors that the pope's

nephew invited boys into the palace for amorous trysts. When the false witnesses were questioned, their claims that they had received such scandalous material on pure hearsay earned them a reprieve. That such political scurrility coursed freely through the city was by now entirely plausible; and its role in discrediting the Barberini administration was well known. Officials had to admit that townspeople were more aware of the political uses of invective than ever before.

But the invective itself was far more worrisome than the patterns of petty criminality that seemed to have spun off from it. The Roman authorities were not alone in experiencing a certain helplessness as they stood by and observed the circulation, throughout the city's streets, squares, and houses, of material attacking the government's reputation and sovereignty, in spite of the late Renaissance system of press censorship. In 1621 in the Republic of Venice, Paolo Sarpi, an adviser to the Senate with the 1606 Interdict controversy still fresh in his mind, conceived the first public policy of information in Italy, one containing considerable originality and acumen. Sarpi was well acquainted with the many avenues for the diffusion of information in the seventeenth-century Italian world, where writings quickly became the subjects of public discussions. "They encourage conversation and provide material for the discourses of the disaffected and the self-interested, who insinuate themselves into the open ears of the simple-minded, seducing them and impressing upon them concepts with pernicious effects." Even the truth could sometimes hurt, Sarpi noted. For the public dealings of a government, based on a calculus of the lesser evil, were bound to appear suspect to an ignorant private person bound to conventional morality, who might recoil, for instance, at the thought of Catholics making deals with heretics. "No state has been nor can be without very great imperfections," he noted—including the Venetian republic. "By no means immune to the human condition, its defects could be exposed and censured and used to condemn the whole government by anyone who wants to offend and create a bad impression; they cannot be defended, can scarcely be hidden, and to make excuse for them is to admit them, even though human malice does not listen to excuses anyway."[90]

Faced with the futility of the alternatives to controlling information, Sarpi made a startling break with the past. The best strategy, he suggested, was to combat information with more information. One could pay attention to events as they occurred and publish a narration of them with arguments supporting the side that fit one's interests and increased

one's advantage. By offering readers their first taste of what was going on in the world and tinting information in the proper way, the government could ensure that information from other sources would be discounted or ignored. However, having come so far, Sarpi drew back. He rejected his own suggestion as soon as he made it; and his reasons reveal still more about ideas concerning information in the world of the 1620s. The gesture of verbal defense and explanation of policies placed the government in an attitude of subservience to the audience and unnecessarily opened up the secrets of state to private persons. This was to be avoided at all costs. "Everyone confesses that the true way of ruling the subject is to keep him ignorant of and reverent toward public affairs," Sarpi noted. When the subject finds out about them, he added, "he gradually begins to judge the prince's actions; he becomes so accustomed to this communication that he believes it is due him, and when it is not given, he sees a false significance or else perceives an affront and conceives hatred." If no information had yet been circulated by any of the parties in contention, the best advice was to keep silent. Otherwise, "the subject would not be kept in ignorance and reverence, but the door would be opened to the contrary opinion."[91] Botero, Frachetta, and Bonaventura could scarcely have disagreed. Encouraging subjects to think about politics could open a Pandora's box. Thus, having rejected his own best suggestion, Sarpi gave up.

In Rome, efforts were made to explore the possible effects of more voluminous political information. Among those who were particularly at risk, at least in the view of Mesenzio Carbonario, an experienced papal administrator, were the governors of the cities subject to the pope. "If the governor's imprudent government gives occasion for eight or ten subjects to detest it within their shops or houses," Carbonario began, "we might call this a bad thing." If he showed himself to be corrupt as well as impervious to complaints, so that the people began to denounce him not only in their houses and shops but outside in the public streets and squares, "we might call this not just a bad thing but a terrible one." If the matter was not settled, and "his imprudence, vice, and obstinacy passes from the houses and shops not only into the public streets and squares but into the rooms of the councils, great and small, and even into the ears of his superiors," in that case, "we would call this total folly."[92] Alas, the only solution, in this rumor-saturated world, was to take Botero seriously once and for all and be a good prince—a bewildering prospect for most seventeenth-century rulers struggling to navigate their troubled states in the midst of economic depression and military threat.

Yet the suppression of information could actually have an effect opposite to the one intended—so said Evangelista Sartonio, writing in Bologna in the 1620s, nearly two decades before John Milton made his plea for freedom of the press in the *Areopagitica*. To wit, "One must never, in any city or place, prohibit people from reasoning, especially about things that one does not want them to know," said Sartonio, "for surely those things will only be all the more diffused because of that very privation, which is a fertile mother of curiosity and appetite."[93] But allowing information to circulate freely was no better policy. Writing in response to the circulation of news in the War of Mantua and Montferrat, one of the most disastrous of the Italian episodes of the Thirty Years' War, he gave the example of ancient times, when the emperor Vitellius prohibited the circulation of information about the war with Vespasian. The rumors that thus emerged were far more cruel and calamitous than the truth.[94] The vulgar crowd, full of impetus and temerity then as now, was prone to judging things without prudence or reflection. Disaster could result. In other words, a war like the present one could be made all the worse if its destructiveness were compounded by the circulation of unfounded reports. Instead of offering a better policy suggestion, Sartonio offered a warning. The public was bound to discuss and reason in whatever way it was able to do, in spite of any prohibitions, and even though its reasoning was defective.

Writers and Networks

No amount of capital punishment, exile, or general harassment of the writers sufficed for the Roman or any of the other Italian governments to get rid of the newsletters. Each new generation of writers seemed to forget the persecutions of the generation before; the problem for the governments surfaced once again, to be confronted by a new series of laws, decrees, and punishments. Indeed, the most likely challenge to the newsletters came not from governments at all but from any other system that provided a similar service more efficiently, more regularly, and for less money—such as the printed newspapers invented in Germany in 1609 and quickly imitated everywhere else in Europe.

When Genoese newsletter writer Michele Castelli began having Italy's first newspaper printed by the local firm of Giovanni Maria Farroni in 1640, he simply transcribed his newsletter sheets.[95] But as he became more adept, he discovered he could squeeze more than twice as much

material on a single four-sided newspaper sheet as he could into his newsletter, and he could sell it for twelve *soldi*—about half as much. After the first newspaper aroused market interest, others followed in quick succession between the 1640s and the 1660s, in Florence, Naples, Milan, Rome (for a short time), and in many locations around the papal states: Bologna, Perugia, Rimini, Fano, Foligno, and Ancona.

However, newsletters were never wholly supplanted by newspapers. First of all, they were recognized to be far more daring and interesting. To be sure, not all newsletters were alike; and an informal distinction was made at the time between the so-called secret and the so-called public sheets. A typical "secret" sheet might add the elements of intrigue, suspicion of scandal, and influence peddling to a story about the mighty's travel plans. The following account of Bishop Francesco Ravizza's travel plans, circulated in Rome on October 15, 1667, gives some idea of how this was done: "Monsignor Ravizza, having left the court, went to Orvieto and divulged the report that he went to enjoy fresh air to cure his tertian fever; but the common opinion is that his departure was forced, and indeed, it is said that besides being chased out of town by the highest authorities, he was forced to renounce his canonry of St. Peter's, however, with the concession that he might choose an ally in his place."[96]

There was a world of difference between such reporting and the account of the same event presented in a "public" sheet, to the following effect: "Monsignor Ravizza, secretary of the Consulta, went to Orvieto, his place of origin, to enjoy some weeks of his native air due to his illness of retention of urine."[97] Reports on the health of the eminent were for anyone; descriptions of political pressure were for the few. Indeed, the main difference between the "public" and "secret" sheets appears to have lain in the reporting of embarrassing news; and when Francesco Maria Vialardi, a writer of "secret" newsletters, specified that he left "the minutiae of Rome to the newsletter writers," he meant that the standard term *newsletter* was far too banal for the sort of deep background he provided to an exclusive audience of high-paying customers.[98] Writers who produced the "public" newsletters, on the other hand, appear to have enjoyed a semiofficial status, signing their otherwise entirely typical newsletters, in total defiance of the common practices of self-concealment. In this sense, Timoleone Mozzi, who sold his signed newsletters about Rome and Antwerp for more than ten years, was only exceeded in his utter respectability by Bartolomeo Dardano, who sent his signed newsletters concerning Rome around to selected customers for at least twenty-

one years until retiring with a canonry in Spoleto.[99] But all the newsletters, of whatever sort, seemed to compensate in quality for their disadvantages with respect to the newspapers in matters of quantity and price. Writers like Luca Assarino, who also wrote newspapers, were explicit about the differences. To justify the higher price of the newsletter, he explained to one correspondent, "you have to understand that it costs me money and risk."[100]

Few of the first newspaper writers possessed the inside sources of information that were the lifeblood of the newsletters, except those who, like Castelli and Assarino, worked in both genres. Most of the time, newspaper writers, knowing they were highly vulnerable targets for the authorities, quietly purchased the newsletters for their own information and kept their distance from espionage networks and embassy snoops. That, no doubt, was the assumption of the compiler of the Genoa gazette, who got his news of Rome straight off a Roman newsletter sheet that carried the same information transmitted to the papal nuncio in Florence.[101] The compiler of the Bologna paper could be as certain of avoiding risky personal contacts when he repeated, almost word for word, the information in a newsletter of Venice as could the compiler of the *Nieuwe Tijdinghen* in Antwerp, who depended on the Venetian and Roman newsletters for its material.[102]

The second reason that newsletters were never wholly supplanted by newspapers was their irreplaceable usefulness for conducting international relations—in spite of their defects. This had been apparent almost as soon as they began to circulate in the previous century. Emanuele Filiberto of Savoy was not alone in holding their writers to be "a race of men more fit for the gallows than the galleys." They were, he added, "all insolent scoundrels, and living very dangerously, they utter a thousand lies." Nor was he alone in conceding that "whoever needs them ought to let them keep lying."[103] Already in the 1590s, the secretary of state of the Republic of Lucca had ordered his Venetian correspondent to "find out, from the master of the post of Genoa and from other friends of mine and experts especially in the matter of newsletters, just who are the best in this genre."[104] By the seventeenth century, papal nuncios all over Italy customarily included the sheets along with their regular missives—hence the vast collections in the Vatican Secret Archives; and so did the representatives of other powers—hence the Codici Urbinati collection in the Vatican Library, originally from the duchy of Urbino. Often, no other sources existed on which to base political decisions.[105]

This leads to the third reason the newsletters persisted: that is, their deep roots in the networks of power, privilege, and patronage in their respective states. Such networks, in early modern societies, passed for what in later times would serve as the articulations of a bureaucratic system for getting things done. In our period, persons enmeshed in them were shielded from the scrutiny or the interference even of the rulers themselves. The postmasters whose offices, by intention or by carelessness, provided some of the first seeds of the stories carried by newsletters were virtually untouchable. The northern routes were controlled by the powerful Tasso family from Bergamo and its various branches throughout Lombardy, Austria, Germany, and other parts of the Habsburg empire, where it became known as "Thurm und Taxis."[106] The central and some southern routes were controlled by the general of the post in Rome and the Papal States, whose horses all the couriers were obliged to use. He belonged by right to the papal household and rented his office from the Camera Apostolica for no less than fifteen hundred scudi per year, a sum grand enough to excuse many peccadillos. Next in importance in Rome was the master of the post of Genoa, who was on such good terms with the secretary of state that he could dare to request a bishopric for his brother-in-law.[107]

Some of the writers of the newsletters and other clandestine documents were themselves highly placed. Early modern societies were densely stratified, and a Milanese adventurer like Francesco Giuseppe Borri, serving as secretary to the Roman representative of the count of Tyrol in the 1650s, could himself be a person of considerable influence.[108] The same went for Francesco Maria Vialardi, who could call himself a "gentleman" in the retinue of the second son of Emperor Maximilian II while living in Turin and received a knighthood for his service.[109] Even more so the abbot Francesco Cattaneo, who was the grand master of the Teutonic Order while serving as a representative of the Archduke Leopold in Rome for thirty years, until 1656.[110] Among the most exalted writers was Uldrico Da Monte, who operated in Milan on behalf of the Venetian ambassadors in the 1680s while serving as bishop of Coira.[111] And Manfrino Castiglione, general commissioner of the Spanish cavalry in Milan, was not only unlikely to draw suspicion but also powerful enough to deflect attacks.[112] Like all the others, he wrote newsletters as a service to patrons and benefactors—in his case, for the court of Urbino from 1629 to 1630.

Few could match, either in length of service or in personal influence, Theodore Ameyden, who was a personal friend of Urban VIII.[113] After

growing up in Flanders, he studied law at the University of Macerata, then came to Rome with recommendations from none other than Cardinal Bellarmino. During the course of his career he became one of the best-known lawyers of his time, eventually publishing a series of important legal tracts. His work as a lawyer for the Datary and other high Roman offices put him into contact with all the most important personages in Rome. He published newsletters for thirteen years, beginning in 1640, and diffused a sea of manuscript pamphlets on topics of contemporary politics ranging from the actions of the emperor to those of Don John of Austria, which are extant in dozens of copies in libraries all over Rome. Considering the favored treatment customarily reserved by the judicial system for those with appropriate connections to the high and mighty, such persons could operate with relative freedom, at least until they managed to make thorough nuisances of themselves, as Ameyden had by the year 1654.[114]

Those newsletter writers who were not themselves highly placed were protected from prosecution by their connections to others who were. For both the freelance writer and the spy, the palace of an ambassador was the source par excellence for gleaning the most precious sorts of news without arousing suspicion. Of course, only ambassadors themselves enjoyed the total immunity from reprisals that was enshrined in the international law maxims of Hugo Grotius.[115] Such privileges extended neither to the newsletter writer with diplomatic connections nor to his embassy informant, all the more so as constant strife with citizens in their vicinity had given ambassadorial staffs of all nations a bad name all over Europe—and the Spanish ones, in particular. But having connections was a distinct advantage.[116]

Other writers appear to have written their newsletters with the connivance, or at the very least the benign tolerance, of powerful employers. Copyists by profession, many of them worked for one or another of the many copy studios that could be found here and there around every large city. In Rome, the largest copy studios belonged to the powerful and elite group of notaries, because of the tremendous volume of work that the latter had to handle.[117] It seems highly unlikely that even in a large office, such as that of Giovanni Maria Antonetti, one of the elite Thirty Capitoline Notaries in Rome, the newsletter writing of a certain substitute notary named Giuseppe would have gone unnoticed, in the midst of business with the high-ranking Borghese, Boncompagni, Piccolomini, and Marescotti families and connections to the patron and antiquary Gio-

vanni Giusto Ciampini and the artist Gian Lorenzo Bernini. For all we know, Antonetti may have furnished the original newsletters himself.[118]

Nor was the newsletter writing of a certain copyist named Giovanni Francesco Faccini likely to have escaped the attention of his employer, Jacopo Simoncelli, even though the latter's operations as one of the notaries of the tribunal of the auditor of the Camera Apostolica were extensive enough to include as customers the Barberini family and Cardinal Jules Mazarin.[119] And if tolerance by these notaries may have benefited these newsletter writers, how much more so must the tolerance of Filippo Pirovano, auditor of the Sacra Romana Rota, have benefited a certain Girolamo, who copied newsletters in his spare time and delivered them to Amadeo and other individuals, who, in turn, also copied them. Nor were the advantages entirely one-sided. These employees' second incomes no doubt took some of the pressure off their employers to provide bonuses, and their employers' connections appear to have rubbed off at least to some extent on them. Girolamo, at least, when caught selling newsletters, appears to have gotten off with a warning.[120]

Still more helpful for some newsletter writers were customers who happened to be among the most powerful people in Europe. Thus, whereas Bartolomeo Dardano might imagine that in difficult times he could rely on the duke of Urbino's secretary of state, who was his customer, Giuseppe Suenzo might imagine that he could rely on the imperial ambassador to Venice and the ducal secretary, who bought his newsletters about Germany.[121] And they were not more fortunate than Andrea Vrlstorff and Gerolamo Galata, who sent their Venice newsletters to the counselor of the duke of Mantua, or Alfonso Lucci, who sent his to Count Fabrizio Serbelloni in Milan, not to mention a certain Giulii, who sent his to the grand prior of the Order of Malta and members of the Colonna family in Rome.[122] Only Abbot Leonardo Carrara and Francesco Bertiroma were better protected than these, in that they both communicated with Cardinal Pietro Ottoboni, future pope.[123] Indeed, if cardinals could be trusted at all to protect their dependents, Antonio Gauteri was in good hands with Cardinal Bernardino Spada and the cardinal's brother Virgilio; and the same went for Timoleone Mozzi with Cardinal Antonio Barberini, the pope's brother.[124] In fact, if vicinity to the pope meant anything, Vincenzo Canatella could say he served Giovanni Francesco Ugolini, Pope Innocent X's auditor; and Vincenzo Regii could say he served the papal-appointed governor of Rome.[125] In any case, the latter was hardly likely to prosecute his own journalist.

What all these newsletter writers sought from such customers was not just money, of course, but protection and favors—one might even say patronage. A military commission for a nephew was not too large a request; Giovanni Domenico Marchesati made this perfectly clear when he turned to papal secretary Flavio Chigi to get one. Nor was special treatment for a relative who had been sent to the papal galleys—such was the plea of Matteo Vincenteschi, another newsletter writer.[126] True, this approach was not infallible. Giovanni Amadeo apparently wrote his newsletters to "do a favor for some of my prelate friends who are in governments outside of Rome," hoping the protection of those prelates would make his disgraceful life more comfortable; it did not.[127] Indeed, this ambition of the writers was so well known that the judges sometimes poked fun at it in the trials, when they forced newsletter suspects to write out fake requests for favors in prose that was excessively unctuous, even by baroque standards—ostensibly to test their handwriting against the evidence.[128]

In two centers, Rome and Venice, newsletter production persisted throughout the century and well into the next and strongly rivaled the production of printed news—for reasons that supply the final contours to the picture of the seventeenth-century world of information sketched out here. First, information in those places was intrinsically valuable. In Rome, in fact, the reporting of certain kinds of news, such as the elevation of a cardinal, was customarily rewarded with a gift, as stipulated in the postal guild statutes.[129] What happened in the relatively provincial center of Bologna, on the other hand, was no more likely to provide sustenance for a newsletter writer and his family than was news from Ancona. Not by chance, unlike Bologna, Ancona, Florence, Milan, or Genoa, neither Venice nor Rome became the site of a regular printed newspaper until the eighteenth century, although news pamphlets appeared in remarkable profusion.

Second, both Rome and Venice supplied sufficiently valuable work to a labor market full of potential newsletter writers and scribes, and this is perhaps where these two cities differed from the larger newspaper-producing centers like London, Antwerp, and Paris. Scribes living on a salary had a notoriously difficult time, even in a good-sized notary's office in Rome. As many as seven scribes might actually live on the premises, along with thirteen substitute notaries. In a master scribe's residence, as many as five workers might live cramped together in the same quarters;[130] and the claustrophobic atmosphere was worsened by hazing and even occasionally by the sexual exploitation of younger by older men.[131] Low

pay and hoarding of the best jobs by the master or the more experienced employee encouraged younger employees and apprentices to seek jobs outside the office. Misery led to crime, and scribes were among the best-represented categories in trial records concerning rowdy behavior. The newsletter circuit provided extra income as well as an avenue, however oblique, for expression of discontent and cynicism.[132]

For those who came from elsewhere, breaking into the job market was no easier in Rome and Venice than in the other major cities. Guilds went out of their way to contain commercial endeavors within their membership and, with the consent of the city government, imposed heavy fines upon anyone outside the guild who dared to set up shop. They favored local residents by refusing to give credit for apprenticeships completed elsewhere and by requiring large deposits from members who did not possess property close by. For the benefit of relatives of current members, they sometimes waived entrance fees, age limits, apprenticeship requirements, and the entrance exam. And as though these regulations alone were not enough to stem the tide of foreign entrants into the local economic world, the guilds imposed still others, limiting the number of apprentices each master might keep and stipulating the minimum distance between shops (more than twelve hundred feet for Roman pharmacies).[133] Lawyers and physicians with foreign qualifications were generally not allowed to practice.

Because the basic requirement for copying documents was literacy, and indeed not even too much of that, the guilds of scribes were able to protect their monopoly only on actual storefront copy shops and on the copying of official documents. Any foreigner looking for easy money could get a job with a notary and earn eleven *baiocchi* per day (just over one-tenth of a *scudo*)—barely enough to scrape by.[134] But a single very good political lampoon could fetch up to two hundred ducats from a private customer.[135] And with a yearly contract for regular delivery of a newsletter to a single good customer running at between twelve and forty scudi, the prospect was very tempting—given that a laborer made around twenty scudi and a master craftsman around fifty. A busy copyist writing day and night, as was the custom, could make a reasonable living.[136] So thought a certain Giuseppe Molella from Subiaco, who had "no profession" but had "studied" at a university; he copied newsletters to keep body and soul together while "looking for some job in the Curia," he told the authorities.[137] Unfortunately, after the newsletters were found on

his person, the only job he managed to get was rowing in the papal galleys for ten years.

Venice and Rome were unrivaled on the peninsula as magnets for intellectual talent. Between them, they accounted for a quarter of all the known Italian literary academies or salons created at one time or another across the century, including the adventurous Incogniti (Venice) and the elite Umoristi (Rome), where malicious gossip was raised to the level of art.[138] Between them, the two cities accounted for well more than half the book production; between them, they accounted for a good portion of the literary employments, as well. Odes and sonnets might be dedicated to and paid for (or, more often, conspicuously not paid for) by a veritable archipelago of little courts, including those belonging to a bevy of foreign princes and their legations, and in Rome, a dozen or so cardinals, including future popes, and a host of high-ranking bureaucrats. And there was no end to the copying of documents.

Writers capable of organizing a large newsletter operation could make up to six hundred ducats a year in profit, from which they paid workers perhaps twenty ducats each. Building a larger list of customers cost little more in postal charges, because mail was paid for on the way in rather than on the way out. And customers could be specially treated by custom marketing techniques of a sort not possible with newspapers. There was no need to send every customer the same sheet. Newsletters could be cobbled together, on request, from all the permutations and combinations that could be derived from a menu of other newsletters from different locations. A customer of Giovanni Quorli in Venice who wished to receive only the Venice-based sheet, for instance, would be charged for just that. On the other hand, a customer who wished to receive the Venice, Rome, Milan, Paris, Leghorn, Vienna, and Cologne sheets would be charged accordingly. Besides providing better service to customers, these practices saved paper, the costliest factor in production. The size of the operation not only allowed better deals on materials but also served to lighten the burden of purchasing and receiving other newsletters from which to crib information. A few simple rules could keep waste to a minimum and scribes' diligence to a maximum: "Your Lordship is obliged, as the director," Quorli advised his successor, "to apportion the jobs each week and draw up a newsletter of each type, so that the scribes copying your original cannot cheat." No city was to receive more than its due space: "Un mezzo [foglio] Parigi, un mezzo Milano."[139]

Therefore, newsletters filled the cracks in a fractured labor market where patronage and guild served different and sometimes antagonistic interests. They offered second incomes to underpaid civil servants and scribes. They offered a promise of something better than working-class life. And in the two cities that were the mother lode of vanity at this time, where rich and influential employers were as abundant as the salacious gossip they craved, the newsletter trade even flattered the vanity of writers by the prospect, however remote, of high connections.

The newsletters became a formidable institution in this period, one with its own codes and its own mechanisms of reproduction. Their very existence testified to widespread disobedience of the most sacred canons of traditional rule. They fed upon and in turn nourished a culture of the illicit and a stance of defiance. And the messages they communicated formed a subversive undercurrent beneath the semiotics of absolutism just then being refined to the last stage of perfection by the best artists, sculptors, architects, rhetoricians, playwrights, and musicians in Europe at the time. These reasons combined to make them as indestructible as they were effective, although not always for the purposes for which they were intended. And their effectiveness, as sources of both information and misinformation, was multiplied by the combined impact of printed newspapers and works of contemporary history.

2

Politics' New Clothes

Print became the dress of political reality for a growing number of Europeans in the seventeenth century. At least in comparison with the previous period, a veritable information revolution was under way. Modern analogies can be misleading; but the replacement in the seventeenth century of the earlier, more desultory system of political communication was surely as difficult to ignore at the time, among those paying the closest attention to technological innovations, as the impact of electronic media has been in our own.

Let us consider some important facts. For one thing, the circulation of pamphlets and broadsheets publicizing battle reports, manifestoes concerning treaties, truces, and successions, accounts of important weddings, funerals, and ceremonial entries, legal proceedings, and critical commentary was accompanied in many cities by the appearance of the first regular newspapers. The pioneering gazettes in Strasbourg and Wolfenbüttel were soon followed by others in Antwerp, Amsterdam, Paris, London, Genoa, Milan, Turin, Naples, Bologna, Barcelona, and hundreds of smaller centers. In Germany, no fewer than two hundred newspapers were initiated across the century. In England, some 350 titles of news publications of all kinds appeared in the period 1641–59 alone. Even where newspapers did not appear, production of printed news of other sorts more than doubled. Wide differences in literacy levels determined wide variations in diffusion. But the general impression of jurist Ahasver Fritsch in Jena, that news publications "get into the hands of everyone," was exactly echoed by engraver Giuseppe Mitelli in Bologna.[1] Indeed, in late-seventeenth-century Italy, as in the Britain of Joseph Addison a half-

century later, the coffeehouse politician, the poor soul who passed his life engrossed in the political trivia of the time, was already the object of raillery. "You who after silly tales are lusting / Anxious to hear rumors and reports, / Quickly, run and look at the gazettes, / And see if the news is good, fine, or disgusting"—wailed a Paduan pamphleteer.[2]

The critics bewailed the obsession with printed news that appeared to be a fashion of the times, but deeper changes were occurring beneath the sometimes gaudy surfaces of the various urban societies. In Italy, as in France, Holland, Germany, and England, to name the main places so far covered in the historiography, the diffusion of new texts for thinking about power, authority, and government administration challenged some basic assumptions.[3] It raised questions about the boundaries between private life and the holy circle of sovereignty and legitimacy.[4] It contradicted apologies for monarchical absolutism that situated rulers in a one-sided dialogue with the ruled. And to the protagonists and witnesses of the political disturbances that challenged encroaching administrative control, it contributed a means of popular communication. In Naples it informed suggestions about radical constitutional change. And in Messina, the first revolutionary newspaper, published by the provisional government, defied the Spanish monarchy.

To be sure, the connection between what circulated in the press and what circulated in the minds of audiences was neither obvious nor direct.[5] Still less was it uniform. Stories about a rain of blood in Argentina or about a fetus in Cologne that screamed audibly from within the womb, or any number of other accounts designed to spice up the otherwise rather dreary fare, excited as much scorn among the more discerning as wonderment among the more credulous.[6] The same went for stories about battles never fought, celebrations that never occurred, or rulers who never ruled in quite the way the press described. In case readers did not already guess that information was often deliberately manipulated by the protagonists of many of the stories for the specific purpose of diverting attention or producing admiration, they were continually reminded, occasionally in so many words, by the writers themselves. What is more, the information revolution affected political life as much by what was left out as by what was said, as much by subtle implications as by direct statements, as much by the artfulness of the invention as by the quality of the information. The more the fabric of political reality came under scrutiny, the more its precise texture seemed to fade from view. And in some quarters, expectations for more accurate pictures of the civic world were over-

shadowed by convictions that the construction of events was just another negotiable aspect of the discourse about power. And if the skepticism that, among some readers, eventually took the place of scorn did not reach to the very marrow of political beliefs, at least it contributed to more profound forms of skepticism resulting from other causes.

The Information Revolution

From what has been said so far, there might be good reason to wonder that any sort of information revolution at all occurred in Italy or elsewhere, even in the limited early modern sense that has been suggested here. The official attitudes examined in the last chapter continued throughout the seventeenth century to regard the distribution of political commentary of any kind as a highly delicate government concern. Officials in Venice, Rome, and Florence subjected manuscript newsletters to strict regulation because of possible benefit to military rivals or detriment to popular sentiments.[7] They refused to issue printing licenses even for works that spoke well of the government, when such works might provoke vulgar tongues, by the mere utterance, to sully the names of the great or when excessive praise might be its own refutation—as Antonio Cartari found out when his encomium of Pope Innocent XI was banned in Rome.[8] They worried that works rebutting criticism might provide enough information about an adversary's argument to furnish ammunition to future critics: that was the case of Antonio Diana's work on ecclesiastical immunities, which was to be reprinted in Florence in 1672.[9] They worried that works published by members of the political elite might give the impression of having been endorsed by the whole group, as was true of Venetian nobleman Giovanni Francesco Loredano's story of the life of Albrecht Wenzel von Wallenstein.[10] And responding to particularly acute crises in the distribution of power, governments occasionally put a tourniquet on the circulation of political material of any sort, as the Genoese government did in 1611 in the wake of yet another dispute between the new and the old nobility.[11]

True, none of these governments' concerns was strong enough to cause political information to disappear. We have already seen that the newsletter networks, through which state secrets leaked to the outside world, were protected by powerful patronage structures and strong incentives guaranteeing a steady supply of new recruits into the industry. An irresistible demand made other sorts of manuscripts also a widespread form

of clandestine publication in Italy, as late as the early eighteenth century, when Antonio Magliabechi turned the Medici library into the hub of a distribution system stretching across the peninsula.[12] Clandestine manuscripts often appeared to imitate printed works, as did a Roman satire on Pope Urban VIII that claimed to be "printed for Marforio" (one of the two legendary statues that served as political bulletin boards in Rome) "in the shop of Pasquino" (the other statue). And a printlike format could suggest prudent withdrawal of a salacious manuscript from the legitimate marketplace, as in the case of a work advertised by the Venetian newsletter copyist Paolo Angelelli as a "scene of the noble whores and the whorish nobles. Delightful entertainment for the present Carnival, 1670," which he claimed had been "printed" in "Calicut, with license and privilege," available for twenty *ungari* to anyone desiring the entire volume of 150 manuscript pages. As he explained, "Noble whores are the prostitutes, servants, . . . peasants, and similar worthless people married by nobles, who cuckold their husbands. You will see first of all a Pesaro who married a whore of his nephew. A Foscarini knifed by a Molino, her husband. A Cornaro who took his messenger boy's streetwalker for his wife."[13] Copied out numerous times by hand, the work was sold just like a printed pamphlet.

In the case of printed material, entrepreneurial ingenuity and the black market ensured that censorship systems would never obtain the results intended. Those censors who did not actually collaborate with the printers and writers complained about being overwhelmed by the sheer quantity of material in circulation.[14] Theories about press control began to change along the lines of notions about information control in general, as examined in the last chapter. To Paolo Sarpi's admission that total press control was "impossible," Fulgenzio Micanzio, his successor as consultant to Venice, added that it was useless, because it served to publicize the works being censored.[15] "In fact, many unnecessary books would otherwise simply be forgotten," he advised the Senate, "that survive because prohibition excites the desire of many to see what is so scandalous about them. . . ; and books that ordinarily might be read by few people end up being read by many."[16] No wonder adventurers of the pen like Ferrante Pallavicino and Gregorio Leti exhorted fellow writers to procure censorship whenever possible in order to achieve popularity. And in making such exhortations they were only repeating a fact already well known to printers such as the Bulifon family in Naples, who recorded the rise in book orders following the prohibition of a work and connived with

friendly importers in neighboring cities to bring in by stealth what they could not bring in by law.[17]

Probably more hazardous for political publication than censorship per se were the internal contradictions and unpredictable variations in the censoring mechanisms around the peninsula. Printers in Naples, who risked imprisonment by the viceroy for printing things authorized only by the archbishop and imprisonment by the archbishop for printing things authorized only by the viceroy, were not even the worst off.[18] Their counterparts in Tuscany bore the brunt of the same kind of tension between the local representative of the Roman Inquisition and the secretary of state. Everywhere in Italy, they had to pay close attention to the local political situation. In Rome, that meant keeping in mind that the Master of the Sacred Palace could get in trouble with the pope for not consulting him first.[19] In Venice, that meant keeping in mind that government authorization alone was sufficient only until the republic's necessities during the Candia war from 1645 to 1669 brought about a tacit agreement with Rome. Then printers had to seek permission from both the government and the Inquisition.[20] Even when they had complied with all the shifting regulations, they were still liable to stumble over questions of pure protocol and deference—as Demetrio Degni discovered when he refused to place the state approval before the ecclesiastical imprimatur on the first page of his newspaper, in accordance with the duke of Modena's new rule. Fortunately, he lost only his license and nothing else.[21]

Nevertheless, in some ways, the printing industry suffered most from a lack, rather than an excess, of regulation, particularly in the area of literary property. In spite of the absence of conventions among the eighteen major Italian states, a few attempts were made to institute pan-Italian privileges to print certain books. The papacy insisted that those granted in Rome were universal. But this was no more enforceable than the Venetian Jewish community's insistence that their privileges covered all Jews.[22] Outside the states in which they were granted, privileges to print were treated just like any other kind of privilege: with indifference. Works printed in Venice about the wars in Candia and Dalmatia were routinely reprinted in Rome to the detriment of the Venetians.[23] Works printed in Rome about affairs connected with the papacy were routinely reprinted in Venice, to the detriment of the Romans. In a typical case, an account of one of the last battles of the War of Candia was printed in Venice, Bologna, and Ferrara, all in the same year.[24]

Nor did the tribunals intervene much in favor of the printers, even at

the local level. Indeed, governments were often the most flagrant violators of their own rules. Consider the example of poor Lodovico Grignani in Rome, who received a privilege from Pope Gregory XIII to publish an almanac only to see it abrogated and awarded to someone else by Urban VIII, a later pope.[25] The court ruled against him. In another case, for years no amount of protest by fellow printers was sufficient to motivate the authorities to proceed against Giacomo Mascardi until he had already reissued their most lucrative books, adding new titles, title pages, and introductory material to disguise the theft.[26]

Newspaper entrepreneurs seemed more exposed than almost anyone else to the constraints imposed by this system—and not just because repeated publication by recognized presses made them easy targets for persecution. Repeated publication also made them easy targets for systematic plundering. The writer of the Genoa newspaper could do no more to prevent his work from being immediately reprinted in Florence than could the writer of the Lucca paper prevent his from being nearly as quickly reprinted in Bologna.[27] And if not entire runs of newspapers, selected numbers concerning key events, those very numbers whereby entrepreneurs hoped to attract orders for the rest, might be pirated by out-of-town firms. Thus the author of the Perugian paper could forget about selling copies in Rome of his October 17 and 20, 1643, issues, reporting the defeat of the duke of Parma's allies by papal forces at Montecorno during the War of Castro; they were immediately reprinted by Grignani.[28] One can fully sympathize with Luca Assarino, a newspaper entrepreneur who conceived the desperate expedient of handwriting the name of a saint on each copy he sent out to his subscribers, as much in order to assure authenticity as, by this talisman, to ward off piracy (no one knows with what success).[29]

In the absence of any likelihood that piratical practices might be reformed legislatively in any near future, Juan Caramuel, a Rome-based cleric and correspondent of Pierre Gassendi and René Descartes, compiled a *Syntagma de arte typographica* (1662), calling upon writers, printers, and entrepreneurs to exercise self-control. Printers, he noted, customarily reprinted any books not regulated in their own states; and they had no reason to suppose that laws passed in another state might extend to them. However, custom was not always the best guide, Caramuel warned; and the continuity of a practice from time immemorial was not necessarily an argument for its perpetuation. In the case of seizing, using, and selling the writings of authors without their permission, custom

clearly flew in the face of the only international convention unequivocally binding on all humanity. "In my view," he said, "what they are calling custom is an abuse forbidden by God in the Ten Commandments under the injunction against stealing. And there can be no human dispensations from that law."[30] Unfortunately, his appeal fell on deaf ears.

Governments made some efforts to prevent the collapse of an industry that suffered, if not entirely, at least to a considerable degree, from their own chaotic wavering between intervention and neglect. Paper, for instance, happened to be a relatively costly item, accounting for about 60 percent of a printer's expenses and so difficult to obtain in large amounts that printers used it for settling debts among themselves as a substitute for books or cash. Some printers took to manufacturing it themselves and gave up printing altogether, as did the heirs of Giovanni Maria Verdi in Modena.[31] Except there and in Genoa and Parma, paper was usually produced in provincial factories close to clear streams and rivers—in Fabriano near Ancona, in Bassano, Salò, and Vicenza in the Venetian state, in Biella in the Savoy state, in Colle Val d'Elsa in the Tuscan state, in Bracciano and Ronciglione in the Papal States, and in the Sardinian town of Cagliari.[32] Moving it to the urban centers of the printing industry combined with local taxes to add as much as a third to its price to the printer. And the price shot up whenever the circulation of rags was prohibited or impeded because of plague or war.

In response, Venice lowered taxes for importing paper from Salò for the benefit of the printers in urban Venice; and the government of Lucca set up protective tariffs on imports from other states. Meanwhile, many of the Italian governments tried to ensure the presence of sufficient raw materials to local paper factories by eliminating duties on rag imports and putting in price controls. This intervention brought about a notorious "rag war" as available supplies migrated to wherever the price was right. Paper manufacturers thereupon began to draw up the first long-term contracts with rag suppliers, ensuring a continuous flow of paper to the printers for the future.[33]

Aids to other industries sometimes redounded to the printing press— notably, the mining industries, whose peacetime uses governments had never fully explored. Yet when the Venetian government began to encourage lead mining in the Vicentine hills in 1667, mainly for the purpose of furnishing the Brescia arms industry with a continuous supply of lead and other metals, the increased productivity made more material available also for casting type. Because the lucrative type-founding trade had

broken off to form a separate guild in Venice, as in most cities with the exception of Modena, where printers Cassiani and Soliani still kept their own foundry on the premises, the only way to control costs was by assuring a plentiful local supply of raw materials.[34] Thus the Venetian printers could hope for at least a few abatements in what usually amounted to the most expensive item, after paper, in their budgets; and this was not the least of their advantages vis-à-vis their counterparts elsewhere.[35]

The most important change in government policies regarding the printing press, at least as far as our modest information revolution was concerned, was the advent of policies of guarded toleration. The change was not abrupt; and its effects varied widely. However, a uniform tendency is unmistakable. For when the government of Naples abolished the law requiring the consignment to the government of a certain number of copies of newly printed works, and that of Tuscany reduced the number of free copies consigned to public libraries, the effects of these actions was the same: policies originally instituted, like similar ones in France, at least in part to discourage excessive book production were no longer in effect.[36] When the Tuscan government allowed news sheets to circulate, at least temporarily, without any supervision at all, it did so for the expressed purpose of encouraging the industry. "[First Secretary Andrea] Cioli gave the order," State Auditor Alessandro Vettori later recalled, "to let them be printed without passing through my hands, so they could go out quickly to Rome by the post from Genoa."[37] Nor was the government of Venice determined to be any less effective in this matter. It tacitly allowed booksellers to ship small packages of printed matter of any kind through private mailing addresses without duty charges or revisers' permissions; and at the same time it stoutly defended printers' rights to reprint works previously given privileges in Rome, resisted new additions to the Index of Forbidden Books, sped up the review process, and stopped harassing the Jewish printers.

That governments intervened for economic reasons connected with the promotion of a flourishing printing industry should come as no surprise. They also acted for more selfish reasons, stemming from a newfound conviction that printing could occasionally be helpful for their own purposes. They too could benefit from spreading ideas favorable to themselves and dangerous to their adversaries. In this period, they rediscovered the usefulness of printed propaganda: The governments of Venice, Naples, and Messina occasionally permitted the publication of books

with false place names and dates. By so doing they could avoid giving the impression of permitting the circulation of certain ideas whose publication could nonetheless prove both lucrative and expedient.[38] Consequently, two editions (1676 and 1683) of Paolo Sarpi's anathematized *Treatise on Benefices,* a book that placed state interests ahead of church ones, circulated with the place name of "Mirandola," though it was actually printed in Venice under the noses of the civic authorities.

To be sure, the publication of officially sponsored political information and comment was no invention of the seventeenth century. But the multiplication of such publications certainly was, and they included patriotic poetry distributed by rulers among their populations under attack, polemical handbills distributed among enemies in the field or in besieged towns, and hefty apologetic tomes distributed to anyone who could read them.[39] Each major diplomatic or military crisis gave rise to a war of words on every side, from the Interdict controversy between Venice and Rome in 1607 to the war in the Valtelline from 1617 to 1626 between Habsburg Milan and allies of France to the War of Castro, rekindled sporadically from 1641, between the dukes of Parma and the papacy. The governments of Florence, Piedmont, Venice, Milan, and Genoa hired the historians Vittorio Siri, Girolamo Brusoni, Maiolino Bisaccioni, Giovanni Francesco Fossati, Pietro Gazzotti, Luca Assarino, and others to analyze their behavior in recent skirmishes in sufficiently encomiastic terms in return for the appropriate rewards. When these governments did not directly commission such works they approved dedications made to themselves in pamphlets celebrating their actions.[40] They thus behaved as active or passive sponsors of a new genre of historiography characterized by subtle exaggerations, judicious omissions, and deviations from the truth. The next chapter shows how this new genre gave further cause for readers' disbelief.

Before printed newspapers came on the scene, governments already recognized the possibilities suggested by the continuous publication of favorable information and commentary. Paolo Sarpi, advising the Venetian government, was not the only one to suggest a series of news books as an instrument of consensus building. A group of petitioners in England, including newsletter writer John Pory, proposed such a series to King James I. The best way to shake people out of their natural torpor and bring them under the right rule of reason, they asserted, was to "[spread] among them such reports as may best make for that matter to which we would have them drawn."[41]

By the mid-seventeenth century, newspapers appeared to be, in the words of Gregorio Leti, the best way to "remind the people about the majesty of the prince."[42] And after the English royal government established the *Mercurius aulicus* and that of France put Théophraste Renaudot on the payroll, the governments of Milan and Piedmont eventually gave their official print shops exclusive rights to publish the local newspaper. The latter government gave the journalist a thousand-lire pension, while the government of France, thoroughly outdone, was giving the same journalist half as much.[43] Other governments took care to deliver appropriate information to the local newspaper from time to time.

Readers of News

If governments began to assume that political information from printed sources reached audiences capable of acting on what they heard, they were right. However, evidence about the composition of these limited but news-hungry audiences suffices only to give a bare impression. Actual subscription lists have survived only for the best-placed newspaper buyers, and without the names attached. They are usually in the form of accounting sheets, like the surviving one for the Mantua newspaper in 1689. Prepared for the purpose of gaining a monopoly from the government, it claimed that of the two hundred or so copies printed every week, "there are always some left over that are not sold, but instead are given gratis to the chancery, to the ministers, and to others."[44] No one knows who may have bought the rest—or whether larger numbers were printed up than the entrepreneur was prepared to admit to the officials. And if, as the owner claimed, the Naples newspaper was indeed printed in lots of up to a thousand under terms that, in 1693, ordered copies to be sent to the half-dozen or so Neapolitan nobles who, along with the viceroy, made up the Collateral, or State Council, that left a considerable number to circulate around the city.

Let us try to imagine just how much circulation Virginio Vangelisti and Piero Martiri in Florence could expect for their paper. After handing out some sixty-two obligatory copies to functionaries in various offices, they were left with some three hundred to five hundred to distribute as they wished.[45] Supposing the lowest possible number of copies and a coefficient of ten readers for each, typical for the period, in a city like Florence with an average population of sixty-four thousand, we can estimate that nearly one in twelve persons may well have seen a newspaper every

week. Yet conspicuous reports of newspaper consumption here and there around the peninsula have been left only by extraordinarily voracious readers like Antonio Magliabechi, a ducal librarian in Florence, Carlo Cartari, an archivist in Rome, and Antonio Bulifon, a printer in Naples.

Occasionally we may catch a rare glimpse of the circulation of news books, the chief prenewspaper version of printed news. News books were among the items lent out by Orazio Morandi at the monastery of Santa Prassede in Rome to the numerous borrowers from his library of licit and illicit, printed and manuscript works. Yet the document does not say what might have been the impact of a work concerning the siege of Verrua, perhaps the one by Matteo Castello, lent in 1627, a year after the event, to a certain Don Stefano Antonietti, to the Apostolic Protonotary Domenico Bandiero, and to Orazio Faliero, a scribe.[46] Similarly, we are left to imagine what impression a work on the siege of Breda of the same year, perhaps the one by Herman Hugo, made upon Antonio Biccari, the procurator who borrowed it, or the *Diario dell'anno 1629* that the same reader borrowed the year it came out.[47] Information about how many news publications may have been solicited by the other borrowers in this circle is as elusive as that concerning its possible effects. We can only make guesses regarding the scholar and philanthropist Cassiano Dal Pozzo, the sculptor Pietro Bernini, and his son Gian Lorenzo. And reviews of more humble types like Pietro Mulier and Ludovico Stella, both painters, Giuliano Finelli, a sculptor, Giovanni Battista Bertollo, a scribe, and Giovanni Poli and Matteo Vincenteschi, both newsletter writers, are as obscure to us as every other aspect of their lives.

In spite of their negligible value, news books showed up from time to time among the inventories of movable goods belonging to persons of many categories. Parish priests in Piedmont were just as likely to possess them as were their counterparts in Venice.[48] In Venice, indeed, the undisputed center of the Italian printing industry, only a small sampling of seventeenth-century death inventories has survived. And the 5 percent that actually include itemized lists of printed works confirm as many obvious conclusions as they raise tantalizing new questions. We scarcely need to be told that nobles like Tommaso Gritti, as might be expected, possessed all the available works on the German and Italian wars along with discourses concerning the Valtelline mountain passes against Philip III of Spain, or that Giovanni Grimani Calergi possessed titles like "Governments and Administrations of Diverse Regions," a "Report on Candia," and the "Distinct Descriptions of the Spanish Monarchy."[49] And there is

no wonder that Giacomo Farolfo, a merchant, listed a report on the court of Rome or that Giovanni Bavella, shipowner, listed a work on the defense of Dalmatia.[50] If they could, they no doubt would have emulated Gaspare Checkel, whose commercial activities helped him acquire houses to rent in the city and villas to enjoy in Maerne and Carpenedo while keeping himself up to date with Loredan's work on Wallenstein, pamphlets from the Piedmont civil war and from the Venetian wars in Dalmatia, and Paolo Beni's reply to anti-Venetian propaganda in 1618. Like him, they might have enjoyed Gerolamo Lunadoro's report on Rome in 1645, not to mention a manuscript, "Description of the Seraglio of the Grand Turk."[51] More interesting are cases further down the social scale, such as painter Pietro Liberi. And almost any guess about what he may have made of his copy of Gualdo Priorato's letters on the imperial wedding would be more plausible than the meanest conjecture over what sorts of news books might have been included in the endless bundles of "books for reading," "bookcases, with books," or "various worthless books, not listed," or the like, generically listed in more inventories than one could count.[52]

The few conclusions that can be drawn about the extent of literacy at least do not refute our notion that in urban areas, there could have been a public for written news. There is no way of counting the number of children who may have benefited from the continuation of the Renaissance system of basic literacy education, administered by state, church, and private individuals. All over Italy, poor students might receive elementary training from the Jesuits and the Piarists. And if the latter were known to accompany students home in some instances to help them withstand the jeers of their less studious contemporaries, we can appreciate the kinds of sacrifices students and families were prepared to make.[53]

For states, an incentive for literacy programs came from the theory that literacy could prevent vagrancy. And for this reason, the Commune of Lucca in 1621 began providing poor students not only with books but also with clothing and shoes.[54] To achieve a male literacy rate of close to 50 percent of the twenty-five-to-forty-nine-year-old age bracket in Naples, and a rate only slightly lower in Lecce, required a considerable structure.[55] In Venice, a structure capable of achieving rates of 30 to 40 percent began, at the most basic level, with literacy imparted by private teachers, both at home and in the numerous private schools. A typical early-seventeenth-century scribe, such as Ottavio Carnevale, might teach literacy to "very low persons" in his school on the Rialto in the mornings

and, in the afternoons, give elementary instruction to the children of a nobleman in a private palace.[56] Next came the six government-funded humanist schools, one to each section of the city, and parallel to these, the church's schools for young clerics. In Rome, state-salaried masters in each of the city districts, or *rioni,* were supposed to teach poor students gratis and were allowed to charge a fee to whoever could pay. In addition, sixty or so independent schools were registered with the government and inspected from time to time.[57] To be sure, literacy was not always the doorway to the world. Sometimes it was the doorway out. And in lonely Morlupo, on the outskirts of Rome, where the four sons of a poor weaver learned to read and imparted this skill to their sister Caterina Palluzzi, the instruction served for the acquisition of spiritual perfection and, eventually, beatification.[58]

Curiosity about news showed evident signs as Italy was swept up in the European wars of the early seventeenth century, and political events beyond the doorsteps of the Italian cities began to take on a new dimension. No one could ignore the fact that distant troop movements and battles often had serious local repercussions in terms of recruitment of infantry by the major powers, impressment of sailors, and fiscal exactions, even when the European wars did not actually spread into Italy—as they did in the territory of Montferrat in 1614 and again in Mantua in 1625. And when pamphlet and newspaper writers behaved as though their readers were anxious to follow the stories they covered, they were not merely indulging in wishful thinking. Pietro Socini could be fairly sure that readers of his *Successi del mondo* were indeed "impatient" to hear the upshot of "the news written two or three times from Paris" in August 1661 about a battle between the Spanish and the Portuguese.[59] Similarly, the writer of *Macerata,* in September 1664, could plausibly imagine that "the letters due in the post the day after tomorrow are eagerly awaited," inasmuch as they were sure to contain information about "some favorable change concerning Imperial arms . . . against the Turk."[60] Already in 1648, a news sheet expressed a conviction rapidly gaining ground, that "great things give occasion to the curious to know them, particularly when the truth about the event is in question," and that this curiosity could only be satisfied fully when "there have been seen not only the reasons but also the means and the ends to which things have been brought."[61]

Although current historiography has yet to agree on a standard for measuring popular attitudes with respect to political affairs, many indi-

cations suggest more than a confused awareness of what was going on.[62] In fact, the presence of Spain in the North and South of Italy generated not confusion but intense concern about the wider picture that determined the permanence or impermanence of this arrangement. In some places, as we have seen, partisanship for France or Spain extended even to the manner of speech and dress.[63] And, far from the epicenter of military combat, printmaker Giovanni Maria Mitelli depicted French and Spanish partisanship in Bologna in his 1690 print designed to demonstrate the connection between journalism and opinion. In this print, a man in spectacles sits on a stump in a city street reading aloud from a newspaper. Around him, characters from different social levels and occupations listen in. One cries, "It cannot be!"; another insists, "Yes it is!" In a corner of the print, a Frenchman and a Spaniard exchange blows, obviously concerning the subject of the story. As they fight and tear at each other's hair, yet another bystander comments, "Oh what folly!," as if to reprove the folly of governments that drag their peoples into useless warfare.[64] It was no wonder that Marc Huguetan, a printer and entrepreneur from Lyons on tour through Italy, found people even in a relatively remote location like Lucca to be so well attuned to what was going on elsewhere that "one encounters little circles of eight or ten persons everywhere on the street trying to discover [the news] or pass it around."[65]

Among governments and entrepreneurs alike, a powerful reminder of what might become an extraordinarily effective way of stirring passions and steering interests was the use of the printed word by rebels against established authority. Genoa was a good example. Here, social tension began building throughout the 1620s as the economy deteriorated; and the non-noble elite grew increasingly resentful of the old nobility's history of profitable deals with the Spanish. This prepared the ground for the so-called Vachero conspiracy of 1628, which the neighboring duke, Carlo Emanuele of Savoy, backed in order to increase his own influence in the area. Supporters of the duke distributed pamphlets enumerating his virtues and condemning the vices of the Genoese ruling nobility, calling for people to judge the affair by themselves and participate in a revolt.[66] Printed in Vercelli, "these writings were sent everywhere," said an observer at the time, "and many of them went to Genoa to the common people, by whom they were read with much pleasure before the Senate had a chance to prohibit them." Even after prohibition, "many did not wish to bring them to the palace as commanded but kept them and, it is thought, frequently read and recited them in groups."[67] In the event, the

uprising failed, and the same non-noble elite tried again in 1648. This time, led by Giovanni Pietro Balbi, they tried to lever themselves into power with French support. News about the scattered flames of discontent along the periphery of the Spanish empire and elsewhere ignited hopes for change in Genoa. Conventicles began to form at every social level, from the elites on down, related Gaspare Squarciafico, a historian. "In familiar conversations," he went on, "they discuss the revolt of Naples, the revolutions of Catalonia, the Portuguese plot and the change of government in England, and the liberty of Holland all in one breath."[68]

The more successful Masaniello revolt, in which a modest fishmonger and his associates held Spanish power in Naples suspended for ten days, and his successors for two years, was attributed by observers, at least in part, to the circulation of information about other rebellions. The one in Palermo a few months before was highly instructive from a Neapolitan point of view.[69] Bad harvests, famine, and plague had induced the nobles in the local government to spend cash reserves on importing expensive grain from abroad. Spanish officials ordered them to recoup losses by raising the fixed price of bread to reflect its actual cost. A popular bread riot ensued, which the disenfranchised city guildsmen used as an occasion to demand the abolition of duties on foodstuffs and the addition of their own representatives on city council to equal the number allotted the nobility.[70] Before the Spanish authorities had a chance to initiate repressive measures in Palermo, Tommaso Aniello, known as Masaniello, and his collaborators made both of these demands the centerpiece of their program in Naples.

Once the Neapolitan revolt got under way, the Dutch provided an even more instructive example. Unlike Palermo and Catalonia, the United Provinces managed to separate permanently from the Spanish orbit. More importantly, they experimented with a new form of government that seemed superficially congenial to the situation in Naples: a powerful States General accounting for the various social and economic divisions in the country, balancing the power of the chief city of Amsterdam against a solid core of delegates from the provinces. To be sure, interest in Dutch affairs began long before Masaniello, as contemporary diaries attest.[71] And for good reason. Every new development in the Dutch revolt called for a new levy of the Neapolitan troops upon which the Spanish monarchy had come to rely; and Naples was the one place in the Spanish areas where commerce with Holland was still permitted.

Apart from word of mouth, information came from newsletters, handbills, and news books, including an account of the treaty of Munster pub-

lished in Naples in 1648. Analyses ranging from Famiano Strada's study of the revolt to Guido Bentivoglio's report on Holland, prepared while he served as papal nuncio in Brussels, were passed from reader to reader.[72] And when Masaniello's middle-class successors to leadership of the rebellion conceived of an assembly or senate, they turned their eyes to the Dutch States General. Such an arrangement, they reasoned, might be far more representative of the kingdom as a whole than the outdated combination of a city council (the Seggi) and a noble Parliament. They made overtures to Henry of Lorraine, duke of Guise, to provide leadership, with a sort of Dutch Stadtholder in mind. In the heat of the moment, no one worried that Guise might not be another Maurice of Nassau or that Naples, a struggling commercial port saddled with a vast agricultural district still subject to feudal obligations, might be a far cry from the Dutch model.[73] Informed decisions, after all, are not always good ones.

While the debates proceeded concerning the organization of the government, the passions of Neapolitans were stoked by printed pronouncements and pamphlets on either side.[74] One such pamphlet, entitled, "The Faithful Citizen," offered "a brief discourse on the just, generous, and valorous decision of the city of Naples" to break away from Spain. It reminded readers that the Dutch had gone from "simple fishermen" to become "formidable among potentates." Just like the Dutch, it recommended, the Neapolitans ought to send deputies to the Munster peace negotiations so the settlement of local affairs would be made part of the international agreement ending the Thirty Years' War. "The Faithful Citizen" assured readers that Spanish power was currently too overtaxed in Europe to mount a successful resistance in Naples. But it warned them about the "bad faith" shown by the Spanish in proceeding from amicable negotiations in Palermo to "bombs and cannon fire." Therefore, any solution short of a violent severing of relations would surely end in the severest reprisals against the revolutionaries, as had recently happened at Cambrils in Catalonia where (it reminded readers) six hundred died.[75]

Not surprisingly, when the Commune of Messina rebelled against Spain in 1675, the provisional government could imagine no better means for galvanizing local support and communicating the goals of the revolution to surrounding cities than to establish a revolutionary newspaper—the first such known outside of England. Published in the newly designated official printing office, it chronicled cases of Spanish soldiers defecting to the side of the Messinese and their French allies in nearly every number. It regarded with high approval the signs that the Messinese

"were becoming very well accustomed" to campaigning under the French generals. And the reinforcement of the fortress of Taormina served, in the revolutionary paper's view, to demonstrate once more the "most exemplary justice" of Vivonne, the interim French viceroy, whom it praised at every occasion. A recent tempest that "ruined" Spanish ships was as worthy of celebration as the anniversary of the French victory at Porta Reale. And the paper brought to the attention of "every good Messinese citizen" information about the "many marriages celebrated between persons of that [French] nation and this nation."[76]

All these developments not only demonstrated the extraordinary power of the printed word; they also persuaded more and more printers, after the first tentative experiments, to invest money, spend time, and take risks for what was beginning to seem a less and less doubtful enterprise. Their productions, like those of the newsletter writers, grew like barnacles on the ship of state but were by no means identical with it. And their efforts helped turn information into a commodity and the peddling of information into a flourishing business involving many different types of publication strategies. Let us now follow them in the reasonings behind the choices they made.

Information Entrepreneurs

When printers and entrepreneurs wished to profit from particular events or series of events without making any long-term promises, they chose to deal in news books rather than newspapers. And to discover what sort of news books people might be buying next, they followed the newsletters—in one case, those furnished by a former Roman bookseller who went to Venice to take up work as an informer to his former comrades.[77] Choosing carefully among the available manuscript reports in circulation, news book entrepreneurs then put out pamphlets offering explanations to readers of whatever happened to be the event of the moment—from "skirmishes between the army of the Tuscan League and that of the Barberini" in 1643 to a "report on the tranquillity of Naples" following the Masaniello revolt. They described the "marvelous and stupendous work of the grand royal canal in the province of Languedoc for communication between the ocean and the Mediterranean" demonstrating the "powerful hand of the august monarch Louis XIV." And to drive home the point about the glory of this monarch they published the "Edict of the Most Christian King prohibiting Every Kind of Public Exercise of

the Pretended Reformed Religion" and repealing the previous Edict of Nantes.[78]

To make sure these miscellaneous tidbits of information whetted the appetite for more, they offered sequels: "The work you have in your hands is . . . just a taste of something more diffuse and more curious that you will immediately receive if you show yourself favorable to accepting this initiative"—a prospect that pamphlet printer Stefano Curti recognized to be practically certain, because "the things about the current wars are sought by everyone."[79] And for longer-term events they put out brief serial publications like Venetian printer Giovanni Pietro Pinelli's semi-annual *Letters* on Venetian naval battles.

To be sure, printers and entrepreneurs who dealt in news books might make an acceptable profit after purchasing the manuscript and deducting expenses, but rates of success varied widely. A brief manuscript might cost a couple of giulii.[80] To have a ream printed up might cost a couple of scudi (a *scudo* is the equivalent of twenty giulii) plus another two scudi for the paper.[81] Thus if the work fetched a quarter of a giulio, an average price, the modest ground-level entrepreneur could pay the rent and eat for a month and still have something left over.[82] Because sales were usually fairly brisk for political works, entrepreneurs often had large numbers printed up; they could then sell the original manuscript to other entrepreneurs.[83] The more ambitious could hope powerful personages might pay up to hundreds of times these amounts for dedications. And for special projects like genealogies of current princes they could expect as much income as their less adventurous colleagues might earn from putting out yet another edition of the best-selling Florentine *Pharmacopoeia* or the novels of Giulio Cesare Croce.[84] However, fashions changed; and as one printer unhappily complained as early as the turn of the seventeenth century, "those [books] that one puts out today might just as well be thrown to the fish tomorrow."[85]

Lodovico Grignani in Rome was among the many printers forced to offset the uncertainties of news book publication by a miscellany of various projects, such as printed handbills and other low-cost items for the university, as well as a series of maps.[86] The temporary Venetian seizure of Negroponte (Euboea) from the Ottoman Turks in 1623 gave occasion for his first newsbooks, and Grignani continued to average about five publications per year until the Treaty of Westphalia, which he reproduced. Not a writer himself, he regularly collaborated with a fixed group of writers for news about urban pageantry, including Alessio Pulci of

L'Aquila and Antonio Gerardi and Gregorio Porcia of Rome. For battle maps and siege reports, a popular form of visual journalism, he worked with Giacomo Lauro, who provided a magnificent plan of Orbetello being wrested from Spain by French forces in 1646, along with numerous maps of ancient and modern cities.[87] To guarantee the best sales, he relied upon the bookshop of Marcantonio Benvenuti in Piazza Pasquino, near where news was hawked and posted. To round out the income from sales of copies he solicited dedications to local dignitaries like Marcantonio Colonna, a Roman nobleman, and Lattanzio Lattanzi, a papal chamberlain.

Girolamo Albrizzi, a printer in Venice, was even more astute at turning news books into profits. Born to a family originating in the minor nobility of Bergamo, he built his printing and bookselling concern virtually from scratch in the 1660s. For his first periodical, he served only as the printer, and the Venetian friar Vincenzo Coronelli acted as entrepreneur. The tourist yearbook and almanac they produced was to remain in print for forty-three years. In the 1680s, when the Habsburg armies broke the siege of Vienna and advanced into Ottoman-occupied territories along the Danube, Albrizzi took the cue to provide an account of the new acquisitions.[88] Next he provided a weekly series, from June to September 1686, recounting the siege of Buda, offering each number to readers on a subscription basis like any other periodical. And if they wanted the "journals of the current wars that I am printing every week," he informed prospective readers, all they had to do was "pay six lire and four soldi in advance for six months." But the arrangement was not the same for every war. Each had its price, and Albrizzi offered a discount for news on the apparently less popular wars in the Levant and in Dalmatia, including a geographical supplement.[89]

Coronelli joined news books with visual journalism to market some of the most successful short-term serial publications of the century.[90] After starting out in Venice as an apprentice carpenter, moving to Ravenna to learn intaglio, and returning to Venice to join the Friars Minor, he gained enough practice and subsequently enough notoriety as a geographer to attract the attention of Colbert. Thus he secured the commission to provide the ten-foot globes now in boxes at La Villette in Paris for which he is chiefly famous. On his return to Venice around 1684, he founded the Accademia degli Argonauti to arrange subscription orders for an ambitious program of geographical works, "particularly, of those places where there are wars." His journalistic publications began with the op-

portunity provided by the capture of Morea in 1684, signaling a new Venetian assault on the Turkish possessions in Greece after the loss of Candia. He then joined forces with the local printer Domenico Padovanino, whose shop was designated by "the sign of Geography" and produced maps of the regions at war along with, optimistically enough, an account of Negroponte, which Francesco Morosini tried and failed to take back from the Turks in 1688.[91] At the same time he offered maps of the places in western Europe where war was raging, such as Mannheim, Franckenthal, and Freiburg. And if his visual journalism did not offer the same opportunities for critical thought as its written counterpart, nonetheless it may well have whetted appetites for more substantial fare.

Newspapers, on the other hand, appealed to entrepreneurs who preferred the greater probabilities of a regular income to the remote chance of high earnings by news books. They could hope for the century's apparently inexhaustible abundance of events to provide material. The regular compilation of similar stock promised savings in time and type, because title friezes, banners, or dedication lines could be left in place for many issues, and formats could be retained and simply filled up with new type.[92] They could hope that a constantly available forum for advertising might help them market other products and at the same time avoid the long periods of unemployment from project to project that plagued their colleagues trying to eke out a living by news book publication. It was not uncommon for newspaper entrepreneurs to demand payment in advance, and the monthly scudo Michele Castelli charged for his Genoa paper, at about half the cost of a newsletter sheet, was an attractive offer. And a hefty 36 percent profit was a reasonable expectation on a yearly outlay of some 170 scudi—that was what the Osanna family reported to the tax officials as having accrued to them from the Mantua gazette.[93]

In spite of their search for distinctiveness by varied type fonts and numbered issues, newspaper entrepreneurs closely imitated the newsletters. Like the newsletters, their publications appeared as weekly or biweekly sheets, one to twelve pages in length, with a brief title frieze and date at the top and divided according to the cities of origin of their stories. Like the newsletters, they often sported as titles just the name of the city of publication and the date, although in this respect *Macerata, Ancona,* and *Bologna* differed from the *Gazette* of Paris and the *Gazzetta di Genova* (not to be confused with another Genoa paper entitled *Genova*) and Turin's *Il sincero*. Again, like the newsletters, they concentrated al-

most exclusively on politics, with some attention to festivities and other occurrences of the sort. And when they, like the newsletters, indicated the sources of their information by phrases like "Letters of such-and-such a date from Utrecht bring the news that. . . ," often the letters in question were the newsletters. More than simple transcriptions of single newsletters, newspapers often amounted to concatenations of several. An average newsletter from Venice, for example, might include two or three pages of Venetian material plus a miscellany from Cologne or Rome. With more than twice the available space, a typical newspaper writer relied on information not only from his home place but from the newsletters of Venice, Vienna, Augusta, Brussels, Cologne, and Paris.[94]

Let us examine an actual example. The one I have in my hand as I write was printed in Bologna by Nicolò Tebaldini on November 21, 1643, and compiled by Lorenzo Pellegrini. It is an exceedingly modest affair. Containing a single folded sheet about twenty-eight by twenty centimeters, it is printed on the cheapest of paper. We are almost tempted to wonder just what the fuss over the new journalism was all about. The title "Bologna" and the date appear centered in tiny lettering in italics at the top. The opener concerns a papal military official on tour to inspect fortifications in Ferrara and Bologna. The closing story is about a Turkish ship grounded off Sardinia. In between, there is information about troop movements outside Modena in the War of Castro and about Cardinal Antonio Barberini's transfer to Perugia, closer to the fighting in the same war. The city of Vercelli is said to be preparing for a possible attack by arranging the arrival of foodstuffs, cannon, and a company of cavalry. Prince Tommaso of Savoy is said to be ill, giving opportunity for his mother, the duchess Cristina, to strengthen her hold on the regency government in Piedmont. Stories are separated only by indentation, and a wide variety of material may be included in a single paragraph. For instance, after the phrase "from Venice on the 14th of this month," we find information about the Archduke Leopold's arrival in Vienna, about Herr Alt's departure for the governorship of Flanders, and about the occupation of Moravia by imperial forces. Single paragraphs normally contain a single sentence many lines long and broken up only by semicolons. The world as seen from Bologna is reduced to three thousand words of breathless prose; and the modern historian, buried in the minutiae of seventeenth-century life, risks losing the thread of the argument.

The first newspaper entrepreneurs in Italy started out as newsletter writers in search of wider audiences. For Michele Castelli, founder of the Genoese newspaper, the necessity to feed a family of ten may have been a powerful inducement to seek patronage at an early stage in his career. In fact, his only known previous publication celebrated the coronation of Agostino Pallavicino as doge and declared its writer to be a "devoted servant" of the new doge's brother Alessandro. This and whatever other similar efforts he may have made apparently yielded unsatisfactory results. Instead, before the newspaper got off the ground, he survived by selling copies of a newsletter to officials in foreign governments. When he got around to compiling his newspaper with the help of his oldest son, he simply made a deal with a local printer named Pier Giovanni Calenzano and began distributing copies as far away as France.[95]

Castelli was soon followed in Genoa by Luca Assarino, whose life exemplified the adventurous search for opportunities that characterized the earliest gatherers of news. To be sure, the purely adventurous side of his personality appeared first. Born in Peru in 1602 of a noble father and raised in the scenic coastal town of Santa Margherita Ligure, he spent the nine years following his sixteenth birthday either in exile or in prison for various offenses ranging from possession of a weapon to desertion from military service to murder. As soon as he was freed for the last time he became embroiled in politics, and after narrowly escaping indictment for complicity in the Vachero conspiracy against Genoa, he dedicated his first literary efforts to improving his relations with the Genoese government.[96] Meanwhile, he gained enough independence by the literary renown accruing from his successful novel, entitled *La stratonica*, to hire himself out to the governments of Lucca and Modena as a newsletter writer about Genoese affairs. The Genoa newspaper, which he entitled *Il sincero*, was an extension of these activities.

In Naples, too, the first newspaper entrepreneur was an independent newsletter writer applying her initiative to new markets. Salomena Antonazzi's husband, Giovan Geronimo Favella, the founder of the newsletter business, started out as an actor, not a writer.[97] After failing to gain a permanent acting job in one of the companies connected with the royal court, or any other sort of patronage position in Naples, Favella went to sea as a privateer. But he soon gave up the perils of piracy for the comforts of home in Naples and began copying the Roman newsletters for sale to local customers. As his business grew, his dream of finding a niche in Neapolitan society finally came true. At his death in 1641 his now-

flourishing newsletter business went to his widow, who ran it for a time with a certain Don Emilio Saccano and then began printing the sheets as a newspaper. Thus was born the *News from Rome and Other Parts of the World.*

As the advantages of newspaper publishing came to be wider known, new entrepreneurs emerged whose backgrounds were entirely extraneous to the newsletter network. Domenico Antonio Parrino came from a printing family in Naples, but family quarrels drove him out of the industry and into acting. After touring Italy as a member of the company of Queen Christina of Sweden and translating Spanish plays on the side, he got help from agents of the duke of Modena to recover his printing patrimony.[98] Soon he turned his shop into a veritable literary salon. In 1684 he struck a deal to supply newspaper stories and half the necessary paper to Camillo Cavallo, a local printer, in return for newsletters, paper, the use of presses, and half the profits. Newspaper publication led to other publications on newsworthy items, like the festivities for the marriage of King Charles II of Spain to Mariana of Austria in 1690, as well as books on local lore and history, with some prompting from the viceroy and collaboration by a local cultural figure, Domenico Aulisio.[99]

When some of the best-established printers in Italy began to take up newspaper production, they turned the typically subservient relationship of printers to writers completely around. In Mantua, the family Osanna, ducal printers since 1588, commissioned a certain Salvatore Castiglioni to prepare the extracts from the newsletters.[100] Only slightly less prestigious were the printers Amadeo Massi and Lorenzo Landi in Florence, who had achieved some renown collaborating on news books, historical works, and engravings and had then opened a subsidiary in nearby Pisa. Together they provided reprints of Castelli's Genoese newspaper.[101] Their success encouraged another well-established Florentine printer, Pietro Cecconcelli, to buy and print a newsletter about Germany, written by a certain Gallacini.

In a relatively close-knit community like Rimini, newspaper printing even managed to gain a certain amount of local respectability. Simbene Simbeni evidently did not regard it as beneath the dignity of a family that had achieved entrance to the local patriciate by monopolies on printing and on the circulation of rags for paper. This was the kind of dignity deeply coveted by Giovanni Felice Dandi, who used newspapers as a steppingstone on the road to social improvement. For him, the short-term *Giornale militare,* covering the siege of Buda from 1686 to 1687 in com-

petition with the similar journal of Girolamo Albrizzi, was merely a means to achieving greater things.[102] After publishing the regular Rimini newspaper for a time, he moved on to Ravenna to work with his brother Giovanni Pellegrino, an aspiring literary figure. Thus they graduated from compiling newspapers to the even more genteel task of compiling a literary journal, largely by cribbing articles from Benedetto Bacchini's pioneering *Giornale de' letterati* in Parma.

Such were the origins of what was to become one of the most influential industries in modern times. But apart from their advantages to writers and entrepreneurs, newspapers were conduits for information; and although we know far more about the information they circulated than about who read them and to what effect, the time has come to test some common assumptions about their role in early modern society.

The Lessons of Information

As the business developed, news publications provided those seventeenth-century readers who read them with what could only be called a political education. Even when reporting what appeared to be dry facts, their accounts of government policies and the actions of ministers showed the most hated features of early modern creative financing at work. In covering the million-ducat loan procured by the Spanish government from merchants in Naples and Genoa in 1641, the Milan paper noted that it was secured on the exploitative taxes and gabelles in Naples and Sicily, while the government demanded cloth enough to make six thousand military uniforms at the same time.[103] The implications of such information were no different from those of an account in the Florence paper of Louis XIV's new sales tax, for which the tax farmers had already offered to pay sixty million francs, while the clergy, stoutly defending its tax exemption, offered a few million one time only.[104] However commonplace such policies may have been, putting them in print drew particular attention to them.

The merits and demerits of public policies offered material for analysis in even the officially licensed press. Let us hear some examples from *Riminio*. The newspaper criticized the Spanish in Milan for increasing grain prices while drawing hands away from the fields for the war with Portugal. It condemned the "inability" of the Spanish governor in the port city of Finale, near Genoa, who raised the cost of foodstuffs and incurred the hatred of the inhabitants. The paper contrasted this with the

situation in France, where Louis XIV combined equity with fiscal prudence in prosecuting the corrupt finance minister Nicolas Fouquet. "The blood of the poor called for vendetta and justice," it proclaimed; and "the king was moved . . . by zeal for good government and by the desire to remove abuses."[105] Readers who might know something about the far more serious depredations of Jules Mazarin were thus invited to side with the paper or perhaps take issue with it. Louis XIV, after all, was no saint.

When discontent boiled over into revolution in the Kingdom of Naples, newspapers all over the peninsula were hot on the trail of events throughout the 1640s. Already at the end of 1644, they registered amazement about the insistence of Spanish ministers on finding new sources of revenue within the struggling kingdom. The people had in fact "lost respect" for the ministers, and disaster would surely follow.[106] Once the Masaniello revolt got under way, the papers referred to the provisional government of 1647 as a "republic" and covered the arrival of French forces to aid the revolutionaries in December of that year.[107] They found the developments to be "exciting," as the discontent spread to other parts of the realm.[108] By the end of January 1648, they reported that the provisional government was offering aid to any city in the surrounding territory that decided to join in rebelling against the nobility and the Spanish. Potential corevolutionaries, they explained, "were asked to chase out all those who were governing and to elect new governors, otherwise they would lose all their privileges and prerogatives."[109] They covered the restoration of order by Don John of Austria and, in 1650, a new outbreak in Palermo, which was swiftly put down.[110] The Macerata newspaper ended its coverage on a positive note: "It is said that the viceroy frequently has meetings about keeping the good government of this kingdom in peace, justice, and prosperity, and for this purpose he has lowered the price of meat and other foodstuffs."[111] Readers were thus invited to consider whether a real modus vivendi between ruler and people had indeed been found.

Events in England provided equally inspiring material for newspapers to expatiate on the struggles between rulers and peoples. The civil war was already well under way when most newspapers started up; and local problems took the lead for several years before the English question got full treatment. Nevertheless, the papers duly recorded the fall of the monarchy and the rise of Oliver Cromwell, and their accounts of the next quarter-century were often even insightful. By March 1659, they noted that Richard Cromwell was in serious trouble because antagonism had

resumed between the army and the new Parliament.[112] During the Exclusion Crisis they reported the king's dismay about the new demands of his Oxford Parliament (1681) and suggested that if he gave in to the exclusion of the duke of York, the House of Commons would not stop until they had reduced him "to a private person."[113] During the Glorious Revolution they noted that Halifax "made every effort to turn the government into a republic, although others wanted an elective king as in Poland but depending on the Parliament."[114] To readers in a kingdom, in a duchy, in a marquisate, and even in an old republic, the spectacle of a people determining its form of rule was extraordinary indeed.

Gaining a general sense of the rise and fall of states, of course, was one thing; and there is no doubt that newspapers provided this. Gaining a clear day-to-day picture of events was another; and here newspapers were of much less help. If readers interested in the affairs of their cities and the world actually expected accurate information from their readings, that is not always what they got; and the elaborate process whereby information became news was partly to blame. Each political event afforded opportunities to scores of writers to offer their "eyewitness" accounts—a "letter" from "N. N.," purportedly "written aboard the Venetian ship *La Capitana*," a "letter" from a "Col. Bortolazzi" at Clissa to his brothers, a "letter" from "G. P. A." at San Teodoro under siege, and a "copy of the request presented in Venice to the Most Excellent Collegio by the Most Illustrious and Excellent Signor Antonio Marino Cappello," admiral of the Venetian armies in the Greek archipelago, "which came into the hands of myself, Captain N. N."[115] Some such accounts were commissioned by or otherwise obtained by officials for use by their governments. All were subject to an elaborate itinerary beginning with personal testimony and word of mouth and ending with the written and printed page.

As soon as such accounts left the battle scene or wherever they originated, they entered the complex ramifications of the newsletter network by the same means as other information: namely, by thievery, bribery, espionage, or commerce. Even reports on local events, by the time they hit the press, were often far removed from authorial control. In a typical case, a certain Fabrizio Benconi in Rome purchased, for resale to local printer Francesco Felice Mancina, a work called *The Tiber Flood* from a Venetian printer named Francesco Pitteri, who happened to be renting a room above a tavern. Where Pitteri got it nobody knows.[116] The work gave such an inaccurate account of papal water-control measures that it

was quickly banned. But this was only a minor example of how such spurious stories might be lurking behind major items in the news.

Newspapers sometimes simply parroted information word for word from the newsletters, and here the serendipitous gleanings of the persistent archive habitué allows us to trace the tortuous paths of this story. An unusual collection of newsletters sent from Bologna, along with the local newspaper, to the papal secretary of state appears to include the same sheets available to the newspaper writer in that relatively small city. For instance, the newspaper of January 22, 1648, referred to "letters from Antwerp of the 3rd of this month" reporting French efforts to block the peace negotiations in Holland and Spanish recruitment of soldiers; and in fact, a newsletter from Antwerp dated January 3, 1648, carried the same information, under the more precise rubric, "from Brussels."[117] What the Bolognese newsletter of March 1, 1648, reported about Venetian action against the Bosnian Turks appeared almost word for word in the Bolognese newspaper of March 4: "From Dalmatia it has been heard that General Foscolo was made to march with the whole army to Sebenico, where he was to decide what to do; and first he routed in battle a troop of soldiers sent by the pasha of Bosnia, who wanted to punish those of Bernissa." Only the last place name was changed, to "Beorniza."[118] Indeed, competing newspapers published in the same city, such as the two parallel ventures in Ancona in 1677, whose stories were based on the same sources, often produced nearly identical accounts.[119] Depending on the local situation, newspapers might modify the wording in their reports: France was merely "France" in Venice; but in Milan, it was "the enemy."[120] If the news in the newsletters happened to be inaccurate, the newspapers, by following the newsletters very closely, at least did not compound the error.

Simply transcribing the newsletters, however, was not without its hazards. The *Napoli* of February 19, 1681, reported under the rubric of "London" concerning the increasing tension created by the Exclusion Crisis in England, when the king sent his last response to the demands of the Parliament. Under the rubric of "Paris" in the same newspaper, apparently based on yet another newsletter, it claimed that "the latest letters of London report the kingdom to be very tranquil." In addition, particularly partial newsletters, adopted by newspapers in their entirety, produced particularly partial newspapers. That was the case of the Venice column of the Genoa newspaper printed on the basis of information provided by Giovanni Quorli, a newsletter writer in Venice, "very inimical to

us," as the Venetian ambassador complained. It repeated, word for word, the newsletter's squalid litany of abuses and mistakes in the conduct of the wars in Candia and Dalmatia, including disagreements between the generals and charges of dereliction of duty hurled between one official and another.[121] The same partiality was repeated in Florence, where the newspaper was nothing but a pirated version of its Genoese counterpart.

Most of the time, newspaper writers picked and chose material from the newsletters and worked it up to suit their purposes. This the Genoa newspaper practically admitted in 1644 when it reported that "the newsletters from Germany contain the following, in substance," thereby justifying a partial resumé, or "the letters brought by the French post are ... all of little moment," thereby justifying the omission.[122] In the course of shortening accounts, newspapers inevitably shifted word order and changed emphasis, sometimes without too much loss.[123] Other times, inconsistencies crept in. The newsletter of Milan of February 5, 1648, collected in the group of documents from Bologna that we have been using, noted that the forces of Prince Tommaso in the Piedmont civil war had evacuated the area around Novara. Supposedly based on the same information, the Bologna newspaper of February 12, 1648, reported that the forces of Prince Tommaso had returned to Milan without ever even entering the area in question.[124] In another case of slippage between one account and another, "seven French privateers from Toulouse" on the way to reinforce the Venetian troops in Candia became ships from "the Venetian fleet."[125] The newspaper compilers faced as formidable a task in mastering the hundreds of tiny details in all these stories as does the modern historian.

For those journalists who occasionally relied on news books for information, the choice of a particular account was as important as the manner of condensing it. Such was the case of some reporting on the execution of King Charles I of England. In fact, a contemporary tract entitled *King Charles: His Speech on the Scaffold,* published hours after the event and now regarded as reasonably accurate, relied (so it claimed) on information from "some gentlemen that wrote," apparently the two clerks of the court, John Phelps and Daniel Broughton. An Italian translation of the pamphlet, probably printed in Venice, modified only the time to suit the Continental clock (10 A.M. becomes "17 hours"), the date to correspond to the Gregorian calendar (January 30, 1648, becomes February 9, 1649), and the title to suit more dramatic tastes *(The Last Words Spoken*

by the King of Britain on the Scaffold, Where He Was Decapitated before His Royal Palace of Vitheal).[126] The title change pointed to an interpretation that was becoming increasingly common on the Continent, namely, that the wide space before Whitehall was chosen as a location for the deed not in order, as the pamphlet claimed, to provide the populace with a better view but in order to add to the egregiousness of the insult.

Not all information concerning this event came from the pamphlet based on Phelps and Broughton, nor did it all originate in London. At least according to Pietro Socini, author of the Turin newspaper, London news was temporarily blocked by the civil war, and the Paris *Gazette* of Théophraste Renaudot was suspended by the Fronde. Apparently he had missed, or else chose to ignore, the February 11, 1649, number of the *Gazette,* which devoted seven short lines to the subject. Thus, he said, his news about the event came by way of Cologne. The supposed version from Cologne was in fact a lampoon circulated in France by the royalist party in the Fronde, with which the Turin government was loosely allied. And the purpose of this lampoon was evidently to discredit the new republican government of England and motivate possible allies to aid the preservation of monarchy. This version had been reprinted in Turin by Franco Ferrofino and dated March 18, 1649, with the title, *Another Account of the Barbarous and Cruel Death of the King of England, with Greater Details Found to Be Truer, and with Information concerning the Revolutions in Scotland and Ireland.*[127]

Socini's unacknowledged source, from which he copied the theatrical sentiments sometimes word for word, imparted an artificial journalistic personality to his own work. "The barbarous death of the king of England," he began, "occurred on the morning of February 9, 1649, on a Tuesday, the day destined to the execrable parricide." The borrowed interpretation passed into every line. "The scaffold was prepared before the royal palace in order to heighten the outrage." Socini then paraphrased a section where the author of the original text invented an episode showing a French role. "The diplomatic corps, alarmed about the hasty decision, especially the French ambassador, tried to avoid a tragedy; but they were not even allowed to speak." Socini gave an ironical thrust to Parliament members' reply to the ambassadors, explaining, "those gentlemen had other very great fish to fry." Unoriginal though it was, Socini's account earned him the approval of early-twentieth-century journalism historian Enrico Jovane for "diligence" and "obvious disapproval of excesses."[128]

Between the original account and Socini's version there were of course the usual choices, changes, and condensations—mainly, it seems, to tone down the polemical ardor of such statements as the following:

My pen falls from my hand, and I am seized and possessed by such horror that I seem scarcely able to arrive at the catastrophe of this bloody tragedy. The king, the best king in the world, is drawn like a lamb to the slaughter, and subject to these barbarous arms to quench their rage and their furor. He is taken from his prison to the place prepared for this execrable act, and there he walks, unconstrained, and Death cannot efface his sacred visage, the living image of God, to replace it with his own.[129]

Wrote Socini, "My pen falls from my hand, and I seem scarcely able to arrive at the catastrophe of that bloody tragedy. A king, the best king in the world, is drawn like a lamb to the slaughter."[130] The rest he omitted. Again, the original: "Having arrived at the scaffold, he asks to speak to the Parliament, saying he had some secret of conscience to reveal to them, but he is denied"; and Socini's version: "He asks to speak to the Parliament, but the executioners forbid him."

Although he modified the narrative, Socini did not modify the basic interpretation. The original account explained why Fairfax, Cromwell, and Lord Say dressed up in hangman's costumes to perform the execution—an invention worthy of modern cinematography: "You should know that the ordinary executioners, though accustomed to bloodshed, were horrified at the prospect of such a frightful execution, and fled." Socini improvised, "The hangmen however were too horrified to proceed to the execution and refused." Socini even cut the king's last words. What appeared in the original as "Take, traitors and rebels, and sate yourselves with my blood, and force the heavens by this last crime to punish you for all the others," became, in Socini's version, "Traitors and rebels, sate yourselves with my blood." The original closed with a moral obliquely referring to the crisis in France: "All the elements will conspire to bring about the destruction of these barbarians, if men and princes do not take this task upon themselves." Socini naturally left that out.

Whatever the sources happened to be, the reliability of news accounts depended to a considerable degree on the scruples of the writers. Yet writers' rush to get a scoop often exceeded their caution about publishing falsehoods, and Italian newspapers were not the only ones at fault. The writer of the London *Protestant Mercury* complained, during the

Stuart Restoration, about rival newspapers, which, according to him, "to make their news sell, take many things in trust from the first reporter."[131] Things could get much worse, as the historian Girolamo Brusoni realized when he showed that a printed letter in circulation in 1657, supposedly from a soldier reporting a battle between the Venetian and Turkish armies before the fortress of Tenedo in Turkey, was entirely fictitious.[132] And when the Venetian ambassador to Genoa in 1680 complained about a report that anticipated the relief of Vienna by several days, his objection joined that of Carlo Cartari in Rome, who noted that the battle of Zhuravno between Polish and Turkish armies in September 1676 was reported more than a week before the fact.[133] And if Roman newsmongers sometimes wrote their accounts even of local weddings, funerals, and pageants beforehand in order to be able to sell copies during the event, as the diarist Giacinto Gigli complained, the practice was also known in England, where the scaffold speech of William Howard, Viscount Stafford, was on sale almost immediately after his death.[134]

The attractions of a good story were sometimes almost impossible to resist, especially where, as in humanist historiography, the words of an important personage could lend explanatory force and emotional realism to the account. Take this example of Mazarin's death scene in *Riminio*. "[His last words were,] 'Sire, I humbly beg pardon for my failings,' and thus [all left the room] with tears in their eyes and sobs on their lips." The account then went into a discussion of heroism: "Here is this great man . . . triumphant not only in life, but also in death, [who] conquered not only himself by his great intrepidity and self-command but also his enemies by goodness and magnanimity."[135] In fact, Mazarin's last words were probably to his surgeons, because two days before he died he forbade anyone else, including the king and queen, to enter his chamber at the palace in Vincennes.[136] But this story was no more fantastic than *Colonia*'s account of the treason trial of Chancellor Hieronym Radziejowscy of Poland in 1656, reporting the conversation between the king of Sweden and the accused man. "The king of Sweden spoke to him as follows: Is this the faithfulness that you promised me; did you not know what the law of justice provides against such perfidy and against disloyal traitors?" Radziejowscy supposedly replied, "I received so many benefits from you that I should have had no reason to conspire against you; but I am a man; and I have sinned."[137] No other document records such an episode.[138]

At least for foreign news, particularly inventive writers could count on the difficulties imposed by seventeenth-century travel conditions to prevent readers from confirming their stories. The tactic was so well known that Girolamo Brusoni noted, "the distance of the places and the lack of information gives journalists [*novellisti*] great freedom."[139] To arrive in Rimini, situated just north of the center of the eastern coast of the peninsula, news might take six days from Milan, nine or ten from Genoa, and ten from Rome or Florence. Compare that with the four weeks news might take to arrive by normal mail from Madrid, and nearly the same amount of time from Paris, London, and Warsaw, or three weeks from Hamburg, two weeks from Vienna, and eleven days from Munich. By the time anyone discovered the fraud, the affair in question was likely to be long past; and newspapers rarely published corrections of errors previously made.

Recognizing the prevalence of these departures from fact, faulty interpretations, and inattention to detail, some writers simply admitted to forming their accounts under the guidance of artistic caprice. No one could blame a certain Nicolo Vellaio for framing his account of the first two years of the War of Candia in 1647 as a message from the afterlife transmitted by a dead writer.[140] Nor could another writer in 1669 be faulted for imagining that the very information being presented in his account had been read by the sultan or for expressing this in a jingle: "Reading the letter the great sultan / With these ill tidings of the war / Took his scepter in his hand / and threw it on the floor."[141] In his news book, "New and True Relation of a Recent Battle in Candia," he covered the last year of the Candia war, on the eve of the Venetian surrender of the island, "in the form of an extraordinary newsletter from Otranto." There seemed no reason not to suppose the sultan might be upset after a battle in which six thousand Turks and two hundred Christians died. And in any case, myth, poetry, and news were often difficult to distinguish.

More frequently, writers simply admitted the hopelessness of their task. They could scarcely deny that "the first information always circulates with some prejudicial effect either from the desire of the listener or the passion of the bearer."[142] And thus, when civil war broke out in England, an apologetic Théophraste Renaudot, founder of the *Gazette de Paris*, noted, "The affairs of the kingdom have never been as confused or in such an unfortunate state as they are at present."[143] His experience was no different from that of Pietro Socini, of *Successi del mondo,* during the Piedmont civil wars, who exclaimed, "the news we have concerning the

affairs of Turin is so rare and uncertain that one might almost with more frankness talk about the affairs of Japan."[144] And from the vantage point of the gazette of Bologna, "The news of Naples [during the Masaniello revolt] is very exciting, and it is contradictory in many things." Writers in this last conflict recognized that tainted news was almost impossible to avoid. And choosing between different accounts could be difficult—especially when "sources on the royal side insist that the Spanish have seized a position of great consequence near the Customs Office," whereas "the popular party says they have seized [three fortresses], without mentioning the Customs Office at all, . . and they say many other things that seem dubious because of contradictions."[145] Similarly, although "the Spaniards insist that there are enough money and provisions for their armies," the popular party maintained that "lack of money is forcing the royalists to petition the Genoese and others who have feudal properties in the kingdom to contribute subsidies."[146] All the writers and their audiences could hope for was that, in the words of one, "time will reveal the truth."[147] More often, time only revealed more versions.

Editorial choices that were not simply the result of faulty sources, unscrupulousness, or artistic caprice were occasionally dictated, like those of some newsletters, by the writers' own adherence to one or another of the parties contending for power. And whereas a pro-Whig paper in England described the murder of a prominent Whig politician named Thomas Thynne in 1682 as a vendetta for a verbal insult, a pro-Tory paper called it a vendetta for a previous attack made by Thynne's men on the future assassin. Similarly, when a pro-Whig paper reported that the duke of Monmouth, favored by the Whigs as a candidate for succession to the throne over the unacceptable future James II, had been welcomed back into the favor of King Charles II, no pro-Tory paper picked up this false news.[148] Far away from Restoration England, two competing newspapers covered the news in Genoa, one from a French point of view, the other from a Spanish one. And what, from the standpoint of the former, was a simple movement of French and Spanish troops in Montferrat became, in the latter, a homily on the senselessness of war. "The people in these areas flee to the other side of the river [Po] to seek refuge with their possessions in [the fortress of] Casale," it reported, "and since the Po is overflowing, and they have trouble crossing, the sight of those poor people waiting on the shore all terrified by the suffering and by the danger of being surprised by the French excites unimaginable compassion."[149]

More often, writers of printed news made their editorial choices in or-

der to content those in power. Critical of policies on occasion, they nevertheless omitted politically delicate newsletter material that could get them into difficulties. No one would have suspected from the following story in the Bologna newspaper that anything out of the ordinary might be afoot in the Venetian envoy's trip to Constantinople: "Letters from Venice dated the eighth of this month say that the Senate sent Secretary Ballerini to Constantinople to care for the interests of that republic, and that for this purpose he boarded an English ship bound for that destination."[150] But the newsletter sent by the papal representative in Bologna to the secretary of state along with his regular dispatch, a newsletter that we may imagine was available to the newspaper writer, revealed a story of espionage and intrigue: "On Monday there was the departure of Secretary Ballerini on an English ship bound for Constantinople, where in order to slip in incognito he will change his name and pretend to be a Walloon merchant; and although it was said that he was going via Leghorn, it has been subsequently understood that he set sail directly for Smyrna."[151] Equally circumspect were the gazette writers who refused to pick up a story in the Roman newsletters during an illness of Innocent XI that "if excommunication were applicable to the negotiations going on outside the conclave, the cardinals would be more embarrassed than the women who go about dressed so scantily."[152]

Concerning local affairs, writers of printed news assumed an encomiastic tone rarely matched in their writing about other places. Otherwise there seems little reason to suppose that the "princely virtues" of the new doge, Giovanni Battista Durazzo, extolled by the *Genova* writer on July 29, 1639, were any more extraordinary than those of his fellow rulers in other states, even though his "piety, prudence, justice, vigilance, reverence," and "a certain affable gravity that awakens love in others," the qualities, in short, that "have elevated him to the supreme dignity," would also "guarantee us a good government." Nor is there any reason to imagine that the "ancient families" or, at least, the "legitimate parentage" of the Bologna writer's local ruling class were any greater than those of, say, the Venetians.[153]

Nonetheless, when not praising the qualities of the personages, writers often expatiated on the beauty of the ceremony, making good use of their considerable space advantages over the newsletters to fill entire pages with, for instance, an account of a Corpus Christi celebration in Naples in 1685. There we find lists of the personages involved, the procession,

the "infinite number of torches" lighting the way, the "most wonderful machines" employed, the "charming and ingenious fountain of immeasurable height" constructed for the occasion, the cannon shots fired from the forts and answered by the galleys in the bay, the "sumptuous altar" prepared in the cathedral, the sermons, and the universal edification of all.[154] To similar affairs elsewhere, the newsletter writers rarely allocated more than a few precious lines.

In recounting military exploits, writers of printed news inevitably sided with the forces allied to their governments, referring to "our armies" and "our battles," whether that meant the local armies or those of all Christianity.[155] Alluding to insufficiently glowing reports, a Venetian news book writer excoriated "the unchristian malice of those who . . . give their conjectures to the vulgar" about the probability of defeat at sea by the Ottoman Turks and "discredit the hopes that everyone must have for the advantageous progress of the justest war."[156] After all, Divine Providence was always on the side of whatever state one happened to be writing from. Thus, a letter concerning the acquisition of Oneglia by the Genoese in August 1672 and printed in Genoa could note, "This is the continuation of our cause, which, because it is entirely just, is promoted by the most partial patronage of the Most Holy Virgin, who does not allow her feast days to go by without adding the glories and benefits of her protection to the Most Serene Republic."[157] And no matter what the army did, it was better than the enemy's—and in the War of Castro, in which the duke of Modena and allies, including the grand duke of Tuscany, sought to prevent the papal takeover of a small fortified town, that meant, according to the *Firenze* writer, better than the papacy's. For "if excesses actually occurred (God forfend), they were introduced by them into this war."[158]

Newspaper writers never forgot that their continuity in print depended to a considerable extent upon the good pleasure of those in charge. Not by chance, the Turin newspaper's most favorable information about the duke of Savoy came out on the day he gave its entrepreneur a monopoly on news publication.[159] Official injunctions to go gently on all governments and avoid interfering in state affairs at home were not limited to Genoa, where compliance with them was the precondition for a privilege to print the newspaper.[160] Once such injunctions became well known, they only served to increase the suspicion that news distribution was being controlled. So noted Gregorio Leti, when he asked, "Tell me, if you please, do the gazette writers write without license from

their princes? Certainly not. Therefore the princes are those who cause the newspapers to circulate everywhere every day; because if they did not agree to this, they could prohibit them with a simple motion."[161]

Indeed, the newspapers, like the newsletters, at least sometimes received their stories directly from the governments in question. And Louis XIII himself was not the only ruler known to be the author of battle reports, in this case, for the Paris *Gazette*.[162] Equally unimpeachable was the probable origin of a notice in the Milan paper calling for all the provinces to supply their military contributions without delay for the next campaign.[163] Official insertions such as a report on the end of the plague in Lecco in the Genoa paper, including a letter from the chief physician, not only provided information for townspeople but also gave opportunities for statements in support of the local regime.[164] And when the Turin paper proclaimed "rigorous enforcement of the new arms control measure," it commented that this "will make the streets safer at night."[165] Similarly, insertions demanded by foreign governments, as by the Milanese to the Genoa newspaper in 1645, provided occasions for statements in support of the allies.[166]

Although privileges for publishing secured from governments often specified payment for official stories, forced retractions usually had to be inserted gratis. An example in Naples occurred in 1693, when the whole city was locked in a three-way struggle between the political establishment under Viceroy F. Benavides Davila, count of Santo Stefano, the ecclesiastical establishment under Archbishop Giacomo Cantelmo Stuart, and the intellectual establishment, including the prominent atomist philosopher Francesco Valletta. Responding to popular outrage against ecclesiastical meddling in civil life, the viceroy took the radical step of abolishing the local Inquisition. The archbishop parried by giving special commissions to the bishops of the kingdom to act as itinerant Inquisition officers and went ahead with some so-called heresy trials. And when he obtained the abjuration of two supposed heretics connected to the intellectual establishment, the local newspaper writer, thinking to score points among those in charge, reported favorably on the archbishop's activity. The viceroy, however, seeking to avoid offense to either the city or the church, forced a highly tendentious retraction in the following number, to the effect that "the deputation of this most faithful city of Naples, because of the inconveniences resulting from the Holy Office of the Inquisition, has expressed intense resentment, because the Most Excellent Cardinal Archbishop did not give [the accused persons] up to the secular

courts."[167] That way, the viceroy would not have to seem soft on heresy while defending himself against encroachments on his power. Readers who understood the Neapolitan newspaper's delicate juggling act could be excused for failing to take its statements too literally.

Generally speaking, early modern readers appear to have been well aware of the defects of contemporary journalism. And from his vantage point in Rotterdam, where newspapers of every sort arrived, Pierre Bayle inveighed against writers who distorted the truth. "Every day they furnish a new comedy," he exclaimed.[168] When the French armies crossed the Rhine in 1672, newspapers sympathetic to the Dutch spoke of nothing but a few skirmishes in which French prisoners had been taken or deserters had been observed. The Paris *Gazette,* on the other hand, spoke of nothing but the enemy's losses and the tribute to be exacted. When the Germans crossed into French territory in 1694, the Paris *Gazette* concentrated on French success in holding the line and pushing them back. On the other hand, gazettes favorable to the Germans, ignoring all this, gave an exact register of the villages pillaged by the German armies, powder magazines burned, and Frenchmen beaten. During the sieges of Namur in 1692 and 1696, gazettes favorable to the League of Augsburg invented so many imaginary assaults, in which the French lost such an infinite number of men, that continuing the attack ought to have been impossible without a miracle. Far from apologizing for these shortcomings, indeed, the gazette writers seemed to glory in them. "There is no gazette writer so abashed," Bayle noted, "as not to hope for immortality from all the absurd falsehoods he invents in his pipe dreams."[169] He conceded that they might fear punishment for publishing unapproved truths. But he added that greed and vanity were equally powerful motives for publishing only what readers wanted to hear. And he classed the gazettes among the libelous and incorrect writings that "spread throughout history an impenetrable chaos of incertitude."[170]

Samuel Butler, the author of *Hudibras,* also attributed the defects of journalism for the most part to shameless greed, and he furnished the century's most memorable caricature of the newsmonger. He is, Butler claimed,

a retailer of rumor, that takes upon trust, and sells as cheap as he buys. He deals in a perishable commodity, that will not keep: for if it be not fresh it lies upon his hands and will yield nothing. True or false is all one to him; for novelty being the grace of both, a truth grows stale as soon as a lie; and as a slight suit will last as

well as a better while the fashion holds, a lie serves as well as truth till new ones come up. He is little concerned whether it be good or bad, for that does not make it more or less news; and, if there be any difference, he loves the bad best, because it is said to come soonest; for he would willingly bear his share in any public calamity, to have the pleasure of hearing and telling it.[171]

For Butler, faulty journalism was just one more example of how little was really known in the world. "Errors and impostures prevail everywhere," he exclaimed, "like the ancient barbarians or modern Turks, that use to invade the civiler part of the world with numerous forces and subdue them," not by superior strategies but "by the brute force of their numbers."[172]

The Lessons of Disinformation

But what was the overall effect of faulty or manipulated information? To find out, we must assume a public of readers who cared about what they read. That excludes the likes of John Wilmot, earl of Rochester and Butler's contemporary, who could only conclude, "The world, ever since I can remember, has been still insupportably the same, that 'twere vain to hope that there will be any alterations; and therefore I can have no curiosity for news."[173] Apparently, too much information sometimes produced a kind of nausea—although in this case the nausea may have come from too many stimuli of other sorts as well. Judging by what he read, the entire population appeared to Wilmot to be divided between "spies, beggars, and rebels" and various permutations and combinations of these. "Hypocrisy is the only vice in decay among us," he exclaimed, because "few men here dissemble being rascals, and no woman disowns being a whore."[174]

From what can be concluded on the basis of our evidence, it seems that no one before the eighteenth century seriously believed that news publications themselves provided much of an indicator of what went on in readers' minds. Indeed, many believed that what circulated among the multitudes must be far more inflammatory than anything anyone would dare to print and that governments ignored such opinions at their peril. When Thomas Hobbes said that "the world is governed by opinion," to which even the powerful were commanded to conform, he was voicing a commonly held notion.[175] Nor was John Milton, in the *Areopagitica*, the only one to view public opinion as a tribunal. Hired historian Vittorio Siri, writing in 1667, claimed, "The generality of men consists of an in-

exorable tribunal instituted by nature to judge with the fullest liberty and to pronounce upon the actions not only of rulers but also of private and humble persons, to allot to them the blame or praise that they deserve."[176]

Gregorio Leti went so far as to suggest that the allotment of praise and blame might be effective in holding governments accountable for their actions. Tyrants, he explained, used to commit crimes knowing their evil actions would never be made public and that, indeed, their very presence would inspire awe and adoration. All this had changed. Now rulers, fearing the circulation of adverse reports, kept their more irresponsible impulses in check. "They see their peoples all set with their tongues wagging ready to spread throughout the public squares the poison of discord that can turn monarchies into republics," he said. "Therefore, if people's silence turned princes into tyrants, peoples' constant jabbering has turned tyrants into princes."[177]

While these writers considered the significance of what they observed to be a better-informed public, initiatives in the area of jurisprudence tended to break down patterns of secrecy and reserve that shielded the instruments of domination from scrutiny and discussion. Here, the exclusive use of the Latin language (except in Venice, where Venetian held sway) not only contributed to the continuation of a distinguished scholarly tradition but also symbolized the sacredness of power and preserved the distance that separated the vernacular-speaking public from the political elites. Nevertheless, in the late seventeenth century the first vernacular commentators began to appear. The pioneer of them all, Giambattista De Luca, a jurist based in Rome, addressed his effort specifically to the need for citizens to know the law in order to protect their rights. Accordingly, he explained in detail each element of the "civil, canon, feudal, and municipal law, moralized in the Italian language," for the benefit not only of princes, whom such knowledge would permit to govern better, but also for the benefit of the litigants themselves. This way, he suggested, "they can, as much as possible, escape the tyranny of lawyers."[178] From publishing the secrets of jurisprudence to recognizing the impropriety, in a world increasingly preoccupied by problems of verification, of the approximative traditional methods of evidence in criminal trials was only a small step, but except in England, it would not be taken until the following century.[179] On the other hand, the public may well have been ready to consider the impropriety of defective journalism.

Far away from proverbially lawyer-infested Rome and Naples, the

University of Padua jurist Giulio Dal Pozzo went still further. He addressed his "Civil Institutes," a work claiming to reconcile Roman and Venetian law with the commentaries of ancient and modern jurists, to the same audience. "To anyone who wonders why I have chosen to write in my native language" (by which he meant Italian, not Venetian), he responded, paraphrasing an argument of De Luca, "since the laws speak to all who have to obey them, they ought to be understood by all."[180] He defended his choice on the basis of the government's need to justify its actions before a reasoning audience, even if he retained the traditional distinction between *public* and *private*. Thus, "When the government imposes a gabelle, this regards primarily the public utility, because the public sustains the armies in time of war or restores the treasury in time of peace. But [such things] comprise the utility of private persons by consequence, because the public maintains peace and religion, which are the most precious capital of Man."[181] The only good reason for keeping quiet about politics was a purely practical one: because public affairs "are infinite . . . not because . . . public affairs cannot be brought to the attention also of him who does not govern."[182] In principle, the discourse of power was shared by all.

Of course, not everyone who picked up a law book or a newspaper worried about whether sovereignty reposed in one or in many, whether the right of rule was ceded permanently by the body politic or only temporarily, whether the public had a just recourse against a tyrant, or any of the other ideas currently making the rounds of the theorists à la mode. But anyone who could think about a law could think about an obligation, and then perhaps about judging the propriety or impropriety of political actions. And anyone who could think that way about political actions might be able to perform them, by participating in a call for change of rulership or in an action to bring about such a change on one or another of the frequent occasions repeated across the century—from expelling the Venetian representative in Arzignano to deposing the Spanish viceroy in Naples, to delivering the city of Messina over to the French, to lynching the governor of Fermo in the Papal States. And the events of the English civil war, the Dutch revolt, and the Fronde, repeated endlessly in the press, were lessons that no ruler could afford to forget, even supposing their subjects might have allowed them to do so.

However, at the time, the constraints imposed by political power upon the publication of pamphlets and newspapers were as well known as their unreliability. Censorship laws clearly defined the difference between

licit and illicit information; and by interdicting the circulation of the latter, they cast into suspicion the veracity of the former. In case any of the connections between news publication and the people in charge might have gone unnoticed, the writers themselves gave obvious indications. Readers of a report on the revolt of Naples could expect the writer, so a certain Gabriele Tontoli promised, "to be unfailingly more truthful in praise than in narration." Let not the critics complain, he continued, about finding encomiums where they expected facts. After all, there were already too many writers in town trying to write simple history. "Therefore," he continued, "I had to resort to invention, and turn my pen into the lance of Achilles; so that, by injuring history it should save discourse."[183] Readers of an account of the celebrations on the occasion of the coronation of Innocent X could well imagine, as Domenico Marcioni, a printer in Rome, told them, that "other things could be recorded. . . . But I have only described what is permitted, so that the superiors would allow this work to be printed."[184]

According to Gregorio Leti, at least, the net effect of news publications among readers who purchased them or heard them read in the town squares was to discredit the governments that tainted the news. "Everyone knows that very frequently princes turn losses into victories in order to terrify the people; and, indeed, to bring them into ever greater affection. Therefore, the people, so frequently hoodwinked, always turn victories into losses, forming squadrons at their pleasure and princes to their tastes." Anyone with any brains, he argued, could tell that many stories were intended to mislead. There could be no other reason for omitting the sordid details of political intrigue, which were the stuff of the better newsletters and the food of gossip throughout the streets and squares, and publishing, instead, useless details about the festive lives of the elites. In this practice the Italian newspapers were not alone. "Now, what difference does it make to the people of France," Leti continued, "to know that the emperor held a dance for the dames? Why do the Germans have to know that the Most Christian King was or was not at the hunt? What effect will it make upon the Roman people, to know that the king of Spain went to see a bullfight? What profit may the English people gain from hearing that the pope went to Sant'Andrea della Valle?" According to Leti, readers could see through a tactic that was evidently intended to busy their minds with matters of little pith and moment while more sinister dealings were going on behind their backs. "Such bagatelles . . . serve for nothing but for making everyone laugh who reads them."[185]

By the late seventeenth century, no one could ignore the advent of printed news that had become politics' new clothes. Nor could they fail to notice that opinions circulating among the multitudes were occasionally informed by and, especially, whipped up in reaction to opinions originating in the world of print. If civic authority was, at least in theory, a public trust and the printing press was one of many mediators between civil society and the sovereign, the deliberate publication of falsehood posed a threat to the very bases of consensus. To the extent that news publications were also major sources for publications of a more weighty sort, they could be agents of still unexplored change in other areas of cultural expression. And the new hired histories of the seventeenth century, in raising disinformation to the level of an art form, produced a crisis of belief from which historiography could be saved only by a radical reform.

3

Snatching Victory from the Jaws of Defeat

From the preliminary episodes of the Thirty Years' War to the conclusion of the War of Castro, from the revolt of Palermo to the revolt of Fermo, from the negotiations between the dukes of Savoy and the Spanish monarchy in 1617 to the negotiations between the Venetians and the Turks in 1699, seventeenth-century Italy offered more material than any aspiring journalist might have wished for. However, journalism was only one dimension of everyday reality, and not necessarily the most intelligible one. The War of Castro, before it got its name, was simply a series of isolated diplomatic maneuvers gone awry between the pope and the Farnese family. In this and any other struggle, a disconnected miscellany of tiny troop movements might make up an attack, a succession of separate decisions might comprise a campaign. But for collected episodes to constitute whole events, for any of these acts to appear united into a single purpose, called for the perspective made possible exclusively by the passage of time. And for everyday reality to acquire a vertical depth to accompany the horizontal breadth of the here and now, called for the labors of the journalist to be accompanied, or indeed replaced, by the more patient and reflective scrutiny of the historian.

The extraordinary opportunities offered to the historian by this event-filled century did not go unnoticed. "The present century [is] so full of news," Pietro Gazzotti remarked, in the preface of his *History of the Wars from 1643 to 1680*, "that previous ones scarcely offer any precedents."[1] So many, indeed, were the writers inspired by these and other events to compile accounts of political and military affairs in their own

times and in the recent past that Agostino Mascardi posited it as a law of nature: "Apparently, the sharpening of intellects is connected to the sharpening of swords. The sweat of combat irrigates the minds of historians; and the ink of writers is purified by military action."[2]

What brought the attention of a new group of writers to the momentous events of the time was more than mere curiosity, however; it was more than the desire for scholarly distinction or even the gratitude of posterity. As in the case of the newsletter and newspaper writers, our story of these historians becomes entangled with some of the larger trends in the development of political structures. The parties in the conflicts demanded interpretations calculated to shore up damaged loyalties, repair breaches of trust, and impress foreign powers. Upon any writer who could provide the necessary material, they were disposed to lavish money and favors, including preferment to the most exclusive court circles. Writers who were attracted to this high-stakes game included professional historians and charlatans, former diplomats and blackmailers. They based their work not just on eyewitness reports and diplomatic correspondence but also on newsletters, news books, newspapers, and simple hearsay. By freely mixing historiography with adulation, deceit, sensationalism, and pure fantasy, these writers turned hired historiography from an occasional strategy into a cultural industry and set the formation of public myths on an entirely new footing. In so doing, they provoked a reaction that was eventually to shake the emerging discipline to its foundations.

Careful cultivation of a particularly edifying view of the recent or remote past, capable of inspiring patriotism and loyalty among the humble and flattering the vanity of the exalted, was, of course, nothing new in the mid-seventeenth century. Renaissance governments routinely encouraged the application, for purposes of adulation and flattery, of humanist historiographical techniques that might just as easily be pressed into the service of mythmaking as that of objective narration. The Venetian government was by no means alone in appointing an official historian of the republic; nor was it alone in assigning to this person the task of promoting the reputation of the state by enhancing the fame of those who made it great—which of course meant drawing a veil of pity over those who made it foul.[3] Giambattista Pigna performed the same encomiastic service for the Este dukes as Bernardino Baldi did for the Urbino ones.[4] And when Scipione Ammirato accepted a commission by Cosimo I to write the history of Florence, he was in good company in avowing "neither the

desire to be considered liberal because of my criticisms, nor the fear of being criticized because of my praises, if I ever have occasion to distort the truth."[5]

The same governments fully believed readers might be misled just as effectively by the wrong sorts of historical works as by the wrong religious ones. They therefore closely scrutinized historians who wrote too freely about sensitive issues, reining them in and steering their accounts where necessary. There was no wonder, then, that the Venetian government should have objected to publication of a first version of Pietro Bembo's account of the battle of Agnadello and its aftermath, in which he was critical of the senators who had approved the policies that led to the debacle.[6] Similarly, the government of Naples was only following suit when it reprimanded Giovanni Antonio Summonte for his unflattering portraits of the Spanish viceroys. Nothing else could be expected from the government of Milan than that it should make Giuliano Goselini insert passages in his biography of Ferrante Gonzaga asserting that the Holy Roman Empire was a steadfast supporter of the papacy, when the evidence to the contrary given by the sack of Rome was there for all to see.[7]

Seventeenth-century governments inherited their predecessors' hopes and fears and added some of their own. Their counselors were among the most impassioned advocates of suppressing the negative historiography and promoting the positive. Thus we find Fulgenzio Micanzio, counselor to the Venetian Senate on matters concerning the printing press, warning about the dangers of pernicious writings in the following terms: "Ingenious authors writing in the cabinets of princes send armies into battle and states to their destruction." For him, the worst was Carlo Pasquale's *Legatio Rhaetica* (1620), which had been powerful enough to turn the French from friends into enemies of Venice during the Valtelline war. Its "conceits and attractive expressions," he explained, made such an impression in the French court, "where it was avidly read by everyone," that later, in the rebellion of the Valtelline Catholics and the occupation of the Valtelline by Spain, "Your Serenity encountered the great difficulty about which unfortunately we are all aware."[8]

If the senators had any doubt about the effect of such writings they had only to recall the words of Paolo Sarpi, Micanzio's predecessor in the same job. For him, one of the most pernicious writings had been a pamphlet attributed to Hermann Conrad, baron von Friedenberg, a Habsburg sympathizer in the Thirty Years' War, who condemned the Venetian

government's deal making with heretical states.[9] Such writings, said Sarpi, "by defaming the authority of the state and portraying its government as weak, undermine the state's reputation both among its neighbors and among its subjects until disdain encourages the introduction of novelties"—clearly, a bad thing.[10] They were matched in their destructiveness only by writings that depicted the government as perfidious to its neighbors and unjust and unloving to its subjects, rendering it odious to both. In the event that any of these works could not be effectively prohibited, well-meaning hired pens might be tempted to refute them in active literary combat. No one knew better than Sarpi that this too had its perils. First of all, the enemy might be more pithy and humorous than the friend. Furthermore, a proper defense might require an extended narrative or discourse. Yet audience attention could not be relied upon for long, inasmuch as "brief and witty expressions impress themselves on and take over the mind, whereas a long discourse tires it to such an extent that it will never open up to the truth."[11] Rather than by refutations, at least as far as posterity is concerned, he recommended, "there is no better way to cultivate loyalties than by writing histories."

The Venetian government, in continuing its earlier policy of commissioning official historiography, was joined by most of the governments of Europe; and Louis XIV was only the most extravagant among them, if he indeed maintained ninety writers on his payroll at any one time, as he is reported to have done, of whom some nineteen were historians, including the poet and dramatist Jean Racine. To ensure proper coverage, he ordered some of them to accompany him on his most important military exploits and offered editorial advice on what to say.[12] His behavior was matched on a lesser scale by the later Stuart monarchs, who appointed, successively, Thomas Shadwell, Thomas Rymer, and John Dryden to illustrate the dynasty's triumphant story in Restoration England. Although the post was regarded mainly as a sinecure, and these writers did not all produce narrative histories, nonetheless, what accounts they did produce provided what should be termed an official version of the dynasty's actions.[13]

To be sure, not even official historiography could always be trusted to convey the proper impression. This was obviously the case when the excessive frankness of such writings or their deep penetration into secret affairs seemed likely to encourage private persons to question the government. The Venetian Senate had no qualms about suppressing the publication of Nicolò Contarini's history of Venice, which it had commissioned in 1620. "In his introductory remarks about the various senators

involved," the censors recorded, "[he] explains much that can allow men to find out how to act politically"—a dangerous prospect, if extended to all and sundry.[14] On the other hand, works that narrated events in a satisfactory way, once they were known to have received the benediction of official authorities, might be ignored by readers as pure propaganda. If not exactly damaging, such works were clearly useless. As Sarpi observed, "Any writer who wishes to seem truthful must tell the good and the bad, because if he tells only the good, he is not believed."[15]

Because outright prohibition rarely worked and official historiography was rarely taken seriously, the only sure way to secure an adequate response against hostile historiography was to encourage the publication of works that appeared to speak well of the government without constraint. Micanzio reflected the views of many political advisers when he noted that "the best remedy is to have well-affected and good writers, especially foreigners, who occasionally, in their works, attest to [the government's] sincerity in religion and integrity in administration and other singular virtues." The example he gave was Fortunat Sprecher's *Historia* of the Valtelline War, fit, in his view, to serve as an antidote to the scandalous polemic by Carlo Pasquale that we have just discussed. Here was a work that defused its opponent by a "very interesting history, full of various occurrences, most important treaties . . . battles, leagues, doubtful expectations, and all those events that can make a history curious." Against Pasquale, it defended the actions of the Venetians and showed, in sufficient detail, the malice of the Austrians. What is more, it accomplished all this "without appearing to do so," Micanzio noted; and this was "the only way to achieve the effect desired."[16]

The Hired Historians

Of course, writers who spoke well of a government ordinarily did not do so out of the goodness of their hearts; they most often expected something in return. And here the history of skepticism begins to descend into the meandering byways of the history of the business of authorship. Historians could always be found who were disposed to offer their services with due discretion, for the right price. The proper approach with writers of that sort, Micanzio argued, was secret payment in money or favors. His words applied wherever such deals were being made. "In general, writers who dedicate their efforts to princes and great personages may seem to do so merely to add luster to their works; but for the most part

they also have another hidden aim—namely, an honorarium or some show of liberality." The many good princes who had recognized this fact over the years showed great wisdom. "Liberality in this matter," he added, "is repaid with interest."[17] Jean Chapelain, adviser to Louis XIV, agreed, adding, in his remarks to one writer, "[the king's] praises should seem spontaneous, and to seem spontaneous they have to be printed outside his realms."[18]

Ministers' well-known anxiety, amid the political trauma of the time, to promote favorable writing and discourage the unfavorable made them easy targets for the unscrupulous. Would-be blackmailers emulating Pietro Aretino, the self-styled sixteenth-century "scourge of princes," might expect higher compensation for what they did not write than for what they did. They were not afraid to declare their intentions even to the most exalted personages. Neither cardinals nor dukes were immune to the threats of Giovanni Giuseppe Arconati Lamberti, a late-seventeenth-century Milanese expatriate, who always seemed ready to hang out their dirty laundry in public if they did not pay up.[19] And anyone who thought Gregorio Leti, the most infamous political pamphleteer of his time, might fail to back up similar threats had merely to refer to such publications as his satirical *Conclave That Elected Fabio Chigi Called Alexander VII*, the sensationalist *Loves of Carlo Gonzaga Duke of Mantua and of the Countess Margherita della Rovere*, or the scandalous *Roman Whorishness*.[20]

The greater the prestige of the writer, the more audaciously he could demand ransom for the reputation of his victims. If Luca Assarino, born in Peru and raised in the Republic of Genoa, was any example, entire careers could be built in preparation for such a role. Assarino's literary credentials originally came from a vaguely pro-French work entitled *On the Revolutions of Catalonia*.[21] Riding a wave of publicity connected with his other works and cultivating his connections with the Turin patriciate, he managed, through Adelaide Enrichetta, the daughter of Victor Amadeus of Savoy and the wife of Duke Ferdinand Maria of Bavaria, to gain appointment as official historian of the Palatinate. The result was the first volume of his *On the Wars of Italy*, covering the years 1613–30.[22] With the second volume, carrying the story up to 1660, the dealing began. First, he sent the completed manuscript around to the Genoese Senate, offering satisfactory coverage in return for a stipend.[23] Next he offered a favorable account of Alexander VII to Cardinal Rospigliosi, papal secretary of state, in return for a benefice for his son.[24]

To the Venetian Senate, Assarino sent a version of the embarrassing War of Candia, showing, in a particularly hostile way, how Venice had lost an important eastern Mediterranean colonial outpost to the Ottoman Turks in 1669. It was a brilliantly calculated move. The war had begun before Venice had fully recovered from the plague of 1630 and the Italian wars of the 1640s, and it postponed full recovery from those disasters for another twenty years. It marked a watershed in Venetian history, polarizing the patriciate and beginning a period of diminished influence in European politics. The passionate concern devoted to it seemed proportionate to the degree to which Venice's reputation seemed to hang on its proper interpretation.

The account Assarino sent as an example of what he intended to write delivered a body blow to the republic's dignity and to the senators' amour propre. He suggested that the Venetians urgently solicited the aid of the other Christian princes only to gain better terms from the Turks, with whom they were secretly negotiating at the time.[25] When the French offered twelve thousand troops, the Venetians, suddenly pressed to make a decisive move, agreed to accept only six thousand but allowed only three thousand of these to land and gave them insufficient provisions. When the duke of Beaufort first arrived in Candia with the last of the French aid to the besieged city, the Venetians, already in the second month of their negotiations with the Turks, failed to give him the necessary support in order to avoid spoiling the process. Whatever may have been their purposes, the Venetians' whole strategy at the end was a failure, in Assarino's view. Not only did they neglect to make more ditches and parapets, but if they had held out for another two days, the Turks would have given up. In spite of the desire to negotiate, they were forced to accept miserable terms, including a huge tribute payment and a promise to refrain from aiding any other powers wishing to make war with the Turks. Indeed, so shocking was the Venetian surrender, Assarino claimed, that Pope Clement IX dropped dead immediately upon receiving word. And the subsequent loss at sea of a huge treasure that the Venetians had been forced to send in order to mollify the Turks was clearly a judgment from God.

The Venetian Senate took Assarino's request seriously enough to have its representative reply point by point to the accusations. To the obvious distortions, fabrications, and unwarranted speculations, the representative replied, "totally false, and based on pure malice"; and rather than blame his countrymen, he blamed the French.[26] In fact, he insisted, the

Venetians kept the allies apprised at all times of any negotiations. They made no deals with the Turks at all until the situation was desperate. And they always insisted on having the largest contingent possible from the French. French commander Philippe de Montault de Bénac, duke de Navailles, had decided on the incomplete debarkation and refused to accept adequate provisions. Moreover, Navailles and Beaufort left Candia of their own accord because they were frightened by the explosion of a few barrels of powder on the Turkish side. In the end, there were not nearly enough men to build more ditches and parapets, and when the Venetians gave up, the Turks still had thirty thousand men. The articles of surrender were not nearly as shameful as Assarino made out. There was no tribute money, nor was there a promise to refrain from military aid to other powers. The pope died not of grief but of incurable diseases. And the supposed gift to the Turks, the Venetian representative concluded, was a normal accompaniment to a new ambassador's entry into Constantinople, lost at sea because of the winter squalls. Fortunately for the representative, for Venice, and probably for other states as well, Assarino died before collecting the money or writing the history.

Authors with less audacity and nerve than Assarino simply advertised their wares, made known their availability, and waited around for appropriate patronage offers. And the parade of exemplary biographies of such figures is impressive indeed. Not all, to be sure, were former Jesuits, like the Genoa-born writer Agostino Mascardi, but most of them adopted similar strategies of self-presentation. After abandoning the Jesuit order, Mascardi joined the best academies of his time in Rome. No sooner had he taken up a position at the University as a professor of rhetoric than he began to seek patronage support for a history of Italy. To the Genoese Senate, he wrote, "I humbly beg Your Illustrious Lordships, to send me the proper information, in the assurance that I will serve you according to the faithfulness and affection I owe you in every respect." Meanwhile, he kept his interpretative options open by promising to "adhere to the Truth prescribed to me by my conscience, my reputation, and my desire to perform a public service."[27] And while he was sending similar requests elsewhere, he ingratiated the Genoese by publishing a pro-government version of the Fieschi conspiracy of 1547. Although the Este government in Modena flatly refused his offers, others accepted them. And when the money began rolling in, fellow writer Francesco Frugoni later claimed, in order to keep up the suspense, he slowed the work down to a snail's pace and eventually gave it up.[28]

What all these writers had in common was their readiness to serve whoever paid them best. This was not always the first prince who came along—as Vittorio Siri recognized while accepting rewards mainly from France. A Benedictine monk born in Parma and operating chiefly in Venice, he soon cast about for other offers. To this end, he let Florentine secretary of state Balì Gondi know that he was working on a history that might include material concerning Florence. To involve Gondi all the more in the work, he requested information concerning the life of Galileo Galilei, engaged in some dispute concerning dates, and asked for documentation of military affairs, especially the movements of the duke of Parma in the last war.[29] He then asked for whatever information Gondi might wish to put in the history, assuring him that all affairs of the grand duchy would be treated to the maximum advantage of the ruler. As soon as he completed the first draft, he sent it to Francesco I d'Este, duke of Modena, to see what information might be added for the right price.[30]

Giovanni Birago Avogadro, born in Genoa and, like Siri, operating in Venice, chiefly accepted rewards from Spain—while taking care not to close other doors. Accordingly, he quickly followed up his more detailed history of the revolution in Catalonia written from a pro-Spanish perspective by a history of all the European revolutions of the mid-seventeenth century. But after he undertook a continuation of Alessandro Zilioli's highly successful multivolume chronicle of current events,[31] he approached the representatives of various governments, including the Florentine ambassador in Venice, explaining his plans and requesting advice and support. To be sure, our authors were not always entirely successful in their proposals for subvention; in this case the efforts of Birago Avogadro were wasted. "I told him I do not have any information with me," the ambassador reported to the secretary of state, "because everything is in Florence." And there the negotiations stopped.[32]

Although Pietro Gazzotti accepted rewards chiefly from his native Genoa, he attempted to content everyone else as well. Accordingly, in his history of the European wars, he reported the 1654 showdown between Spain and Genoa in terms as favorable as possible to the latter. He told readers how the Genoese had required Spanish ships sailing out of the port of Finale to pay tribute to Genoa as they entered the Ligurian Sea. This provoked the Spanish to sequester Genoese property. But the Genoese preferred to "place the conservation of the public dignity before their private convenience."[33] He later treated readers to a description of the Della Torre conspiracy sponsored by Duke Carlo Emanuele II of

Savoy against Genoa in 1672, celebrating the duke's defeat at Castelvec-chio "with shameful disintegration of his armies and consternation of his people."[34] No doubt he knew that Genoa's practice was to reward writers richly for attributing heroic deeds to the republic—and in this case, it rewarded Gazzotti. Pleasing the Spanish at the same time was no easy task; he tried by tempering any negative accounts of Spanish arms and alluding to the "generosity of the king" toward France in 1660. To content the papal government he could only think of noting, in Pope Clement IX's favor, that "few pontiffs have been better loved than he."[35] So that no one would be disappointed in this panoply of praise, he tried to content the duke of Modena, in return for a fee, by a favorable account of his father, Francesco I d'Este, who died in 1658.[36]

But try as they might, none of these writers could match Pier Giovanni Capriata's reputation as the Italian writer most easily purchased by anyone who could afford him. Perhaps he owed some of his negotiating prowess to his law practice in his native Genoa. No sooner had he completed a work covering the first War of Montferrat from a pro-Spanish viewpoint than he managed to gain the confidence of the Spanish ministers. The first volume of his next work, an *Historia* covering the years 1613–34, was so entirely favorable to Spain and the pro-Spanish nobility in Genoa that it left little room for the sensibilities of any other powers.[37] Reactions ranged from threats of violence (from Venice) to fury (from Rome); and in the course of negotiations between Rome and Genoa concerning church payments to the treasury, Urban VIII made the correction of certain passages in book 7 a condition of the pact. Genoa agreed and put the work on its Index *donec expurgetur* (subject to correction) in 1639 and authorized its representative in Rome to make sure the favor was properly returned.

Meanwhile, Capriata cast about for better offers and published a second volume of the work more favorable to France. Seeking patronage for the continuation, he approached Mazarin, who recognized the value of the work as well as the venality of its author. "The sort of people who make a profession out of writing false histories must be rewarded," he admitted; "the good thing is that the Spanish have already paid six hundred scudi to have six pages changed, so we are in time to pay more to have them changed again."[38] Nevertheless, the payment was apparently sufficient only for volume 2: for volume 3, covering the period to 1650 (and published posthumously in 1663), Capriata returned to Spanish favor. And the impulse came from the viceroyal government in Naples, un-

der specific instructions by Philip IV to send Capriata all the information necessary for writing the definitive account of the Masaniello revolt of 1647–48, provided that he should write what Philip himself might deem a "proper and truthful history, as it ought to be," not necessarily as it was.[39] And so he did.

Not all the hired historians were satisfied with monetary compensation. On the other hand, not all of them were in the same desperate straits as Giovanni Francesco Fossati, a Milanese writer who sought a reprieve from the exile imposed on him by the Venetian government for criminal activities he alleged were committed, rather, by his relatives. Nor could they all offer information on a plot against the state, which Fossati claimed to have gleaned from obscure sources and was prepared to divulge while providing appropriate coverage of Venice in the history he was now writing "by order of His Majesty" of Spain, whose pensioner he claimed to be.[40] But the ambitions of all of them extended to the kinds of protection and favors that money could not buy. Galeazzo Gualdo Priorato, a Vicentine nobleman, sought preferment within the elite circles to which his military and diplomatic activity already gave him some access. Soon his history of Queen Christina of Sweden earned him a position at the queen's court in Rome. By the time he had completed more than thirty-nine books, many of which became the seventeenth-century equivalent of best-sellers, he received from Mazarin a commission to write the history of the French civil wars in 1652 and a position as field marshal and commander of the French armies in Italy.[41]

What most of the hired historians had in common, furthermore, and what they proposed to use to help their customers and damage their victims, was a persuasiveness born of their deep understanding of political affairs. They would have been the first to insist that their hands-on practice in diplomacy and other public roles was essential for effective analysis of recent events. "The history written by a person with practical insight is more substantial than the sort that offers nothing but the facts."[42] So said Maiolino Bisaccioni, and he was an example of his own maxim. Indeed, if sharp swords made sharp intellects, as we heard Mascardi suggest at the beginning of this chapter, Bisaccioni ought to have been one of the most incisive historians of his time. Born in Ferrara in 1582 and graduated from the University of Bologna, he fought in the armies of Venice and the Habsburg empire before serving in governorships under the princes of Scandiano, Corregio, and Trent; and he completed diplomatic missions for the princes of Savoy before finally settling down to finish his

career as a novelist and historian. Galeazzo Gualdo Priorato was not far behind. He followed his father into a military career at an early age and took time off to write history while fighting in Flanders under Maurice of Nassau, prince of Orange, against the Spanish at Breda, and elsewhere; he subsequently served the count of Mansfeld while the latter was in England and, finally, as a diplomat for Queen Christina of Sweden.

By these standards, Capriata's experience seemed relatively tame, as a participant in the Vachero conspiracy to deliver Genoa to the Savoy dukes in 1628, for which he was forced to take refuge in Spain. His later experience was not far different in kind from that of Bisaccioni. Sent back to Genoa by Philip IV's first minister, the count-duke of Olivares, as legal counsel to the Spanish ambassador in Genoa, he there began his historical writing. Even Girolamo Brusoni, who began as a novelist, took up diplomacy and political intrigue in Venice and finally put his political experience to use for himself by composing newsletters and writing histories.[43] Vittorio Siri served as the representative in France of the duke of Parma and wrote newsletters for that duke as well as for the rival duke of Modena, and Pietro Gazzotti served as a secretary to the duke of Giovenazzi, the Spanish representative in Paris.

The better to persuade their readers of the veracity of their accounts, the hired historians claimed to put evidence from sensitive diplomatic documents at the center of their historical investigations. History, they never tired of repeating, should be a work of scholarship. Indeed, "Reports from the most authoritative archives of great princes must . . . be the most significant recourse for anyone who seeks to delve into the most dubious ambiguities and emerge with a true narrative."[44] Assarino's sentiments in this passage were echoed by Girolamo Brusoni, who, to confirm his accounts of the Turkish wars, included, among many other examples, what purported to be a letter from the Grand Turk to the pasha of Bosnia in 1660, the entire peace treaty following the War of Candia, and a "letter concerning the life of Sultan Iachia written by Count Luca Fabroni to Signor Balì Gondi, first secretary of state of the grand duke of Tuscany, March 14, 1646," supposedly "delivered to the resident of the Republic of Venice."[45]

In addition to political knowledge, personal experience, and access to documentary sources, the hired historians offered a rhetorical persuasiveness born of a more than passing acquaintance with the standard models of historical writing, from Thucydides to Guicciardini. In achieving perhaps greater success in this latter effort than in any other, they en-

sured that their rolling periods bore not the slightest resemblance to the terse prose of those other cultivators in the fields of history, the erudite antiquaries. They had no interest in compiling densely detailed works of consultation on this or that aspect of classical antiquity, such as Ottavio Ferrari's on Roman dress and funerary lamps, Fortunato Liceti's on ancient rings, and others on gems, furniture, art, pottery, and fortifications.[46] Rather than esoteric disputations, the hired historians offered narrative; rather than descriptions of objects, they offered brilliant character sketches; and rather than mere instruction, they offered instruction and entertainment.

Consider, for instance, Capriata's analysis of the reasons for Spanish general Don Filippo Spínola's vacillation before the attack on Mantua in 1630. There he showed how Spínola arrived in the state of Milan at the end of August and was quickly persuaded by the dubious progress of the war to consider the safer course of securing peace. He imagined the great general contemplating Milan, the principal basis and support for any new enterprise, exhausted, consumed, and too weak to stand under the weight of the troubles of a war. Anyone could see that Mantua and Casale were very strong, the first because of its site along the water, the second because of the powerful fortifications; thus, any siege would be difficult. And anyone in Spínola's position would have recognized that the planned operation would infuriate the rulers of Italy, their populations, and the French. The French were ready at the slightest provocation to come back across the Alps to protect the Mantuan devolution to a French dynasty, that of Nevers. No amount of expense and equipment was likely to suffice for achieving objectives even in small battles against much weaker foes than this. Worse yet, Capriata supposed, Spínola was confounded by the changing inclinations of the duke of Savoy, whose friendship he purchased at great expense with no guarantee of continued fidelity once the situation became more critical. Finally, the soldiers sent by the emperor were a constant source of preoccupation, both from a financial and a strategic point of view, given Spain's long-term interests in Italy:

But more than any other consideration, what worried him was just what seemed to offer the most reason for satisfaction and consolation—namely, the German army. Although its help would be of great assistance to him in this enterprise, in the height of the fervor of a campaign, the pride, arrogance, and rapacity of that naturally insatiable nation, impatient with military discipline and inclined to mutiny, could cause the gravest accidents. Worse yet, the expense of supporting it was great, and the money proceeding from the royal treasury was scarcely suffi-

cient after such long wars. And worst of all, the Germans fought in Italy not as auxiliaries or mercenaries of Spain but as principal parties and in the name of the emperor. So, considering the emperor's authority in Italy and the superior quality, quantity, and preparation of the forces, Spanish authority seemed likely to be forced to defer to imperial authority, and the ambitious imperial captains seemed likely to force the Spanish to fight their own way.[47]

No one who paid heed to this elaborate and finely argued tour de force of special pleading, Capriata must have thought, could possibly resist redeeming the hero from the charge of cowardice levied against him on the basis of a much more obvious conclusion that he was afraid to fight.

Like their Renaissance forebears, the hired historians believed history should be a branch of eloquence as well as a branch of scholarship. They thus agreed with the literary theorists that unlovely writing does not persuade. They took to heart the pronouncements of a Sforza Pallavicino in favor of literary embellishments as a route to understanding. "If men could manifest their ideas immediately like the angels," Pallavicino noted, "words would be superfluous. But since in order to understand one another it is necessary to paint those ideas with some perceptible colors, why choose the sordid dinginess of coal rather than the more gracious tints of ultramarine?"[48] Accordingly, the hired historians spent nearly as much effort carefully selecting their palette, coloring their expressions, and framing their arguments to please the aesthetic sense as they did gathering information.

Moreover, like their Renaissance forebears, the hired historians believed rhetorical persuasiveness went hand in hand with literary imagination, and not just where evidence failed or proved to be inconvenient for one reason or another. Antonio Santacroce was not alone in believing that novel writing was a way of honing his historiographical methods, whether the themes in question were historical or not.[49] What was true for Santacroce was true also for Luca Assarino, best known for his novel *La stratonica,* and Girolamo Brusoni, best known for *La fuggitiva.* Anyone in doubt might refer to the example of Machiavelli, who, although he published works of comedy as well as serious compositions in political theory and historiography, may have found creative writing to be a helpful preparation when it came to putting dialogues and orations in the mouths of historical personages, as was the current practice, or in describing a good scene.[50] And if such fictive dialogues and orations might occasionally give historical works more of the character of imaginative writing than of history, noted Agostino Mascardi, that was to be chalked

up to the necessary transmutation of reality in the course of its presentation to a public. No one would dare find fault, he suggested, with ambassadors who, charged with reporting the proposals of their prince, used his exact meaning rather than his exact expressions, polishing and perfecting what came from his mouth in order to render his ideas more attractive to the minds of others. "The historian must indeed adhere to the truth when recounting facts," he noted, "but in reporting words he may allow his pen greater freedom as long as he does not drift too far from the substance and concept."[51]

Fact and Fiction

What distinguished the seventeenth-century hired historians from their Renaissance forebears, however, was the greater extent to which they allowed rhetorical fancy and scholarship to overlap. Fiction was only a matter of degree for Maiolino Bisaccioni, writer of histories of conspiracies and civil wars as well as of a tragedy based on a true story about the so-called false Dimitri, an adventurer who tried to seize the throne of Muscovy by impersonating the heir of Ivan the Terrible.[52] Gian Paolo Marana, a Genoa-based historian, could only agree. In his famous novel, the *Espion turc,* he used the device of a found manuscript in order to make a veiled and imaginative comment on his contemporary times. And in his best-known historical work, an account of the 1672 conspiracy of Raffaello della Torre in Genoa, he brought the action to a close with the revelation of a "manuscript memoir of Della Torre," of Marana's own invention, supposedly demonstrating the conspirator's admiration for such notorious lovers of violence as Cesare Borgia and Niccolò Machiavelli, along with instructions on the use of explosives.[53]

Not surprisingly, the hired historians made frequent use, in their historical works, of metaphors concerning literary creativity and the language of Baroque poetics. On this view, there was nothing incongruous in considering illustrative digressions in historiography as expressions of poetic license. After a long reflection on how the Neapolitan fishmonger Masaniello humbled the pride of the mighty viceroy in the revolt of Naples, Bisaccioni exclaimed, "I have purposely kept better conceits inside my pen in order not to make my own vileness proud and arrogant"[54] —something most of his readers would have found hard to believe. Nor was there anything incongruous in Gabriele Tontoli's approach, in which he offered his own account of the same events as a "combined historical,

poetical, declamatory, and familiar discourse." Let pedantic critics object all they wished, he went on. Sooner or later, they would have to admit that "modern intellects cannot be prevented from inventing" and that the capricious events he had to relate demanded for their exposition a capricious style of writing.[55] It was only a matter of time before the straightforward concept of "history" in itself was viewed as being far too dull. Accordingly, the anonymous writer of a work on recent Venetian conquests preferred "episodes that could be history." He told his reader, "I know you do not like foods unless they are very delectable." In any case, "in these times, fables are histories and histories are fables."[56]

Indeed, a common theme running through both the historical and the imaginative works of the hired historians was the relation between fact and fiction in everyday life. Let us examine in detail a typical literary treatment of the theme by Bisaccioni. His famous novel entitled *The Gentleman of Genoa* shows how a well-intentioned bystander becomes an object of manipulation in events that soon prove to be far different from first impressions.[57] We will postpone until the next chapter a discussion of the extent to which Bisaccioni and his fellow writers faced similar problems in their relations with their patrons.

The novel begins when Ansaldo, the gentleman in the title, sees a distressed lady, Eurispe, walking along the shoreline at the edge of the city. At first, he assumes she is in trouble, a supposition immediately confirmed by the appearance of Costanzo, a youth with whom she appears to be having an altercation. Ansaldo responds to her request for protection and soon concludes that he is witness to an ordinary lovers' quarrel. To help reconcile the two, he refuses Eurispe's entreaties to send Costanzo away. Suddenly Eurispe becomes the aggressor rather than the victim when she inexplicably stabs Costanzo with a dagger, leaving Ansaldo utterly confused.

Ansaldo continues to be misled about the reality behind the quarrel between Costanzo and Eurispe while Costanzo, to save Eurispe, deceives the police by saying his wound was received in a duel. Not only are first appearances deceptive in Bisaccioni's novel; indeed, the depth of deception seems to reach every character. When Costanzo sends wines and delicacies to the church where Ansaldo has hidden Eurispe, the priest, supposing them to be gifts from Ansaldo, compounds the deception by concealing them to prevent a budding relationship damaging to the latter. To guard against his own passions, the priest asks the housekeeper to be present when he administers confession to Eurispe. But when Eurispe

asks permission to leave the church, he breaks his promise to Ansaldo and lets her flee to Lucca, later feigning surprise at her absence when Ansaldo inquires.

Finally, Costanzo reveals the true story between himself and Eurispe. He first met her years before, he says, when she redeemed him from slavery to some pirates who had abducted him. The episodes he relates are another tissue of deception, compounded by his evident intention to demonstrate Eurispe's treachery more conclusively. His love grew day by day, but he concealed it, partly for fear of being rebuffed and partly to avoid harming her reputation. After she finally liberates herself from other suitors, he declares his love for her, and she hers for him. However, when the moment comes to finish the courtship and exchange vows, she insists that for reputation's sake he ought instead to marry her pretty ward, Lesbia, of whom she has grown very fond. He refuses at first, thinking this is a test of his constancy. Only after Eurispe's repeated insistence does he finally comply, and eventually he transfers his love for Eurispe over to his new bride. When Eurispe shows her utter despondency about this apparent change of heart, he dissimulates his own lingering affection for her and persuades her to transform her own love into a hatred so powerful as to provoke the desperate act Ansaldo witnessed at the seashore.

In his historical work, too, truth, fiction, deception, and dissimulation were major themes for Bisaccioni, as for many other hired historians.[58] Writing about the Masaniello revolt in Naples, Bisaccioni went even further than his printed sources in attributing events to self-interested falsehoods, extending from the lowest levels of territorial administration all the way up to the ministers closest to the king.[59] Such was only to be expected, he noted, where the monarch relied on others for crucial information. Similarly, ship captains who try to steer a ship by compasses while shut up in their cabins may not know that the first mate is outside using a magnet to move the compass needle wherever best suits his interests. Thus, the tax farmers and others in Naples, especially among the nobility, who had bought the tax farms and other revenues and drew large incomes from them continued to deceive Viceroy Rodrigo Ponce de Leon, duke of Arcos, into thinking that still more revenues could be extracted; Arcos in turn led the king to expect more, dismissing any official who complained about the growing misery of the people. As an antidote to deception, Bisaccioni recommended that kings rely on descriptions written not by conniving or fawning courtiers but by foreigners, perhaps even himself.

In the high-stakes game of transforming recent events into confirmations of the political ideals of their employers, the hired historians combined attention to the sources, rhetorical technique, and sheer invention. In order to apply a French point of view to the chain of events leading from fiscal pressure to the Masaniello revolt, Bisaccioni ignored the standard notion, repeated by his mostly pro-Spanish sources, that the Neapolitans were primed by news about a previous rebellion in Palermo. Instead, he fabricated, out of whole cloth, a new story about how popular demands for fiscal relief received a "barbarous response" from the viceroy—to wit, "if you cannot pay, go and sell the honor of your wives and daughters and then pay." The spread of news about this, according to Bisaccioni, created a climate of tension throughout the kingdom.[60] On the other hand, Bisaccioni followed the sources' story of how the viceroy, complying with a demand made early in the rebellion, commissioned the duke of Maddaloni to bring to the people assembled in the Piazza del Mercato a copy of Charles V's ancient pact confirming the city's privileges; and when Maddaloni arrived, Masaniello forced him to dismount and take the document into the Church of the Carmine for authentication. But in order to give due emphasis to the tragic plight of his hero and the perfidy of Spain and its allies, Bisaccioni artificially placed Masaniello's lieutenant Domenico Perrone at the scene and invented a treasonous conversation between him and the duke of Maddaloni, to the effect that Masaniello must be assassinated at all costs.[61]

The sources claimed that the rebellious crowd, searching for explosives, came upon the store of a powder maker allied to the viceroy; but Bisaccioni rejected the hypothesis that the store accidentally blew up, before they were able to supply themselves, because of children playing with a lighted fuse. Instead, he had the lighted fuse placed deliberately by the loyalist store owner before fleeing.[62] Nor did Bisaccioni have much use for a version claiming that Masaniello, at the height of his power, was warmly received on first meeting the viceroy, especially if that meant, as in one account, that Masaniello threw himself down to kiss the viceroy's feet. Apparently he found more value in a version in which Masaniello, overcome with emotion and fatigue, supposedly collapsed before the viceroy, whereupon the latter attempted to reanimate him by wiping his brow with a handkerchief. Bisaccioni situated the episode at a later meeting and had the viceroy attempt to assuage the crowd's fears for Masaniello's safety by bringing him to the palace balcony and wiping his brow deferentially, in an ironic demonstration of the vanity of greatness:

"Pride and human extravagance are but a vile smoke."[63] Finally, Bisaccioni ignored his sources' suggestion that Masaniello gladly accepted a valuable gold chain and accompanying title from the viceroy. Instead, in order to acquit his hero of charges of foolishness, venality, and corruption, Bisaccioni claimed that Masaniello adamantly refused the chain and accepted the title only out of humility.[64]

History and Persuasion

The greatest challenge for the hired historians was to help snatch victory from the jaws of defeat on behalf of a beleaguered employer involved in a disastrous war. Here is where the care and repair of public myth, as the task of the historian has been characterized even in our times, was required most urgently; and new interpretations capable of justifying civic pride were most in demand. Here is where the gratitude of a ruler to the savior of a reputation might receive its fullest expression. At the same time, all the deft reinterpretations, clever omissions, and embellishments of the truth, characteristic of this literature, received their freest reign; and eventually those who were aware of the manipulations conceived reasons for historical skepticism and cause for alarm.

Among the most remarkable of its kind in the late seventeenth century was Girolamo Brusoni's effort to restore the reputation of Venice after the loss of Candia, followed almost immediately by Vittorio Siri's attempt to restore the image of France, which was involved in the same defeat. Brusoni's was a formidable task. The spectacle of the two decaying titans, Venice and the Ottoman Empire, locked in a struggle for which their outdated weaponry was exclusively qualified, did not appear to furnish the stuff of legends. Brusoni was not deterred. His treatment of what in anyone else's hands might have seemed a hopeless subject constituted a model of the genre. His methodological and rhetorical choices contributed a new historiographical variation. We now embark on a full investigation of his procedures, his conclusions, and their significance for prospective reformers of sagging historiography.

To find material for a suitable interpretation, Brusoni did not have to go far. Battle reports commissioned by or in one way or another inspired by the Venetian patriciate customarily recounted events in the most favorable light. By compiling all these into one seamless account without acknowledgement and dedicating it to the Venetian procurator of St. Mark's, Giorgio Morosini, he managed to produce a work that gave the

appearance of originality and that converged completely with a well-accredited view; that by the very abundance of details appeared to be based on authoritative documentation; and that preserved the breathless quality of journalistic prose while portraying Venice as a victorious power, in spite of the dubious support of its contentious and perfidious allies. "From the sincere narration of these events," he told his readers, repeating one of his sources word for word, "the accounts divulged by vulgar rumors are clearly shown to be false."[65] What is more, he managed to accomplish all this in time for the argument to be useful to his patrons, by virtue of appearing in print before some of the most searing criticisms of Venice began to circulate.

The first setback for the Venetians in the war was the failure to retake Canea, a principal fortified town on the island and the Turks' first prize. No account of this episode was nearly so worthy of imitation, Brusoni found, as that of Antonio Santacroce, a Paduan nobleman connected to the Venetian patriciate.[66] Like Santacroce, he pinned the blame for the failure not directly on the Venetians but on the French soldier of fortune de La Vallette, hired by Venice—a relatively unimportant player, according to modern scholarship.[67] Borrowing Santacroce's description of the disagreements between Venetian commanders concerning de La Vallette's excessive caution, Brusoni also borrowed Santacroce's negative judgment of the resulting damage to the war effort. He practically repeated the same words: "Although the Senate had been contacted so that the various claims could be examined, and a clearer order was awaited, nonetheless considerable bitterness remained, with much damage to the public cause."[68] However, he slightly modified Santacroce's explanation for de La Vallette's controversial belief that the town could not be taken. Santacroce's assertion that de La Vallette despaired of being able to rely on the townspeople for any support—"because they were Greeks and therefore well-regarded by the Turks"—cast Venice in an unfavorable light. Rather, said Brusoni, de La Vallette supposed the townspeople were naturally worried about the growing power of Venice—a far more flattering conclusion.

To divert the attention of his reader from the Candia debacle, Brusoni included information about Venetian successes against the Turks in Dalmatia. For an account of the taking of Sebenico (Sibenik), in which the Turks lost some six thousand men to Venice's eight hundred, he found a work by a certain Virginio Dalla Spada, dedicated to the Venetian patrician Pietro Ottoboni, auditor of the Sacra Romana Rota and later pope,

to be a worthy source of ideas as well as of words.[69] So satisfied, indeed, was he with the descriptions of the site of the city and the fortress of San Giovanni that he adopted them lock, stock, and barrel. Like his source, he recounted how the Venetians built the fort on a rise outside the city at the request of the inhabitants. "The republic (as has been said concerning the last campaign) responded to the supplications of the city of Sebenico," Brusoni explained, "for the construction of the fort of San Giovanni, recognized to be necessary and of great benefit to its safety, and they provided money for the work." In pointing out that the fort had been designed by a Franciscan friar according to the standard star-shaped plan, with breastworks and counterscarps, his interpretation and even most of the phrasing were faithful to the source.[70]

Fitting the borrowed narratives elegantly into his own account tested Brusoni's sensitivity as a literary stylist as well as his skill as a polemicist. The campaign of 1651 opened with a new assault by Turkish forces on Candia; and Brusoni found a virtual treasure trove of information in a *Lettera di ragguaglio* of Giovanni Carlo Serpentino printed by state printer Giovanni Pietro Pinelli. He plundered the entire description of the Turkish strategy: the pasha, he said, precisely echoing his source, "had orders from the Porte to besiege the port and starve it into surrender if the captain general happened to be inside, and if not, to attack him immediately."[71] But he had no use for the pamphlet's complication of the otherwise starkly simple religious situation, so he left out an account of how the Turkish captains' quick provisioning of a fleet had been carried out by means of some sympathetic Christians. Apparently the pamphlet was too dry in its version of how the Venetian commander had decided to hurry to Santorin, an island in the Cyclades, on the basis of new information about the whereabouts of the Turkish fleet. So Brusoni thought to spice it up by adding that this information came from two Greek slaves left behind by the Turks.[72]

Yet another work published by Pinelli, describing the fortress of Volos on the Gulf near Mount Pelion during the campaign of 1655, Brusoni found to be so irresistible that he simply transcribed it word for word: "almost square in shape, surrounded by walls pierced to accommodate cannons, adorned with a beautiful facade toward the sea, defended by two towers and a very strong citadel, all furnished with many cannons."[73] But it was not enough for him that the people of Volos defended themselves by order of the Turkish commander, as his source suggested. Instead, he said that the doughty denizens acted spontaneously and not by

order, making the enterprise of the Venetian attackers appear the more challenging.[74] He found no such fault with his source's account of the Venetian naval victory in the Dardanelles in 1656, the one that modern accounts credit with having inspired Grand Visir Mohammed Kiuprili's final push into Candia. Where he found the reminder about the importance of the war "against the most powerful potentate in the world" and praise for the Venetians' "constancy in defending the faith and the state, even with the treasury emptied, the blood of citizens and subject spilled, always constant in its ardor and most pious zeal," he repeated it verbatim.[75]

Portraying the final defeat of Venice as the unimaginable outcome of a valiant effort required all of Brusoni's powers of selection. Fortunately, he chanced upon the account of a battle won by Venice in March 1668, on the eve of the loss of Candia, "in the waters of Fraschia" between the cities of Candia and Canea.[76] He could find no fault with the account's assertion that, unable to collect enough forces to take the fortress of Candia right away, the Turks had resorted to the desperate measure of sending a reinforcement of two thousand soldiers from Retimo (Réthymnon) under cover of darkness. So he faithfully transcribed his original's portrayal of how the Venetian commander Francesco Morosini prevailed with a contingent of only six hundred men, changing only the length of battle from five hours to seven. Any problems the Venetians encountered in subsequent weeks ought obviously to be attributed in part to the Candiots themselves, who failed to defend the place with adequate ardor. Most of all, he blamed French commander Navailles, who stormed away from the battle scene in August 1669, ostensibly to protest against the conduct of the war but actually out of fear, Brusoni suggested, leaving an inadequate contingent of Frenchmen to help with the fighting. Even with the defense reduced to a few soldiers, Brusoni insisted, "they generally behaved themselves well; indeed, they could scarcely do otherwise, on such a serious occasion, when the common glory and welfare were at stake."[77] And in deciding upon the ultimate surrender of the island, the Venetian war council concluded, after due deliberation, that if they kept up the defense for a few more days they would lose the entire armada as well as the island; so they decided to come to terms, as Brusoni said, "for better service to the prince."[78]

When senator and diplomat Andrea Valier set out to write the first semiofficial history of the whole war, as a member of the inner circle of the Venetian government and emissary to Constantinople in the last

weeks of the war, he found that his own reputation coincided with that of the republic. And he found in Brusoni a ready-made interpretation that perfectly suited his needs. The similarity between his conclusions and Brusoni's was by no means casual. In fact, for writing about the period before his own personal contacts with the war began, he apparently used Brusoni from time to time as the basis for his own account. Readers who had read Brusoni could thus be excused for sensing something familiar when they came across lines like this in Valier: "The Venetians, having acquired Turlulù, turned their artillery against San Teodoro, where the frightened defenders raised a white flag to signal their surrender." The sentence was simply copied from the original.[79] Valier mostly added new details drawn from privileged sources unavailable to Brusoni, concerning, for instance, the inner workings of the Turkish government, his own observations of the end of the war, and a sweeping new overall interpretation.[80]

By placing the War of Candia in the larger context of Venice's struggle to prevent the universal monarchy either of Austria or of the Ottoman Turks, Valier was able to add a new dimension to the republic's reputation. The difference between the wars against the two empires competing for the territories that stood between them, which belonged to Venice, he explained, was that Venice scarcely lost anything in the struggle with the Austrians, even though most of the powers of Christendom were ranged on the Austrian side. In the case of the Ottomans, however, every struggle cost the republic dearly. Thus, charges that the Venetians kept the war going solely to benefit from foreign contributions were wholly baseless. Indeed, he added, Venice had succeeded brilliantly as a world peace-keeper in the seventy years between the Wars of Cyprus and of Candia. And the Candian episode, far from being a sign of decadence, was the ultimate confirmation of Venetian heroism: "This war, . . . for length of time, for variety of events, . . . for the constrictions on the Christian world, and for the disparity between the princes who fought, will remain not only memorable but marvelous to all posterity."[81] And with more reliable help from the allies, especially the French, things would have turned out differently.

For anyone who was aware of the unreliability of the sorts of sources Brusoni and Valier were using, the two accounts were easy to dismiss. Writers of battle reports commissioned or inspired in one way or another by the Venetian commanders could not be trusted. Their main concern was to help the subjects of their accounts achieve prestige in the Senate or

pursue private vendettas with other families. Yet all they risked, in embellishing their accounts, was the possibility that their inventions might by chance conflict with those of other equally partial writers. Otherwise, they were unlikely to be gainsaid, because the Senate never solicited reports except from its own officials. Such were the criticisms of Vittorio Siri, who compiled an account of the same events on behalf of France, Venice's closest ally in the war. He himself professed to prefer "sincere memoirs, unadorned by lies," although he admitted that such accounts were "difficult" to find, "not to say . . . impossible."[82]

From Siri's point of view, the only acceptable sources were those that fit his intention to reinterpret France's misfortunes in the war. He based his account on the unfavorable evaluations originating from the rumor mill and diplomatic leaks rather than on the encomiastic progress reports coming off the Venetian presses. Although most of his sources are forever lost to us because of their ephemeral nature, we have been able to discover some of them. His view of the beginning of the 1650s campaigns appears to have derived from that of a clandestine Venetian newsletter reprinted in Genoa and Florence, which found the Candiots to be "abandoned because of the lack of concord between the authorities . . . and such negligence threatening, that constituted a great detriment."[83] In his view, too, disorders caused by unreliable hired commanders or allies were compounded by competition between the Venetian commanders themselves, especially between Captain General Alvise Leonardo Mocenigo and Captain of the Ships Giacomo da Riva.[84] In each of the relevant sections of his serially published volumes of contemporary history, he chose material that represented the events as the consequence of an injury by perfidious Venice rather than as an embarrassment for Louis XIV. Having begun his investigations when the war was already half over and concluded them when it was already lost, he was able to read back into the earliest events the disasters that were to come. And having decided from the outset that the Venetians were deceitful, greedy, and incompetent whereas the French were honest, generous, and skillful, he was able to show that at every stage, the Venetians either arrogantly scorned or irresponsibly misused French aid.[85]

From the structure of authority to the carrying out of orders to the character of individuals, Siri tried to show the Venetian military and political establishment to be rotten to the core. When the Turks attacked Canea in 1644, Captain of the Ships Marin Cappello pusillanimously ordered his ships to remain at port near Suda (Souda), in spite of the objec-

tions of Andrea Cornaro, governor of Candia, and of Antonio Navagero, governor of Corfu. Yet when the Turkish fleet came back toward Suda, Cappello simply left the port that he had claimed to be committed to defending. Siri proved his point by long excerpts from what purported to be a correspondence between Cornaro and Navagero; and he reinforced his argument by a further series of letters from Giovanni Battista Grimani, a regional governor who claimed, against many "Venetian imprints and reports," that he had sought to offer his own help to Cappello but was advised by a flummoxed Senate to back down.[86]

Even where the bravery of the individuals was not a question, according to Siri, the coexistence of various ill-defined levels of command made victory impossible. This Prince Nicolo Ludovisi discovered when he arrived with fleets from the pope and from Malta and found that his plans conflicted with those of Venetian commander Francesco Morosini. As if this were not bad enough, each of these champions was supported by one or another of the parties in the Senate. The same again occurred when Camillo Gonzaga provided a report on the defense of Candia to the Venetian officials, which Siri claimed to include. General de La Vallette opposed it so vehemently that pressure from supporters of the latter forced Gonzaga to resign. All the Senate could agree on was to accuse Navagero of gross dereliction of duty in the loss of Canea, forcing him to defend himself at length in another document Siri claimed to include.

Most of the time, Siri claimed, the Senate was hopelessly divided. On the question of whether to enrich the republic's coffers by offering nobility to those willing to pay high prices for it, two factions emerged: the most wealthy viewed the new measure as an easy way to deflect the republic's search for funds away from their own private resources without costing them any loss of personal prestige; the less wealthy regarded the prospect of new entrants to the nobility as a dangerous threat to their own hard-won status. Siri even included what purported to be copies of applications for nobility by the Labia and Widman families with the admonition "to be cautious when reading such appeals, which are mostly not turned on the lathe of Truth."[87]

For his severest indictments of Venice's behavior in the loss of Candia, Siri adopted a variation on the novelistic device of the found manuscript. Having "unfortunately lost, during a trip," a "detailed memoir made at my bidding by [French general] Modana Gildas," he claimed to rely instead on the account of Brusoni, corrected "by a noble Venetian who was in the battle," presumably one even more partial to France.[88] To this spe-

cial source he attributed the view that the Venetians, during the final Ottoman siege, sought to deceive both the French ambassador in Constantinople and the Turks by assuring the former that they needed French help in a battle that could only redound to the greater glory of France and aid in French expansion throughout the Mediterranean, while assuring the latter that a peace treaty was the only way to halt such expansion and frustrate the aims of the French. The rest of the war, Siri insisted, echoing anti-Venetian polemicist Gregorio Leti, proceeded on a mutual understanding between the Turks and the Venetians (still unconfirmed by recent scholarship) that the latter would put up a mild show of resistance in order to fool the world into thinking that they wished to keep the island; whereas they were really from the outset willing to give it up in exchange for diplomatic and commercial advantages.[89] Far from offering further proof of the dignity and valor of the Venetian patriciate, Siri asserted, the War of Candia was an unfortunate consequence of errors, lies, and manipulations, further evidence of the failure of Venetian leadership and the defects of republican government. And the reputation of France was secure.

In serving up for his readers a mixture of invective, fantasy, and truth in the attractive guise of contemporary historical narrative, Siri and the other hired historians fully agreed with the governments employing them that sometimes the actual facts about an event were less important than the beliefs about them that fired readers' imaginations, whether or not such beliefs were true. In the realm of politics, the most important beliefs were those notions about the power and glory of the state that could inspire affection and allegiance. Without the affection and allegiance of at least a good portion of the people, they agreed, there could be no legitimacy; and in an age of continuous threats to consolidated power, legitimacy was the sole aim and limit of much that went on in political policy making.

Governments in turn may well have recognized that the hired historians themselves constituted a small but noisy category of subjects to whom careful attention must be paid. When disturbances occurred, hired historians were rarely far from the scene. Purchasing their allegiance both at home and abroad could retard the formation of dangerous pockets of resistance. Along with other intellectuals, they were looked upon by fellow subjects with a kind of awe. Guaranteeing the reproduction of such salient examples of loyalty and deference among the population at large might inspire imitation by others. That the hired historians could be

an important part of such policies was proved by their engagements throughout Europe.

However, the very success of the genre of hired history was the policy's own greatest threat. The historians themselves were among the most vehement protesters. Siri referred to his Venetian counterparts as "murderers of the public" because of their application of the historian's craft to the adulator's task. Moreover, he claimed, "they dare to attack princes who have emptied their treasuries and depopulated their states to aid the republic, and they rob soldiers and captains of the fame and glory due from memorable actions." All of this, according to Siri, provoked "a hue and cry" against them "almost everywhere in Europe." Of course, mutatis mutandis, the same applied to Siri himself, whose work was as antagonistic to the allies of Venice as the pro-Venetian works were to the allies of France.[90] For a time, the hired historians might safely ignore such complaints and be consoled by the popularity of the genre, apparently even to the detriment of sales in the works of the ancient historians.[91] Buoyed up by the defiant words of the likes of Luca Assarino, they need not concern themselves with the skepticism of the learned. "The glory of authors comes from the majority, not the minority of the audience. Even if the majority is made up of those less learned and less capable of judging," Assarino continued, "one must follow the current whenever the current, however contorted, leads to the journey's destination."[92] And more often than not, that destination was, in the imaginations of the historians, the early modern equivalent of fame, fortune, and romance.

When even among the majority in the audience, the conflict between myth and antimyth noted by Siri began to erode whatever credibility the hired historians may have acquired by calling themselves historians at all, then not only the genre of hired history but the whole discipline of history stood to lose. Something of the kind began to happen at the end of the seventeenth century—or so some critics believed. But by then, the abating confidence in historians' writings became mingled with the epistemological debate about the nature of historiographical truth, to force a reexamination of research methods with a view to putting the investigation of the past on an entirely new footing.

4

Veritas Filia Temporis

Any study of the effects of the information trade in early modern times calls upon the historian to perform a remarkable conjuring act by attempting to read the minds of the people of the past. Fortunately, for the argument we have been advancing here, there is no need to read the minds of all readers, nor even a majority of them. We are only interested in the most attentive and vociferous of observers, those more or less close to the cultural elite, whose views were heard and heeded. How many of these seventeenth-century observers worried that the newsletters appeared to be concocted from malicious gossip? How many worried that the newspapers just might be published at the bidding of powerful political interests with little inclination to tell the truth? And how many worried that histories of recent events might be based on faulty sources even when the writers endeavored to procure faithful accounts?[1] Among those whose views have been recorded, our evidence suggests that few had any illusions about the reliability of political information imparted by the sources newly minted or voluminously increased during the course of the century.

Nor did the information specialists themselves offer much in the way of a defense. In admitting that "truth is by nature elusive and slippery," Agostino Mascardi, the history theorist, could recommend nothing better to exculpate the inaccurate historian than the injunction against throwing the first stone. But "Omnis homo mendax," the expression attributed to King David, was likely to offer readers little more in the way of consolation than the reminder that "those who are such harsh critics of historians' involuntary lies may well be astute trammelers of perfidy and de-

ceit in their own lives."[2] Mascardi had no answer about historians who deliberately distorted the truth. Yet, just when readers might have desired it most, from the earliest days of the Thirty Years' War to the last days of the Turkish wars at the end of the century, the possibility of gaining a realistic picture of the contemporary world seemed to be getting more and more remote.

The time has come to analyze the cultural consequences of this late-seventeenth-century trend. Our inquiry now ascends from the ground level of the writing business to the airy realm of theory. For the time being we must leave behind the world of the writers, literary hacks, and charlatans we have been describing to join the company of contemplators and philosophers. To this, the previous chapters will seem but an essential prelude; and the tale we now have to tell reveals an unexpected dimension of some of the best-known trends in the intellectual history of the age. As often happens, these trends have an internal as well as an external history. And the series of events leading to the late-seventeenth-century crisis from within the history of ideas itself has been told many times—most notably, years ago by Paul Hazard in a groundbreaking work. The external history has yet to be written. Our concern here, in undertaking a first attempt at providing this, will be to sort out, from amid the complex of causes that led to an outcome of skepticism, just what may have been attributable to intellectual dynamics and what may be attributed to social, political, and economic dynamics embodied in the system of gathering and peddling political information.

There is no need to exaggerate. To some of the readers, writers, thinkers, and theorists of the age, the unreliability of information about their own time or about the past, however compounded by contemporary political and social circumstances, was nothing but a minor nuisance. To others, it was a hint about the bad faith of the governments that influenced writers. To still others, and these are the ones whose views preoccupied the historiographical reformers of the last decades of the century, this same unreliability raised deeply troubling questions about human nature and existence. It provided social and political reasons for historical skepticism, quite apart from one's familiarity with Sextus Empiricus or the elite intellectual fashions of the moment.[3] It placed everyday social and political reality in a new light, thus adding a more mundane element to the uneasy feeling induced by the new science and cosmology—the feeling, that is, of being borne along on uncontrollable currents whose exact configuration the best minds nonetheless seemed in-

capable of understanding. It added to the disquiet produced by confessional disputes, suggesting that truth might be beyond human capacity to grasp. This was no ordinary skepticism, of the sort that, for example, a casual listener might have evinced in hearing an improbable story. Pierre Bayle and Lorenzo Magalotti, two of our main characters, were riven with doubt of a most fundamental kind. Our object is to show why it extended to journalism and historiography.

Not only in Italy, but throughout Europe in the late seventeenth century, existing methods of ascertaining facts in political and military affairs both in the present and in past times came under a new sort of scrutiny as part of what Hazard has regarded as no less than a wide-ranging "crisis of consciousness" at the threshold of the Enlightenment.[4] In fact, the crisis was resolved at least in part by a corresponding movement for methodological change and by a reform of ideas about the proper place for intellectual improvisation in the formation of narrative, in order to make historical writing persuasive and civically useful again. If the product of error and fraud was skepticism, the product of skepticism was modern historiography.[5]

History and Experience

The elusiveness of political truth that contributed to the late-seventeenth-century crisis was no novelty of the age. What passed for information about contemporary events was already notoriously unreliable in the sixteenth century, when Ludovico Ariosto made that the subject of his verse.[6] Any exceptionally gullible person paying heed solely to the newsletters could be sure of gaining a highly peculiar view of the surrounding world. Such a person, reading the best-accredited Roman newsletters of the year 1588, would have been wrongly convinced of the death of Henry of Navarre, the future king of France, and of Giovanni de' Medici, natural son of Grand Duke Cosimo I of Tuscany.[7] The same person would have believed Anne de Joyeuse, the favorite of Henry III of France, was murdered by Henry I of Bourbon, prince of Condé, whereas he actually died in battle. And the reader would have found information about a key event like the defeat of the Spanish Armada notoriously difficult to confirm. Affirmations like, "We have news from the court of His Highness that the Spanish and English armadas joined battle and the English one was ruined and destroyed," shortly followed by, "From an extraordinary courier arrived in France . . . there has been news that the

Catholic armada landed safely in Scotland," were likely to produce considerable disappointment later on. That the newsletters constantly alerted their patrons to the problem was small consolation. Variations on the dictions, "they say that . . . but others say. . . ." or "although some believe . . . nonetheless the last letters from Utrecht affirm . . . ," emphasizing the uncertainties, only made things worse.

In addition, deliberate misinformation was a fully recognized political strategy at least by the time that Machiavelli made it an explicit part of prudence during the small break in the Italian wars that brought the return of the Medici to Florence. No one would ever forget his admiration for Pope Alexander VI and Ferdinand I of Spain as the best liars of their time. From his time onward, good appearances were to be cultivated by keeping in mind his famous phrase, "Everyone sees what you seem; few perceive what you are."[8] And if Francesco Guicciardini, Machiavelli's contemporary, disagreed about recommending such policies, this was not because he believed they were little used or, when used, were ineffective, but simply because true evil could not long be hidden.[9]

Anyone who was scared away from the works of Machiavelli by the official denunciations of his unconventional morality could find his insights smuggled into any number of other works wrapped in the slightly more acceptable dress of Cornelius Tacitus. By 1574, they could refer to the scholarly edition of Tacitus prepared by Justus Lipsius, ostensibly in order to bring the strategies and tactics of princely rulership to the attention of more readers. What Lipsius purveyed to his Dutch readers in the way of political advice in his *Politicorum libri sex,* in 1589, Guy de Pibrac purveyed to his French ones, and Arnold Clapmar to his German ones. That such theories went to support causes as diverse as the Dutch revolt against Spain, the St. Bartholomew's Day Massacre, and the adjustment of Habsburg relations with the German towns made no difference. The writers all agreed that means justify ends.[10] If not explicitly, at least implicitly they all agreed with the extreme formulation of the Piedmontese writer Giovanni Botero who, exploring these Tacitist perspectives in his *Reason of State,* expressed the fewest reservations about insisting on the propriety of a policy of state secrecy and misinformation. He frankly admitted that "dissembling is a big help";[11] and he suggested that "two things are necessary" in deciding what to dissemble: "The first is to know one's own weakness; the second is to show one's greatness without ostentation." The only limits on such a policy were that it ought not to be pursued to the extent of damaging credibility; for "although it

may go beyond the bounds of truth, it ought to be contained at least within the bounds of likelihood."[12]

Scipione Ammirato, a political theorist and historian in Florence, provided a philosophical basis for what was becoming a more and more openly accepted counsel. In his treatise *On Secrecy*, he took as his point of departure the Aristotelian distinction between bodies of knowledge like logic, philosophy, and metaphysics, where complete certainty could be attained, and others, like rhetoric, history, and what concerned the world of sense and experience. In the latter areas, he explained, only probable truth was at stake.[13] Indeed, even concerning the most basic problems of the observation of nature, he noted, such as the size of the sun, there had been many different opinions. So much more, then, he argued, might we expect to encounter doubtful matters in morality; and the many variations in national customs concerning a basic institution like matrimony bears this out. Let no one then be scandalized by the proposition that political policies might be acceptable or unacceptable according to the circumstances or that policies could be unethical from the standpoint of the ordinary citizen but praiseworthy from the standpoint of the state. Given the difference between private and public morality, persons informed about such policies, he suggested, ought to learn from the example of nature, which leaves the ears wide open to receive sounds but places a lid on the mouth. Secrecy is not just good counsel; it is also natural.

Practices of secrecy and dissimulation made for a historiography that often appeared to be caught between guarded enlightenment and hypocritical encomium. But what distinguished the Renaissance critics of faulty information from their seventeenth-century counterparts were the conclusions they drew from their observations.[14] Pietro Bizzarri and Benedetto Varchi's critiques of Paolo Giovio, Giovanni Battista Leoni's critique of Guicciardini, and Gian Michele Bruto's critique of Florentine historiography were never any more damaging, at least from a methodological standpoint, than Cesare Baronio's attacks on the Magdeburg Centuriators or Isaac Casaubon's critique of Cesare Baronio: namely, that historians distort the truth because of their own interests and those of their employers, quite apart from whether or not they have mastered the evidence.[15] Leoni set the tone for all the rest when he complained that "the truth, which is the only soul and animator of history," was, in Guicciardini's work, "corrupted and defaced by passion and artifice" because the author had wished to be "a very loyal citizen of his country rather than a good historian."[16]

When Bruto chimed in, "as the history [i.e., historiography of Florence] comes closer to our own times, you will find it full of perpetual praise for the Medici and full of calumnies, libels, villainies, and brazen lies concerning the whole city,"[17] neither he nor any of the others suggested that historical knowledge as such might be impossible. The only observer to hint in that direction was Cornelius Agrippa von Nettesheim, the German scholar who made Italy his home. But even he was more of a "fundamentalist anti-intellectual" than an authentic Pyrrhonist. After repeating the common complaints about the defects of secondhand information and the vices of malicious distortion, he concluded that the light of truth, dimmed in human nature by original sin, might shine again when all the disciplines had been reformed according to the teachings of the occult sciences.[18]

The most famous historical skeptic of the late sixteenth century was Francesco Patrizi, a Neoplatonist philosopher and professor at the University of Padua. According to him, bad historians and faulty works of history existed in part because of unreliable sources. And unreliable sources existed, he had one of the characters in his dialogue suggest, because the persons most likely to possess the most accurate inside information about events were ministers informed about the secret counsels of a prince. Yet ministers who received such counsels were precisely those most likely to transmit them in a modified form.[19] Given the pressure of reputation, on both the prince and the minister, manipulation of the truth was almost inevitable.[20] Even when there was no outright manipulation, the documentary or verbal accounts of a particular event were subject to an endless process of substitutions and omissions caused by the defective or selective memories of those involved. The most reliable such accounts were likely to be by eyewitnesses who maintained a neutral position regarding what was going on. But those who maintained such a position usually did so because they simply did not understand. Therefore they were likely to miss important details that helped explain the interests and the actions in play. Furthermore, general narratives were more likely to be truthful than specific ones. Yet the more general an account became the less useful it was likely to be. And when, in the absence of necessary evidence about specific episodes, historians sought to add details and causal hypotheses to their excessively general accounts, they risked sacrificing truth on the altar of didacticism.

In spite of all these difficulties, Patrizi himself, appearing in person in his dialogue, concluded that history per se was safe. Historical research

was capable of attaining a sufficient degree of certitude for the discipline to be classed among the sciences rather than among the arts of rhetoric, where Aristotle had put it. Whatever might be its actual record of achievements, its object was the attainment of true knowledge by the faithful exposition of things, unlike poetry, whose object was the attainment of probable knowledge by way of plausible representations. History shared with philosophy a concern for understanding the effects of the forces in the earthly sphere, and although it did not accompany philosophy in the search for the higher causes of those forces, it did seek to elucidate the human causes of events. As such it was an essential handmaid to philosophy, showing what could be done by what had been done before, teaching what, in Patrizi's words, "may make life happy and eternal."[21]

Melchior Cano, a Spanish theologian writing around the same time, came to similar conclusions. In his inquiry about whether historical accounts could be relied upon in forming theological arguments, he concluded that they might, to the extent that they satisfied one of three conditions: The most trustworthy of all were of course those that were regarded as authoritative by ecclesiastical officials. But accounts did not have to be revered as scripture for them to be granted a high degree of probability "and sometimes even certainty."[22] They could also, and this was the second condition, be written by writers known for probity and veracity—such writers as might be expected to tell the truth in any circumstances. Finally, they could be written with sufficient attention to the correct evaluation of testimony. And in offering their results, they could distinguish proven fact from conjecture.

Some apparently unrelated intellectual breakthroughs in this time actually served to reinforce the notion that the historian might be in a particularly favorable position to discover the facts.[23] For toward the end of the sixteenth century few members of the ideal audience we have been hypothesizing here were entirely unaware of the new fact-finding procedures being tried at least in the study of nature. The cadaver-scrutinizing followers of Andreas Vesalius were not the only ones whose new focus on empirical investigation appeared to bring their research down from the lofty heights of philosophical speculation. Nor were the methodological implications of their work later recognized only by Francis Bacon, whose words are most familiar. "The mind is fond of starting off to generalities," he proclaimed, "that it may avoid labor. But the true method of discovering the truth constructs its axioms from the senses and particulars."[24] He proposed a program of natural history designed to apply the

method of experience and observation systematically by collections of particulars.[25]

Similarly, the tomb-scouring emulators of Onofrio Panvinio seemed intent on bringing the study of history down to the level of everyday experience. As the study of the past, not only in theory but also in practice, moved away from the arts of rhetoric and toward the arts of scholarship, natural philosophy and scholarship seemed to intersect, and not only because descriptions of natural objects by Ulisse Aldrovandi and others bore at least some resemblance to antiquarian researches, with appropriate citations to the ancient and modern authorities. No encyclopedic collection worthy of the name could afford to be without its coins, medals, inscriptions, and architectural fragments—"tamquam tabula naufragii," Bacon called them, "like the planks of a shipwreck."[26] Even before the narrative historians began to incorporate the results of antiquarian research into their work, the new opportunities for empirical verification seemed to reinforce the notion that the study of the past was a science of verifiable truth.

These intellectual breakthroughs encouraged at least one theorist, the early-seventeenth-century Calabrian philosopher Tommaso Campanella, to attribute a new importance to historiography.[27] Going beyond Bacon's formulation, Campanella claimed that not only all cognition but all motion in the universe was grounded in individual sensual perception by discrete subjects. All bodies reacted to sense perception by directing desire and effecting change.[28] Human beings attained knowledge of the universe by organizing sense perceptions into descriptions of experience. "The senses, then, our own and others', are in a certain measure narrators and witnesses for the soul, which is the inventor, builder, and master of the sciences."[29] And history being the true description of experience, in both the natural and the civic worlds, as Ludovico Castelvetro had noted in his commentary on Aristotle's poetics nearly a century before, its objects were more real than those of mathematics, which dealt in figments of the imagination.

Campanella thus made historiography one of the five parts, along with grammar, dialectic, rhetoric, and poetry, of his comprehensive *Philosophiae rationalis*.[30] "Although history precedes and is the base of doctrine," he explained, "nonetheless to place the base under this edifice and adapt it to the latter is the work of a wise architect; therefore I place history before logic and grammar and I consider it to be the first part of every philosophy."[31] To civil or "moral" history belonged the task of un-

locking the truths of the civic world in the fields of ethics, politics, and economics; to natural history belonged that of unlocking the truths of the natural world. He proposed to direct further progress by ambitious new projects, anticipating Francis Bacon's, for a universal civil history and a new universal natural history along the lines laid down, yet imperfectly fulfilled (so he said), by Pliny.

Alessandro Tassoni, the Modenese poet and historian, agreed with Campanella, his contemporary, at least regarding the notion of history as a science of truth. Ranging in his *Thoughts* over a host of problems in contemporary arts and sciences, from the self-propulsion of shrimp to the causes of gout in humans and capons, he looked provocatively to Sextus Empiricus for a definition of history. It was, he agreed, "the true narration of things done in the past."[32] But he ignored Sextus's claim that historians could not confirm their knowledge because they were unable to use empirical methods to trace events with anything like the same assurance with which doctors diagnosed diseases or musicians perceived dissonance. Historical truth, Tassoni insisted, could indeed be discovered; and the proper method was precise attendance to sense experience. For "the objects of the senses are real and certain," and sense provided the material for knowledge. But the path from sense to knowledge was not a simple one. Indeed, "the intellect does not speculate without images; and images do not detach themselves from or present themselves to the intellect without the imagination, which draws them out of the senses."[33]

In contrast with the objects of the senses, Tassoni maintained, "those of the intellect are fantastic and imaginary, because the intellect works only on what is furnished by the imagination."[34] Errors in history and in any other writing came from the excessive intervention of the imagination in the process of writing or reading. Persons of lively intellect, he argued, could not prevent their minds from straying off into fantasies, more or less related to the words before them, faster than eye or hand could follow. The eye or hand, in the meantime, being physically detached from the imagination, could easily take these fantasies for something other than what they were and draw upon them, generating errors. Thus, "before we finish writing or reading the first word," he pointed out, "the imagination presents the letters of the second and confuses them together or causes the first to be left out or transposed."[35] However, the errors thus generated were not serious enough to invalidate the process of gaining and communicating knowledge. As long as the imagination was grounded in sense, it could never deceive the mind entirely. If it did, and

the imagination delivered fantasies that had no connection to the reality of the senses, the result was the condition we call insanity.

The discussions about new foundations and new methodologies that helped redefine historiography as a science of truth rather than as an art of rhetoric raised an exciting new possibility: that modern historians might be at least the equals, if not the superiors, of the ancient historians. If historians were to be judged on the criterion of veracity, which the new methods seemed to suggest might be attainable by attending more precisely to experience, rather than on the criterion of eloquence, still the undisputed preserve of the ancients, then the quarrel between the ancients and the moderns might be settled in favor of the latter. And so it was in the mind of Secondo Lancellotti, who touted modern achievements in science, technology, commerce, and engineering in response to the "today haters" who put the ancients on a pedestal in all fields. According to his perspective, the tall tales told by some modern historians ought to be regarded as the exception, not the rule. "Every writer," he claimed, "especially of history, has either erred somewhat or failed to give total satisfaction."[36] Anyone who doubted this could refer to his treatise on the great mistakes and improbabilities of ancient historiography—one hundred in all, including Valerius Maximus's preposterous story about Zaleucus's self-mutilation, Diodorus Siculus's report about Xerxes drying up the rivers, and Plutarch's account of Mark Antony's eloquent speech before his would-be assassins.[37] The moderns who erred were at least in good company; and now, as ever, some acted in good faith: "Not all historians are adulators, nor is sincerity entirely dead."[38] Moreover, only the moderns had given such attention to the histories of countries other than their own, from Famiano Strada on the Low Countries to Enrico Caterina Davila on France.

Honest Dissembling

While Campanella, Tassoni, and Lancellotti contemplated the prospects for a future ordered by science and scholarly inquiry, still other readers, writers, thinkers, and theorists in this period worried that a severe deterioration of conditions in the political and social realms could threaten any methodological advances that had been made.[39] The revolts and rebellions of the 1640s were still a long way off. But pressing concerns seemed to impinge upon the half of the peninsula that, nominally ruled by Spain, shared in the debacle of the Spanish empire. And danger-

ous forebodings seemed to beckon in the other half of the peninsula, where city industries and civic institutions that had been a chief strength in the Renaissance were now, in the seventeenth century, becoming a chief weakness. All over the peninsula, economic disasters led to biological disasters just when the Thirty Years' War required the consolidation of precious resources. The plague of 1630 raged through Lombardy, the Venetian republic, Tuscany, and the Este states, cutting down populations by as much as 40 percent. The exigencies of state governments in a time of rising costs, fiscal drain, increasing discontent, and heightened dynastic competition widened the gap between what was promised and what could be accomplished, between words and the things spoken of, between representations of power and effects of power on an international as well as on a local scale. A reevaluation, more incisive and profound than any in Machiavelli's time, came about of the relation between the ideal and the real, both in public and private life.

Torquato Accetto, a Neapolitan lawyer inspired by a society he viewed as increasingly polarized between the powerful and the powerless, between rich and poor, between the custodians of truth and their beneficiaries, suggested that in cases in which political and social reality could never measure up to the ideals, "dissembling" was not only an "honest" practice among both the great and the humble, it was also a duty.[40] Indeed, from his vantage point as a servant in the powerful Carafa household within the politically troubled and financially addled Kingdom of Naples, it seemed to him that "dissembling cures all ills." The very art of civilized life itself, he argued, calls for fleeing ugliness by taking refuge in formalized patterns of behavior and aesthetic embellishment of the interior and exterior environments in which people lived. Dissembling saved reputations; it protected the feelings of loved ones. There could be no evil in this.

Nor could there be any evil in using lies, subterfuge, and hypocrisy to escape impossible demands and obligations self-imposed and imposed by others, Accetto argued. "Dress may be changed occasionally to suit the season of fortune, with the intention not of doing but rather of avoiding harm; and this is the only reason to tolerate dissembling, which thereby is not fraud." Much less should anyone be scandalized at the use of deception by the powerful. As the positive counterpart to the negative policy of secrecy expounded by all the political theorists, deception was the essential accompaniment of the exercise of power. "Crowns of gold have no brightness that at some time does not need your shadows," he said,

rhetorically addressing his subject, "and scepters not carried by your hand are often susceptible to vacillation. Flashing swords, if they do not use any of your cloud, shine in vain. Prudence, with all its virtue, possesses nothing better than you."[41] In the midst of this general game of fictions and counterfictions, the only certain knowledge one might have was of oneself; beyond that, the truths of life will be revealed only on the last day, "when reckoning will be made and there will be no art of making black seem white."[42]

Perhaps the most extreme formulation of the same view came by way of the Spain of Philip IV. "Deceit rules the roost," noted the famous priest Baltasar Gracián in a treatise published just three years before Accetto's and later admired by none other than Arnold Schopenhauer. "Things are judged by their jackets and many things are other than they seem."[43] In the midst of this general game of fictions and counterfictions, the individual had little choice but to play along. Human life, Gracián explained, involved constant warfare against the malice of others and called for constant shifts in strategy. "Sagacity now rises to higher flights on seeing its artifice foreseen and tries to deceive by truth itself, changes its game in order to change its deceit, and cheats by not cheating, and founds deception on the greatest candor."[44] No wonder historical works could be confusing.

Among the first to suspect that deception was a condition of politics and not an optional strategy, as Machiavelli and his disciples had maintained, was Traiano Boccalini. To reach this conclusion he did not have to look far. Apart from his scholarly commitment to the writings of Tacitus, he served as a curial lawyer in Rome and governor of several of the subject cities of the Papal States in the time of Paul V. Thus, he was aware of the perils of provincial administration by a distant central government as well as the dangers of serving a prince whose mental imbalance and fiscal irresponsibility rendered him ill equipped for leadership in a newly polarized Europe. In his *Reports from Parnassus*, Boccalini reflected upon the ironies of the age. All of politics, he concluded, was an elaborate game of deception: "The courts of princes are nothing but costume shops," he suggested, "where everything on sale is fake, made for the service of falsehood";[45] and the behavior of princes toward their subjects was an extension of the same practices. Unwilling or unable to win hearts by policies tending to the public good, they sought vainly to prevent discord by keeping their populations uninformed.

To show modern policies in action, Boccalini imagines that Tacitus,

the master of deceitful "reason of state," has been invited to apply his insights to the government of the island of Lesbos. No sooner does Tacitus arrive than he puts his own precepts into practice, subtly insinuating discord between the people and the nobility in order to weaken both. Using "very secret techniques," he then incites the people to take up arms against the nobles.[46] After publicly offering himself as a mediator, he exercises this role in such a way as to let the ill feelings smolder. He then gains the support of the people for recruiting a foreign militia to save them from the nobles. At the same time, he cements the loyalty of the militia to himself by allowing it to commit atrocities against both sides. After causing false accusations of treachery to circulate against the nobility, he confiscates the property of some of the most powerful and gives it to the accusers; he sends others to squander their resources in expensive missions far from Lesbos. Finally, he builds a huge fort under the pretext of the threat of foreign invasion but actually arms it against his own subjects and throws dissenters into its dungeons. But because the people of Lesbos retain, during all this time, some vestiges of their ancient freedom (unlike the inhabitants of so many contemporary polities in Italy, Boccalini wishes to imply), they eventually chase him off the island.

Among the same rulers who sought to conceal their own misdeeds, fear of historical truth ran rampant, Boccalini believed. And to illustrate this, he imagines, in another passage of the *Reports,* that Tacitus has been brought up before Apollo, the judge of Parnassus, on charges of having exposed the secrets of political behavior to the gaze of everyone.[47] Boccalini conveys this concept by means of an extended metaphor referring to the disenchanted analyses of the Roman emperors (and, by extension, all politics) in the *Annals* and *Histories.* Tacitus, he says, has been creating a new and dangerous type of eyeglasses that allow the wearer not only to see the actions of princes more clearly but also to see through all the artifices used to disguise the real nature of power. And what is worse, the distribution of the eyeglasses has extended far beyond the restricted circle of political adepts, ministers, and princes themselves, to all and sundry. It is well known, the indictment claims, that princes often commit evil actions in order to maintain their authority and represent such actions in the false light of the public good in order to maintain their reputations. With the new eyeglasses, not only might these reputations be destroyed, but the people, learning the rules of politics, might discover how to wield power for themselves. Then even good princes might be encouraged to give up the problems, frustrations, and perplexities of rule,

and monarchy would be no more. In the event, Apollo acquits Tacitus, on the condition that the new eyeglasses will be distributed only on a limited scale. Censorship and dissembling win the day.

Some readers, writers, thinkers, and theorists were less interested in the cultural significance of fraud than in the possible utility of it. Whereas Paolo Sarpi, adviser to Venice, encouraged governments to hire historians and propagandists to carry their messages to present and future generations, Virgilio Malvezzi, political theorist and adviser to the grand duke of Tuscany, encouraged the spreading of falsehood.[48] When all political acts were shrouded in secrecy, Malvezzi argued, curiosity might lead to the revelation of things that could be damaging to the state. Let the prince select the most damaging truth, transform it into a flattering or at least innocuous lie, and allow this to leak out. By placing false rumors in circulation, the government could satisfy curiosity and protect itself from excessive openness at the same time. In case anyone had any doubts about such a policy, he suggested, all they had to do was to consult the example of Scipio, the ancient Roman hero who made people believe that a message he had received from Syphax, the Numidian general, had been an invitation to go into Africa, whereas it had actually been a threat. Scipio thus distracted the multitudes while avoiding a possible cause of unnecessary preoccupation within the army. No modern ruler could avoid pursuing policies of this sort.

With political actors spinning ever more complex webs of deception and dissembling, the possibility of arriving at the bedrock of conviction about politics appeared ever more remote. Among the early-seventeenth-century figures who worried about the consequences of this on historiography was Agostino Mascardi, writing in Rome in the 1630s. Picking up where Patrizi left off, he observed that historians often rely on official correspondence or diplomatic documents. Yet the most important information in military and diplomatic affairs, in order to avoid discovery, was communicated by word of mouth, not by writing.[49] Moreover, interested parties jealously protected the documentary sources; and to guard against espionage they often used deliberately convoluted or cryptic language even when they did not resort to cipher.

Supposing the historian succeeded in acquiring such material and understanding what it said, Mascardi continued, this still did not guarantee full comprehension of events. Ministers were often mistaken about what went on; and even when they were not, they often modified their reports to correspond to their own interests. Princes, on the other hand, routinely

deceived their ministers whenever this suited their purposes. "Princes proceed in their affairs with such secrecy that penetrating to the heart of them is harder than interpreting the words of the Sphinx."[50] He concluded by reminding readers that, according to the intellectual categories that had held fast at least up to the time of Patrizi, history did not belong to the exact sciences at all but only to the probable ones. Fact could hardly be separated from opinion; and there was no use demanding of scholarship more than it could deliver. "The credit one gives to histories is human credit, that is, always joined to doubt," he reminded readers. "Those who require infallible certainty based on incontrovertible proof are asking the impossible."[51] The best that could be expected was that history, far more than any philosophically derived science of civility, could teach practical political prudence by providing a repertoire of relevant historical examples.

In discussing the present state of historiography, even Mascardi dropped his dispassionate facade. He found the number of unreliable historical works in circulation to be a cause of grave concern. "Anyone who knows how to register credits and debits in a ledger book indiscriminately and temerariously takes up history writing."[52] Nevertheless, the writing of history, he pointed out, was not merely a leisure-time activity. It required "very long study" and the perfection, through experience, of "a mature and perfect judgment," not to mention specific techniques for gathering evidence concerning political behavior. No one, he said, would be so foolish as to commission a sculpture from a cobbler or a suit of clothes from a baker. Yet something of the kind was happening in historiography. As a result of current fashion, "an entire population of writers has arisen, who are filling the world with paper and putting printers to work."[53]

Among the many causes that tipped the scales in the late seventeenth century toward a more radical historical skepticism than Mascardi and his contemporaries were earlier able to muster, the spread of misinformation and falsehood certainly played an important role. A few specimens of untruth circulating among a relatively restricted audience was one thing. The commercialization of error and its spread to a broad audience raised some serious questions. Professional writers hired themselves out to governments to provide the necessary accounts of recent historical events: Raffaelle Della Torre to Naples, Luca Assarino to Rome, Genoa, and Venice; Mascardi himself to Genoa; Pietro Gazzotti to Genoa and Modena; Galeazzo Gualdo Priorato to France, Capriata to Genoa,

France, and Spain; Vittorio Siri and Giovanni Birago Avogadro to Florence; Giovanni Francesco Fossati to Venice and Spain; and a host of others to all the major governments of the time.[54] We have already met them and seen them in action.

By the time political authorities began to use newspapers as vehicles for official notification about events, information had already become a major commodity of governments. Newspaper entrepreneurs in Milan and Piedmont agreed to print the local papers in the official government printing offices; and those in Piedmont accepted government pensions.[55] Here and everywhere else they accepted government-planted stories when asked and covered political affairs at home and abroad as favorably as possible to local interests. No one could ignore the possible effects of such practices on historical credibility. "Those who are too accustomed to lies," commented the anonymous author of a work on Venice, "will never believe or heed the truth."[56]

The newly invented or newly voluminous sources of political information promised far more than they could ever deliver. They promised to bring reflection upon everyday experience out of the murky realm of oral tradition and myth and into the clear and bright realm of published print. For the first time, printed information seemed to fix the unfixable, to render permanent the ephemeral, to put a hard finish on the ragged edge of early modern time. It seemed to hasten closure of the itinerary of a rumor, to dam the fluid boundaries between various versions of reality and myth within the rigid terms of a single conclusion. News in printed form no longer seemed to be, like the manuscript traditions, in a dialogue with the world outside, part of a context of writings and rewritings, but seemed rather to propose itself as something in a state of completion.[57] Hard copy seemed to promise hard fact. That, at least, was the expectation; that was the ideal; and that was the intended impression.

How wrong these expectations could be was proven by the result. What the spread of political misinformation in more massive quantities most powerfully underscored was the considerable degree of uncertainty at which individuals as well as governments had been accustomed to operating—and would continue to operate. The medium of print not only diffused the truth in many cases; it also put casual misinformation into a deceptively permanent form. The results could be supremely unsettling. Seeing a lie in print was not the same as hearing it from a neighbor or seeing it in a manuscript newsletter. A lie in print was an invitation to join the community of the deceived. Moreover, the rich variety of versions

and variants in anonymous accounts of an event that was the aspect whereby preprint political information most resembled rumor and myth went from being a creative tool to being an annoying impediment to comprehension in the world of print. Printed news permitted the comparison of accounts in a way never possible before. Accounts of the same event were in sufficiently available abundance to be present at the same time in the same place. The inaccuracies were easy to detect even when the writers themselves did not continuously direct attention to them.

Open party conflict gave a particularly powerful impetus to the proliferation of divergent accounts, and Italy and France, with their frequent rebellions and wars, were by no means the only places where such divergences occurred. Consider the case of England, where a whole generation of readers and writers was reared during the civil war. This, according to Thomas Fuller, a church historian writing at the end of the 1650s, could only lead to a fatally damaged historiography, as in fact occurred. All one had to do was to compare historians who wrote before the struggle, when "there was a general right understanding betwixt all of the nation," with their later counterparts, who "are seldom apprehended truly or candidly, save of such of their own persuasion, while others do not . . . understand them aright."[58] If Thomas Hobbes, a historian in his own right, agreed with this view, Samuel Butler extended it to all historiography. Modern historians, he insisted, far outdid those of classical antiquity only in their partiality, because the ancients, at least, recorded divergent opinions dispassionately by placing them in the mouths of historical characters in the form of staged speeches, whereas the moderns passed off their own tendentious interpretations as facts.[59]

More and more writers began to adopt, as an opening gambit for presenting their productions, the new notion that the public had been duped, rather than the Guicciardinian concept that a given subject was intrinsically important. Capriata offered his work as containing "more truth" than contemporary Venetian accounts of the years 1634–44.[60] Authors entitled their works *True Relation, Faithful History,* and the like not simply in deference to a literary topos but rather in reference to a mark whereby they claimed to distinguish themselves from the myriad accounts that, as they explained in their prefaces, did not live up to these standards. With ostensible sincerity, Luca Assarino claimed that "seeing not only the variations but also the manifest contradictions in accounts of the same event, with too much damage to posterity, has persuaded me to enter the fray."[61] This claim was no more extravagant than that of

Bisaccioni, who recommended his account of the Masaniello revolt as a "foreign" work, that is, not Neapolitan, and therefore more likely to be "dispassionate."[62] Thus, when Birago Avogadro introduced his suggestively entitled *Mercurio veridico* by noting that his work was more reliable than Vittorio Siri's, he could scarcely expect more credit than his adversary.[63] Siri's work bore an engraving by Gabriel Le Brun depicting Mercury, the god of eloquence, at the entrance to a cave on a hill with people bringing him gifts, while Truth lies naked on the ground. The tableau was adorned with the motto, "Hoc tantum ditior in antro" (loosely, "Mercury gains more by sheer verbal chicanery than Truth does by veracity").[64] No one who read these histories would have dared to disagree.

That they protested too much for their own good was confirmed at mid-century by the papal lawyer Francesco De Rossi, who declared that historical works were no longer acceptable as proof in legal disputes among the Roman families or among the Italian states. No one, he believed, should confuse works of modern history with works of canonical devotion, whose historical accounts were confirmed by revelation and tradition. Nor should they confuse them with the ancient compendium of law in the *Corpus juris civilis,* whose historical accounts were confirmed by generations of legal practice.[65] After all, he argued, modern histories are only private writings, not officially guaranteed by any authoritative body or method. Generally, they consist only in the opinions of the writers, and not often of writers of the best kind. They could scarcely be regarded as superior to the opinions of jurisconsults, which are themselves not regarded as authoritative. And because they are often at a considerable distance from eyewitness accounts, they could claim no more veracity than public documents, which are not necessarily believed without proof. Indeed, more than any other documents, histories contain falsehoods that are difficult to separate from the truth.

The New Skepticism

Historiography was not the only field to experience a new wave of skepticism toward the end of the century. The questioning of methods and approaches that went on in science and philosophy had powerful collateral effects on the way readers, writers, thinkers, and theorists in this period viewed contemporary accounts of the past. For one thing, the new experimental and experiential science that had been a model for his-

toriography became in some ways the victim of its own success.[66] Even Galileo's erstwhile enemies, the Jesuits, began to abandon Aristotelianism for a more eclectic and experience-oriented intellectual system by this time.[67] Yet excessive confidence in observation and experiment, the same confidence that earlier had been an inspiration for the theorists of historiography as a science, began to give way to diminished enthusiasm for the empirical attitudes of the Galilean and Baconian schools.

In order to see a promising new field like microscopy as an example of the new caution about observation, there is no need to belittle its remarkable contributions to the developing sciences of embryology, subtle anatomy, and botany nor to find skeptical sparring matches in every disagreement between Robert Hooke in England, Jan Swammerdam and Antonie van Leeuwenhoek in Holland, and Marcello Malpighi in Bologna.[68] Seized upon in the second half of the seventeenth century by enthusiasts throughout Europe as the tool that would force nature to reveal its innermost parts, just as the outermost ones were coming into view in telescopic astronomy, the new field gradually began to give way to disillusionment and doubt. The closer the observer appeared to get to the tiny structures that were the object of his researches, the more those tiny structures seemed to reveal the existence of still-invisible aspects. Imperfections in glassmaking and lens polishing combined with entoptical irregularities to create appearances of the most unbiological sorts. Even when the observations were correct, verbal description seemed as inadequate as graphic representation to convey what the researcher claimed to have seen.

Leeuwenhoek himself cautioned against the multitude of fallacious viewings that were pouring in even to a respected organ like the *Philosophical Transactions* of the Royal Society—"for it doth happen that people looking through a Magnifying-glass, do say now I see this and then that, and when I give them better instructions, they saw themselves mistaken in their opinion." He was able to unmask fraudulent researchers who loaded their instruments with devices to produce special effects. But he was unable to dispel the skepticism surrounding his own supposed observation of the microscopic man-shaped beings—the so-called homunculi—forming the active agents in human sperm. And when the observation results were not impugned, explanations of even the most accurate observations of the invisible structure of things seemed to provide the researcher with only a larger, closer-up version of the same in-

scrutable appearances, without arriving at truths about the purposes of those structures or how they functioned.

To be sure, many practitioners in fields of natural knowledge, probably including the ones mentioned in the previous paragraph, were not too bothered about the lack of an agreed-upon explanatory scheme. Nor did they worry that, in the absence of such a scheme, new observations, even of the most unexceptionable sort, might seem to dangle in a chaos of divergent interpretations. They experienced no sense of disorientation, knowing that the utter discrediting of long-standing philosophical and epistemological traditions—the Aristotelian, the Galenic, the Platonic—with no comfortable substitute in sight left practitioners with nothing to depend upon for theoretical support. To them, if many of the problems with which the new science began to concern itself—the generation of life, the organization of matter—were simply not susceptible to the kinds of empirical verification permitted by available techniques, this was exclusively a matter for the epistemologists.[69]

However, some protagonists in the changes we have been analyzing began to believe that no research program could proceed without a new cognitive structure to put in the place of the now discredited traditions. In this context, they found new meaning in Galileo's reliance on geometry and mathematics. They paid renewed attention to his famous dictum in the *Letter to Christina* that the book of the world was written in mathematical language; they now saw this as proceeding from a conviction that mathematical laws were prior to sensory experience and capable in some cases of arriving at a greater degree of certitude than unaided observation.[70] They then set out to establish reason and logic as the essential bases of knowledge, implicitly relegating historiography, a mainly experiential science, to the realm of pure opinion. No one yet noticed that empiricism and deductive laws could be combined to form a powerful historiographical method, first theorized by Hermann Conring in Germany and later, in a different context, by Giambattista Vico.[71]

To be sure, these intellectual trends did not proceed in the same way in every part of Europe. They were more pronounced in Italy and France than in Holland and England, although the latter is likely to be by far the more familiar context to most readers of these pages; and the different ways in which the trends were worked out did not depend solely on episodes in the realm of ideas. In England, for instance, the Restoration reinforcement of the gentlemanly ethos, an ethos that valued the common

sense and good judgment of privileged persons, is reputed to have induced Robert Boyle to believe that the light of reason itself, without the
aid of structures or paradigms, might provide an antidote to the uncertainty of the evidence.[72] Thus, English empiricism may well have kept its
tenacious hold for reasons as much concerned with the history of social
and political life as with the history of ideas. A complete social history of
skepticism would account for how such causes contributed to linking the
spread of political information with the spread of disbelief in all its different settings.

Here we focus on the Kingdom of Naples, which provides an unusually revealing set of examples of how circumstances combined to gener-
ate a movement for refining processes of verification in the natural sciences but not in historiography. We provide a rather in-depth exploration
of the Neapolitan context, because it is the least known. Specialists on
the history of southern Italy have described well how the cultural elite,
including such figures as Tommaso Cornelio, Francesco D'Andrea,
Domenico Aulisio, Gregorio Caloprese, and Gian Vincenzo Gravina,
drawn mainly from professional groups excluded from political power
and well known to modern scholars of Giambattista Vico, quarreled with
a local power elite composed of members and clients of the landed aristocracy.[73] They have shown how the cultural elite objected to the way the
power elite had connived with the Spanish crown over the years to build
private wealth at the expense of the kingdom by buying up alienated
lands and revenues, creating a fiscal crisis of vast proportions.[74]

In Naples, hopes for reform were to some extent inspired among the
cultural elite by the Masaniello revolt, which had briefly put the government of the whole city into the hands of the citizens. The elite's determi-
nation was galvanized by the subsequent wave of repression in the midst
of plagues and epidemics that served only to demonstrate the inadequa-
cies of the system. In this scenario some traditional structures were more
vulnerable than others; among the most vulnerable were the medical and
educational establishments. This is where reform and renewal appeared
most likely to produce solutions to the most pressing problems, and this
is where the cultural elite took the initiative to launch their assault. In
various impromptu cultural associations, such as the Accademia degli Investiganti and later the Medina Celi, they sought to build a solid common
intellectual ground, one that took advantage of the methodological advances of the century.[75] The solution they eventually hit upon, drawing
from a Neapolitan tradition dating back to Bernardino Telesio and Gior-

dano Bruno, was a radical investigative technique involving rational interpretation of sense data with reference to a sound philosophical basis and a skeptical attitude with regard to both traditional and modern ideas.[76] Their movement for methodological renewal, which formed the context for Vico's thought, spread rapidly to intellectual groups throughout the peninsula.

Let us now embark upon a survey of these important but now half-forgotten thinkers. The first on our list is the Neapolitan physician and naturalist Lionardo Di Capua. Like the others, he had a practical, we might say, social aim in mind. His purpose, in his most important work, was to undermine the cultural qualifications of the government-backed medical establishment once and for all while showing the new investigative technique in action. He accordingly attacked pure empiricism and demonstrated how the experiential world could be examined by reference to a far more accurate map than the traditional approaches offered.[77] He conceived of reality as fitting into a mechanical model whose existence could be intuited but not proved.

Concentrating particularly on the natural world, Di Capua followed Robert Boyle in hypothesizing the existence of corpuscular principles in matter, undetectable except for the evidence from their action in the physical properties they imparted to objects. He insisted that such presuppositions, beyond the realm of sensory perception, were essential to important scientific tasks like curing disease and maintaining public health. Writing about the errors of late-seventeenth-century medical practice and updating an ancient quarrel between the elite physicians and the low-class barber surgeons, he excoriated the so-called empirics, who medicated simply on the basis of the success of a few medicines. He praised the Dutch physicians for their use of experimentation, but he insisted that sense experience could be deceiving and must be accompanied by a complete theory.[78] Such a theory, he believed, must be based on solid erudition in all the ancient and modern authors and a thorough argument about how the materials of the body functioned together.

Gian Vincenzo Gravina, a Neapolitan lawyer and virtuoso residing in Rome, examined the essential conditions of truth and belief about the same time as his distinguished contemporary John Locke. But he entirely repudiated the sort of cautious empiricism in which Locke appeared to place such confidence. The ability to distinguish truth from falsehood and to judge the nature and essence of things—in other words, those mental functions that constituted true wisdom—Gravina claimed, could never

depend on information originating outside the subject. In fact, he suggested, information arising from outside the subject could never transmit anything but the bare and distorted traces of things, refracted and modified by the senses and the imagination before reaching the conscious mind.[79] Indeed, even if sensory perception could be trusted, the interference of mental images, of all sorts and from all origins, might entirely impede the distinguishing of truth from falsehood. True and familiar things cannot communicate their entire properties to us, he argued, because as their images combine with other images, the mind is drawn from one to another in more and more confused fashion. The imagination thus occupied by many objects at once cannot collect its forces to concentrate on one alone. Contrary to Tassoni, he asserted that the closer things are to our senses, the more the mind is distracted by the variety of images and unable to analyze any of them properly.[80]

What was necessary was a mental discipline and a method for ordering all such images according to their value for acquiring cognition; and at least one example of such a mental discipline Gravina found in the reading and writing of poetry. Far more than factual prose accounts, he believed, poetry was capable of mastering the passions and collecting them around truthlike images, if not around the truth itself. And most of the time, that was the closest anyone could get to effective communication.

Gregorio Caloprese, Gravina's uncle and another prominent member of the Neapolitan intellectual elite, demonstrated that a precise science of cognition invalidated a good part of the *soi-disant* politically astute historical writing of his time.[81] Historians attempting to show off their own powers of political analysis attributed the actions of princes, for good or ill, to deliberate policies of intrigue and deception. However, he pointed out, the human will is inconstant and subject to many conflicting influences. It is scarcely able to sustain any particular policy for a long time with constant calculation. Even if a prince were able to muster all his energies for such a policy, there was little likelihood that the historian could penetrate to the inner reaches of his soul, where motivation lies.

To many of these thinkers, as Giambattista Vico recalled much later in his *Autobiography*, Descartes answered the appeal for a philosophy that might offer epistemological justification for the predominance of reason over sensory perception.[82] Starting in Naples, the ideas of Descartes, along with the commentaries and critiques by Antoine Arnauld and

Nicholas Malebranche, began spreading throughout Italy in the second half of the century.[83] However, in borrowing Descartes's ideas, these thinkers also borrowed Descartes's antihistorical bias. They had no use for a science grounded in defective methods and oriented toward pursuing information about affairs of no enduring moral significance. If certainty was to be obtained by way of methodical doubt and the systematic unveiling of truths, beginning with those already present in the mind, historical knowledge would have to be relegated to the realm of fable.

Typical of the trend was the Sicilian philosopher Michelangelo Fardella, who shared some of the same experiences as the Neapolitans and knew Malebranche personally from a sojourn in France. For him, methodological introspection for attaining clear and distinct ideas seemed to offer a kind of rigor lacking in any haphazard program for the collection of miscellaneous facts of the sort undertaken by the Accademia del Cimento and the last holdouts of the Galilean school. "The main result of this new method," he maintained, "is to render the mind attentive and recollected in itself, using its reason, detached from all other things not belonging to its nature—a most potent technique for finding the truth."[84] From this discipline the mind learned, first of all, to concentrate only on problems and concerns that were within its capacity and to avoid vainly trying to understand matters extraneous to itself and to its being. For instance, it might intuit the existence of God by contemplating the idea of perfection, but it could never intuit his nature or actions. Secondly, it learned to avoid relying on the knowledge of others, particularly the traditional authorities. Those things that could be comprehended only by individual meditation it would seek by using insight and reason, turning off the senses and thinking by itself.[85]

Following the same line of reasoning, at least in his theoretical work, Paolo Mattia Doria, a Genoese political philosopher who spent most of his career in Naples, conceived of a new system of civil society without reference to any historical examples at all. Although he gave due credit to Machiavelli for having founded political science, he broke with the Machiavellian tradition, most recently reformulated by Virgilio Malvezzi, of defining political prudence in terms of what had been done in the past. The time had come to start anew, he argued; and that meant recognizing how people had been drawn away from their civic nature by faulty and erroneous sensory experience.[86] As soon as infants left the womb, he contended, they became enveloped in the world of sense. Yet the images

brought into their minds by sensory impressions concerned only things and events in their immediate surroundings. From these they could never learn the principles of civil society. As they grew up and began to read histories, they might learn to imitate actions; but they would never attain true civic knowledge. "These pictures, which represent only the things that have been done, and narrate only the most immediate reasons for things, without providing any sort of science or principles, may excite the heart to love the virtue of states but do not teach how to form and maintain and restore them."[87] Moreover, for discovering these latter principles, he insisted, no Machiavellian compilation of historical examples would suffice—particularly as such examples could be formulated only according to unreliable historiographical methods.

Doria proposed instead to deduce the principles of civil society from the philosophy of human nature. Here he found much less help from Descartes, who eschewed the classic moralists and their concerns with civic duty only to retreat to a solitary position of noninvolvement in the human comedy. All human conduct, Doria argued, proceeds from the use or abuse of the four principles of love of truth, love of glory, love of self, and love of pleasure. Any of these principles could be exaggerated to produce a vice; and any number of individuals with such vices could be joined to produce a defective society. But defective societies were not inevitable, and, contrary to Bernard de Mandeville, whose complete theory was yet to emerge, society, in Doria's view, did not have to consist of a balance of vices. Instead, let the members of the intellectual elite—the same elite to which Doria, Gravina, Caloprese, and the others belonged—endeavor to attain self-knowledge and achieve a balance of the four principles within themselves. Next, let them bring clear and distinct ideas about these principles to the attention of others. Then all individuals will share a new level of social harmony, and skepticism about politics will disappear.[88]

However, the sheet anchor of reason and introspection provided by Descartes was not for everyone. And in England, those who failed to be sustained by the sheet anchor of empiricism offered in response to Descartes by a defiant tradition proceeding from Robert Boyle to John Locke found themselves in dangerous waters, indeed. John Wilmot, the earl of Rochester, harking back to the skeptical tradition of Agrippa von Nettesheim in the previous century, spoke for all those with no sufficient answer to the apparent impossibility of gaining secure knowledge about the world:

I'd be a dog, a monkey or a bear
Or any thing but that vain animal
Who is so proud of being rational.
The senses are too gross, and he'll contrive
A sixth, to contradict the other five.
And before certain instinct, will prefer
Reason, which fifty times for one does err.[89]

At least according to Gilbert Burnet, his biographer, the earl doubted absolutely everything.[90]

Whereas the earl of Rochester doubted everything, the Florentine diplomat and virtuoso Lorenzo Magalotti began by doubting Descartes. And for all his agreement with the *cogito* principle concerning the foundations of certitude about the existence of the mind, he followed Malebranche in returning to St. Augustine for a psychological theory. No thinking substance, Magalotti reasoned, could be so complex as to will and not will at the same time, to divide itself, as he said, into "ego" and "io" (the Italian equivalent) and to operate from both simultaneously.[91] Clearly, the correct analysis was that the corrupt human will was in conflict with the original purity of human nature. Descartes's theory of animals as machines, derived from clear and distinct ideas concerning the nature of the mental substance, was no less improbable than the vortex-filled cosmos he derived from the properties of matter in motion; and neither was any more persuasive than the accepted views he claimed to sweep away by systematic doubt.[92] For Magalotti, all this was yet another proof that the moderns had vastly exaggerated their superiority over the ancients. "I still wonder whether they come any closer to the truth than someone who starts at the number one and keeps counting to infinity."[93]

In fact, for Magalotti, the absence of certainty about the world, about contemporary and past affairs, about the nature of the elements, the organization of the cosmos, and the cures for the simplest ailments, was not just a reminder about the weakness of human reason. In such circumstances, he concluded, the safest harbor for the troubled soul was in the truths of faith.[94] He took contemporary historiography as an example. Harking back to arguments made previously by Patrizi and developed by Mascardi and many others, he noted the damage done to the truth by passions and interests. Even the most scrupulous and insightful historian, recounting things he did himself, might have to deceive and dissemble in order to save his own skin. Supposing he wished to tell the truth about

events in his immediate vicinity, he was likely to encounter some of the most serious problems of verification. He could not rely on the news. "I think you know how difficult it is to discover the truth about a solitary battle that is no more than four leagues away from the court in which one writes."[95] And within the courtly environment where he did his writing, all his influence and all his acquaintances among the powerful might not suffice to help him discover the truth about a conspiracy going on before his very eyes. The actors themselves were often uncertain about their reasons for making decisions. "I had the fortune," he explained, "to be admitted to the secret dealing about a peace treaty, and a war, in our century, whose real reasons are perhaps . . . unknown even to this day to those involved and likely to remain so forever." One could scarcely hope for particularly accurate accounts of such events, even by the protagonists. "Therefore," he concluded, "we must consider, there can be no human history," either of the past or of the present, "that is not false in many circumstances."

All this uncertainty about historical reality was, for Magalotti, a buttress to faith, not an incitement to skepticism. Because of it, the research of Benedict de Spinoza and Richard Simon showing the absence of references to biblical events in civic histories was no longer any cause for alarm. Magalotti's reasoning went like this: Existing civic histories were obviously full of falsehoods; thus, divinely inspired history could scarcely avoid conflicting with them. Indeed, because of this very conflict, ecclesiastical history might be true. "This [conflict] may not be a proof of the divinity [of these accounts]; but it is at least an indication of the possibility of their divinity." With no better information, belief, he said, echoing Pascal, was the best bet. There was no need to resort to the more intricate rational arguments for faith suggested by Vitus Erbermann, Johann Musaeus, and so many others.[96]

Magalotti was not alone. His Rotterdam-based contemporary Pierre Bayle also turned skepticism about a system of political communication dominated by the passions and the interests into part of a much broader questioning of the usual sources of knowledge.[97] Concentrating his attention on the wars of words between late-seventeenth-century Catholics and Protestants, Bayle wondered if the truth about any event described by one or the other side could ever really be known. And when the errors of historical works were compounded by reliance on reports and documents spread about by newspaper writers seeking fast gain by sensationalism and flattery, the unreliability of the result was enough to lead the

serious reader to distraction. "There is no greater mischief," he remarked, "than that which can be exercised upon historical monuments."[98] Consequently, he supposed, many of his contemporaries had stopped believing history at all. "And their conclusion begins with the newspapers, and extends to the whole range of civil historians, who compile their rhapsodies out of nothing but these miserable sources."[99] The only mistake of the true skeptics, he believed, was in taking the lack of proof about the existence of worldly things as a cause for atheism rather than an incitement to fall back upon fideism. The truths of faith are probably not, he argued, susceptible to rational understanding at all.[100]

The same line of reasoning led to one of the strangest episodes in all of late-seventeenth-century intellectual history. For in the work of the French Jesuit Jean Hardouin, skepticism about the authenticity of historical documents did not stop at skepticism about the various available accounts of the past. It could provoke doubt about the very existence of the past. Using the methods of the historians against the historians themselves, Hardouin set out to prove that all the texts known from the ancient world except works by Cicero, Virgil, Horace, and Pliny the Elder were actually forged by a fourteenth-century scholar named Severus Archontius and his collaborators. Such was the only possible conjecture he could imagine on the basis of what he regarded as faulty and incomplete literary evidence, mainly from medieval manuscripts, which appeared to contradict the nonliterary evidence from archaeology and epigraphy. Favorite medieval texts were subject to similar criticism; and according to him, the *Divine Comedy* was written in the fifteenth century by a Wycliffite heretic.[101] What went for secular texts applied similarly to religious ones. The teachings of the church fathers, including Augustine, Bernard, and Thomas Aquinas, Hardouin argued, were to be rejected as apocryphal compilations of heretical doctrines. All the poor believer could do in such circumstances was to repose his faith in church traditions as interpreted by the Roman authorities and in the truths contained in the Latin Vulgate—especially because, according to Hardouin, the Hebrew bible was a forgery.

The New Historiography

The very techniques of criticism employed by Bayle, and to less effect by Hardouin, signaled to others a way out of the tunnel of Pyrrhonism. Whereas the Cartesians questioned the certainty of sense experience and

the fideists sought to replace it with faith, a new breed of historians sought to combat skepticism by directing attention to historiographical methodology itself. To be sure, they did not have to start from scratch. Far beyond the influences that the critics condemned, the traditions of literary and historical scholarship formed in the time of Pietro Vettori and Joseph Scaliger and earlier had continued into the time of Jean Mabillon and his Italian disciple, Benedetto Bacchini.[102] Their efforts to refine and develop previous traditions brought about a veritable movement for methodological reform.

The new methodologists agreed that history, like any empirical science, was only as good as its fact-finding procedures and that a distinction could be drawn between reasonable and unreasonable doubt. Mabillon himself set out the rules for distinguishing reliable from unreliable testimonies. He discarded Melchior Cano's primitive and question-begging criteria of the "probity," "veracity," or "authoritativeness" of the witness. Instead, he proposed the more certain criteria of proximity to the event in question and agreement with other testimonies. He showed how the study of the physical characteristics of documents and the script used in drawing them up could be employed in distinguishing, classifying, authenticating, and dating them. Indeed, his and his contemporaries' systematic efforts to form a history of scripts by comparing known dated examples to other undated ones brought about what has been termed a Galilean revolution in the science of diplomatics. Jean Le Clerc conveniently summarized the whole science of textual and historical criticism and the associated discipline of hermeneutics in a comprehensive manual, the *Ars critica*.[103] He concluded that anyone who, after following all the correct procedures, still routinely doubted the truth of all histories must be "a madman."[104]

Meanwhile, the new historians brought their methods to bear on some of the most ambitious projects yet conceived for recovering the records of the past. Even the achievements of Gottfried Willem Leibniz in Germany and, in England, of Thomas Hearne, Henry Dodwell, and the collaborators on the augmented edition of Camden's *Brittania* paled in comparison with the tasks taken on in the quiet of the cloisters by a few regular priests and monks.[105] The first such projects were mainly intended to prevent historical skepticism from eroding the foundations of ecclesiastical authority. Such was the inspiration for the Jesuit fathers known as the Bollandists in Antwerp, as they went about assembling the fundamental *Acta sanctorum* of their order. By the time the Benedictines of St. Maur,

including Mabillon and Bernard de Montfaucon, got around to assembling their own *Acta sanctorum,* the purpose had shifted to creation of a reliable historical account for anyone studying the Benedictine order. Bacchini in turn transmitted the modern science of history to Ludovico Antonio Muratori.

Muratori, applying the new methods to the history of Italy, produced the most ambitious project of all. The twenty-eight volumes of the *Rerum Italicarum scriptores* contained up-to-date editions of the main documentary sources of each area of the peninsula, from the Middle Ages to the Renaissance. Including documents ranging from Landolfo Sagax's ninth-century compilation from chronicles by Eutropius and Paulus Diaconus and late Roman and Gothic history up to Charlemagne's partition of his empire, Poggio Bracciolini's fifteenth-century history of Florence, and Benvenuto di San Giorgio's early-sixteenth-century discourse on the marquises of Montferrat, the collection situated the lives of each place in a real past that could be viewed from multiple perspectives. It provided the raw material for the next generation of historical narratives, for which a good part of the scholarly footwork had already been done—the identification of sources and the comparison and evaluation of manuscripts.

Without ever having pursued Vico's intricate philosophical arguments, Muratori, Jean Mabillon, the Maurists, and their admirers implicitly agreed with his proposition that the past was truly verifiable because it had been made by men. This was one reason that the collection and the critical edition and publication of original documents was such an important part of their endeavors. Just as their method books insisted on testing the authenticity of testimony by the agreement of many witnesses, the authenticity of the past itself might be tested by an overwhelming array of verified texts. The antidote to the skeptic's denial of the past was to place the past before him in such overwhelming profusion that he could not deny its reality without evident contradiction. Muratori's vast *Rerum Italicarum scriptores* was not only a compilation of documents in editions that are still consulted today; it was, as well, a compilation of the reports of witnesses to the existence of a past that each could confirm by actions as well as words.

For Bacchini, the modern science of historiography was not just a science of diplomatics and textual criticism: by joining diplomatics with the craft of narrative history, he believed, the historian might be free for the first time to properly balance documented historical conclusions with cre-

ative hypotheses.[106] To produce good writing, there was no need to resort to the tools of the novelist or the ruses of the rhetorician—contrary to so many seventeenth-century examples, particularly including those who wrote at the behest of powerful employers, from Maiolino Bisaccioni to Pier Giovanni Capriata to Vittorio Siri. With the sources for historical ideas fully exposed to the view of the reader, the task of filling in the interstices by learned suppositions could hardly be called dishonest. Let the historian inform the reader exactly when a conclusion was a proven fact and when an educated guess. And when the listener made an educated guess, let him make it responsibly, not merely for effect. "Poets create realistic things, historians produce them," he argued; "the former employ them by choice, the latter by necessity."[107] For this reason, in his history of the monastery of San Benedetto Polirone in Mantua, he corroborated both his true and his realistic conclusions, his facts and his educated guesses, by an appendix of documents nearly as long as the text itself.

Still, documents could deceive even the responsible researcher. A major methodological breakthrough of the late-seventeenth-century historians was to bring the study of antiquities—that is, the nonliterary remains of ancient civilizations, including coins, inscriptions, pottery, iconography, and the like—back out of the realm of erudite curiosity and into the realm of historiography, where they had been in the time of Flavio Biondo and Angelo Poliziano. Indeed, so deep was the skepticism into which late-seventeenth-century scholars had been thrown by the contemporary abuse of documents for purposes of political interest and personal advancement that they began to regard nonliterary remains as nearly indispensable for discovering the truth, in spite of the formidable problems of interpretation. Even Montfaucon was eventually persuaded that the mastery of texts had to be supplemented by mastery of visual evidence, and he began publishing a corpus of it.[108]

In Italy, Francesco Bianchini proposed an entire universal history in which literary evidence would be systematically corroborated by other sorts—refuting Hardouin's claim that the two were incompatible. For "every historian agrees that the most difficult and important problem is to make his account authoritative by the signs of validity that distinguish true narrations from the fables of the romance writers."[109] For Bianchini, those signs of validity, the very "figures of the facts," could be found in the archaeological record. Their inclusion in historiography would "perfectly fit the tastes of our age"[110] because most people, at the end of the Baroque century, were more accustomed to a figurative mode of presen-

tation than to a strictly logocentric one—as the reception of Claude-François Menestrier's history of the medallions of the reign of Louis XIV had recently demonstrated. Moreover, it might help cure the skepticism that plagued contemporary intellectual life. Accordingly, covering the period from the ancient Egyptians to the Greeks in the time of Lycurgus, he accompanied his text with a judicious selection of images and inscriptions from vases, coins, and architectural remains.

By shielding themselves from the skeptics, the new historical methodologists also shielded themselves from the area of historiography that most closely affected readers—namely, the history of modern and recent times. A method that privileged the study of vases, coins, and archaeological remains could scarcely be expected to be of much use for periods when such objects were not the main records of the past. Even the new methods of textual criticism and emendation could offer little guidance where the most authoritative testimony to an event might just as well be transmitted by word of mouth and hearsay as by a written document.

However, in the field of recent history, the real cause of the malaise was not faulty sources; nor was it faulty methods. The real cause, as Bacchini began to suspect, lay in the social relations of historians—as he put it, "the excessive desire of the learned of Italy to get ahead."[111] Those very writers who would otherwise be the most capable of discovering the truth, he argued, depended for their livelihoods upon satisfying powerful patrons and finding customers for their works. Attracted by the hope of great rewards, they made their writings conform to a flattering view, even contradicting their most emphatic statements in subsequent publications according to which way the winds of favor blew. It was no wonder that the more attentive readers had begun to adopt "a certain attitude of skepticism." His view summed up the course of reflection on the communication of political reality over the previous century. In his opinion, no amount of scholarly innovation was likely to have much effect until independent cultural bodies could be instituted so as to ensure that at least sometimes truth would be placed before any material advantage. Clearly, the seventeenth-century academies would not do, as most of them were sold out in one way or another to powerful patrons. The same went for the universities of the time, whose political attachments made them unreliable arbiters of intellectual taste. Exactly what Bacchini had in mind, he does not say; and we are left to wonder whether any of the institutions in present-day experience would have precisely fit the bill.

Conclusion

By the early eighteenth century, when Giambattista Vico wrote his *Autobiography*, the skeptical crisis of the seventeenth century seemed to be little more than a bad dream, and not just in the field of philosophy, where George Berkeley no longer found the radical critique of experience to be a cause for despair. In political affairs as well, problems of communication no longer excited the same indignation or caused the same disappointment as they had in the time of Pierre Bayle. And in historiography, the promise of the new methodological advances was enough to lighten the shadow cast by inaccurate narrations. It was in this context that Giambattista Vico completed one of the most remarkable itineraries of philosophical and historiographical theorizing of any in the century. His conclusions draw attention to the paradox of the public sphere revealed in these pages.

Admittedly, our story has already proceeded far beyond the original questions posed. It began by asking why the emerging information trade in the seventeenth century was not greeted with the same general enthusiasm that has accompanied almost every other advance in information technology in modern times. The answer drew the narrative into the labyrinthine ramifications of a long-gone system, from the composition and survival of the manuscript newsletters in a world of censorship to the incorporation of the newsletters into the newer genre of printed newspapers, through the changes wrought in news products by printed reproduction and by the influence of patronage on the purveyors of news.

Our heroes, sometimes our antiheroes, have been writers or merchants of ideas, in a very literal sense. Their lives have formed a good part of

what is interesting here. But they were caught up in processes that were as far beyond their control as were the consequences of their actions. Our inquiry, for instance, has identified a new connection between their publications and the emergence of the modern state. The transition to a more modern form of state began with a move toward administrative centralization. But administrative centralization produced conflicts both outside and within the states of western Europe. Conflict, warfare, and revolution in turn produced material for the creation of news and the writing of history, just as it called for more effective programs of public appeasement and consensus building. While governments and officials sought to promote ways of representing power that might further their interests, writers sought high rewards as a hedge against economic turmoil and change. The result was the first wave of historiographical entrepreneurialism in modern times. Neither the governments nor the officials nor the writers could have foreseen the profound significance that might be attributed to what they were doing.

The emerging state structure allowed writers to subject political information to the money economy, and the money economy allowed them to detach information from its ceremonial bearings within the practices of courts. The same cause allowed them to depersonalize such information by separating the doer from the expression of the deed and turning the deed into an object upon which commentary might be made. Applying their innovativeness to the formation of strategies for the exchange of information, they modified or withheld it to enhance its value in the marketplace. From that moment, their creation—the commodity information—became a social fact, and a social fact of enormous power and significance. Such commodities in this story have acted as switchmen, narrowing the number of options for intellectual change, moving ideas along new tracks.

Given the particular cultural conditions of the late seventeenth century, skepticism concerning the faulty sources of information could scarcely be avoided. Long-term trends—such as the widening of Europe's frontiers through geographical discovery, the emergence of ethnography, the spread of religious heterodoxy, and the release of scientific and scholarly investigations from the thrall of authoritative texts, both sacred and secular—came together to prepare a climate of dissatisfaction with received opinion. In this sense, our story has added a new episode to developments within the course of European civilization that have long been known. At the same time, the demise of a premodern mythic mentality

brought with it a diminished tolerance for error and inaccuracy in the reporting of data.[1] Rulers and governments were supposed to live up to the expectations raised by their symbolic programs or else change their programs to reflect what they were actually able to accomplish; because of this, their utterances were subjected to a new and often devastating scrutiny.

Already before Vico began to write, a movement for historiographical reform had begun to combat the pervasive sense of uncertainty and disillusionment. We have traced some of the most important results. As we have seen, the Maurists, Bacchini, and Muratori were not alone in recognizing that to assert the validity of their claims to impart knowledge their procedures must differ dramatically from those their contemporaries condemned. All who undertook to institute the new science of history did so with a view to raising it to a higher ethical plane. Their methodological statements and critical studies, they hoped, might stand as reminders to subsequent generations of what could be accomplished when the desire for accuracy was joined to the most refined technical proficiency. And the desire for accuracy was to be inscribed on the minds of writers as part of their moral and civic responsibility.

What the new methodologists failed to do was to provide historiography with a more appropriate epistemological grounding; and this is where Vico's contribution forms a fitting epilogue to the story told in the preceding chapter. He fully recognized the obstacles. Late-seventeenth-century philosophy had provided an unfriendly environment for the historian in many parts of Europe, especially in Naples. Simply because he remained unaffected by the Cartesian craze, he perceived himself to be "a stranger in his own land."[2] Nonetheless, whereas Gravina, Caloprese, Di Capua, and the rest groped among the wreckage of late-seventeenth-century philosophical systems, he struck out on his own. In Vico's estimation, at least for the general climate of doubt, Descartes's cure was worse than the disease. Here was a philosopher who, in Vico's words, "disapproves the study of languages, orators, historians, and poets" and trusts "only his metaphysics, physics, and mathematics."[3] But for Vico, Cartesian doubt was the last refuge of intellectual sloth. Doubting was easy, he pointed out; achieving true understanding was not. The application of clear and distinct ideas to the physical universe, which the Neapolitan intellectuals undertook following Descartes, served for little more than to apply new adornment to a body whose main contours had already been sketched out in antiquity.

In the whole line of reasoning that culminated in the *New Science,* Vico turned Descartes's *cogito* on its head, along with the tradition of Renaissance philosophy and rhetoric.[4] It was not true, he came to believe, that philosophical and metaphysical knowledge were alone susceptible to truth seeking. Indeed, these fields might be more open to doubt than many others. Moreover, if Descartes truly believed that his method had answered all the objections of the radical skeptics, he was sorely mistaken, although he was correct in believing that empirical verification and experience were not per se guarantors of certainty. In spite of Descartes's theories, history could give a kind of certainty available nowhere else. It was not even damaged, in its fundamental propositions, by historians' proclivities to overvalue their own countries and to judge the past in modern terms. And the late-seventeenth-century advances in critical method made its verification procedures ever more uniform and systematic.

What made historical truth possible, according to Vico, had to do not with how history was written but with how it occurred; for history occurred unlike any other phenomena in human experience, by the operations of the human mind. In every age, changes in mental processes have brought about radically different forms of behavior and social intercourse, incomprehensible by the standards of other ages. By modifying our own minds to enter into the minds of the past, we can achieve true historical understanding. "The rule and criterion of truth is to have made it," Vico postulated, not because truth was a convenient convention nor because truth, or what passed for truth, changed from time to time. History can be known because the doer, within a reasonable degree of certitude, knows his deeds. Thus, humans, who produced the past, can be just as certain about its truths as God may be about the truths of the universe that he created; and for humans, with their notorious limitations, the former was a far more appropriate object than the latter.[5] The object of history itself was saved once again.

However, a new epistemological grounding was no more effective for solving the problems raised by the late-seventeenth-century critics than were the new methods of verification. Although the object of history might be safe, the actual products of the political information press seemed forever subject to corruption and deceit. As the European states were plunged once more at the turn of the century into the tangle of dynastic affairs, even the best scholars, when writing history for political purposes, occasionally committed the abuses of a century before. Muratori, commissioned to defend the Este dynasty's jurisdiction over the city

of Comacchio in the midst of his work on scholarly compilation, was nearly as capable of manipulating the evidence as was his antagonist, Giusto Fontanini, on the side of the pope.[6] For every Muratori and Fontanini, hundreds of hack writers with no more scruples than what it took to avoid the wrath of some by ingratiating others arose to take the places of Brusoni and Siri. And while the Spanish succession war placed a new emphasis on getting the story out rather than getting it right, a new generation of newspaper entrepreneurs placed themselves at the service of their princes for the purposes of flattery and adulation. For the time being, the "care and repair of public myth" could proceed as though reality and myth were occasionally indistinguishable, at least for the necessities of civil life.[7]

Ever an attentive observer of his contemporary world in spite of his reputation for estrangement from it, Vico apparently perceived these problems, too. At this time he was engaged in formulating the theory of historical cycles for which he is best known.[8] Although his conclusions are often highly abstract and his main intent was to propose a method for studying ancient, not modern, societies, nevertheless, some allusions to events in relatively recent times can be discerned, especially in the final controversial chapters of the New Science. Indeed, that he explained the Latin Middle Ages in terms of a throwback to the "heroic" or most archaic age of aristocratic leadership has been interpreted as a deliberate reference to the oppressive vestiges of feudalism in his own day, destined, in his view, to disappear before the advance of a civilized or "human" form of life.[9] It should not appear too hazardous, then, to suggest yet another allusion to his own day in his explanation of the pattern of change within civilized society itself. Nor should it seem out of place to conjecture that, from the vantage point of Naples, one of the areas hardest hit by the problems of information, the defects in historiography, and the rise of historical skepticism, Vico might have tried to direct readers' attention to these issues in some of his most enigmatic passages. Let us see whether this interpretation really holds up.

Of course, these brief pages can scarcely do justice to the richness of Vico's insights or even attempt an adequate summary of his results. But let us recall the basic structure of his argument. In the course of his research, as we know, he came to understand civilization as a developmental process leading to a stage where reason held sway. Reading back into the earliest periods of ancient society, he posited an initial "poetic" stage of primitive cruelty, without rational thought or articulate speech, in

which authority was believed to proceed directly from divine fiat. Next came a "heroic" stage. Here he defied contemporary admirers of Homer, who associated the first heroic poetry with a lost age of advanced philosophical wisdom. Similarly, he debunked the notion that the Twelve Tables, the oldest record of Roman law, were a product of advanced jurisprudence imported from Greece. Both texts, he argued, were formed during periods of violence and struggle for domination in their respective countries, periods in which economic and political status were allotted on the basis of the valor of warlike heroes. Finally there came the "human" stage, which in Greece corresponded to the classical age, and in Rome, to the early republic. In this stage, the maturity of human reason and the softening of customs permitted the formation of institutions based on equity, impartiality, and utility. Vico discerned a repetition of these developmental stages in Europe following the decline of ancient civilization.

Changes in political behavior played an important part in the movement from one stage to the next. Vico noticed that a transition to more open communication, to what we might call a wider public sphere, had previously occurred in antiquity, during the passage from what he called the "heroic" governments of the kings of Rome, considered to be divinely ordained and based on the right of the strongest, to the "human" government of the Roman republic, based on reason, benevolence, and equity. A comparison between this change and the passage from the modern equivalent of "heroic" government, namely, feudal aristocracy, to the beginnings of "human" governments in modern times yielded one of the fundamental patterns in history. In the "heroic," or aristocratic, stage, political discourse was intentionally concealed from the purview of the general population and kept as a sort of professional monopoly among the ruling elite. "Naturally continuing to practice religious customs, they religiously continued to keep the laws mysterious and secret (this secrecy being the soul and life of aristocratic states)."[10] Discussing political interests only among themselves, the aristocrats decided generally for the good of the territory because of their private interests as proprietors. In the "human" stage, by contrast, everyone was required to know the law and to judge private utility in relation to society. "Naturally open, generous, and magnanimous (being commanded by the multitude, who naturally understand natural equity) . . . [the nations] went on to make public what had been secret." Such had happened in Europe within recent memory.

If Vico had stopped here, with the civilized imperative to make public

the secrets of rule, later advocates of freedom of the press might rightly have claimed him for their patron saint. Was his failure to do so a symptom of the temper of his times? Like the late-seventeenth-century critics, he may have recognized that more-open communication practices, in the form of the rise of public eloquence, could be a mixed blessing. Consider the following passage. Vico is speaking specifically about the Roman republic, but his comments refer generally to a stage in universal history. "As the popular states became corrupt, so did the philosophers. They descended to skepticism. Learned fools fell to calumniating the truth. Thence there arose a false eloquence, ready to uphold either of the opposed sides of a case indifferently."[11] Could the implicit allusion to hired historians have escaped Vico?

In the event, the results were devastating. "And as furious South winds whip up the sea, so these citizens provoked civil wars in their commonwealths and drove them to total disorder." In his own time, just as human frailty and hero worship in the philosophical realm could lead to philosophical skepticism, so the passions and the interests in the political realm could hinder true communication between the ruler and the ruled. What began as an encouragement to confidence in political power could then easily furnish an incitement to cynicism and ill will. In the next passages, Vico illustrates the most incisive ancient solution to the problem: "And the few survivors in the midst of an abundance of the things necessary for life naturally became well-behaved and, returning to the primitive simplicity of the first world of peoples, are again religious, truthful, and faithful. Thus Providence brings back among them the piety, faith, and truth which are the natural foundations of justice as well as the graces and beauties of the eternal order of God."[12]

In considering the significance of these insights, Vico turned to Thomas Hobbes. In mid-seventeenth-century England, the costs of internal political dissent were civil war and the destruction of society. Hobbes's solution had been the social covenant replacing individual sovereignty with absolute monarchy; Vico placed this solution in the perspective of world history. After the door to popular participation in political discourse had been opened in the "human" stage of governments and the principles of equity upon which the people naturally judged political actions had been established as the principles of government, that door could once again be closed.[13] Gradually within the nation there would form a consensus for the achievement of objectives attainable only by joint effort and of sovereign power as both expression and guarantor

of this. Because the multitude thus made the sovereign the author of its acts, all dissent, criticism, and contention—in other words, what passed for internal politics in the polities of his time—could safely cease. Politics having ceased, public eloquence too could safely terminate. Publicity being no longer necessary, secrecy in government could safely be restored. Public and private being reduced to harmony, philosophers would, in essence, be kings. And skepticism would disappear.

However Vico's observation of contemporary circumstance may have influenced his analysis of the stages of political behavior, he stopped far short of applying his ideas to modern governments in any direct way. Nor did he offer any hints to others. And it is by no means clear just what sorts of policies might have been conceivable along the lines he suggested. One thing is certain: by the time Vico wrote, the market for political information was rapidly spinning out of even the most absolute sovereigns' control.

Indeed, once political information had become a commodity, intellectual and social life in Europe would never be the same.[14] Book sales and readerships increased dramatically everywhere across the eighteenth century, not only in England, where a relatively free press and a thriving economy spawned a multitude of printing initiatives designed to take advantage of what was perceived as a burgeoning interest in political affairs among the middle classes, but also in France, where the Enlightenment became a thriving publishing enterprise and the first veritable press baron, Charles-Joseph Panckoucke, made a fortune in newspapers. Meanwhile, busy Grub Street writers, unable to work their way into the more lucrative patronage networks, survived by peddling satires on recent and current politics to a growing public. In Italy, the increasingly dangerous course of European affairs was refracted, as through a prism, Franco Venturi has said, in thousands of publications from one end of the peninsula to the other. And it was in Naples that Gaetano Filangieri, as the century drew to a close, noted that public opinion had become an immovable fixture of life all across Europe. This "tribunal," as he called it, "stronger than magistrates and laws promulgated by ministers and kings" and "unable to be thwarted or dominated," stood as a demonstration that "sovereignty is constantly and really in the hands of the people."[15]

There can be little doubt that all these developments contributed, in different degrees according to the place, to forming a separate sphere of public reasoning about political affairs, outside the official sphere of the

representation and enforcement of authority.[16] Nor can there be any doubt that one effect of this reasoning was to bring about an increasing awareness of the political and social environment and a critical stance vis-à-vis the traditional institutions of power. What Vico reminds us is that the new institutions of public opinion could also have more baleful consequences.[17]

The entrepreneurial strategies of writers working to improve their market positions and the political pressures upon rulers to get their messages across led equally often to manipulations, distortions, and, ultimately, interruptions in the development of the ideologies necessary for civil society to flourish. We may wonder, as Vico suggests, whether the public sphere is indeed too important to be left to its own self-regulation; some recent debates in political and social theory raise this very question.[18] At the time, a new sense of responsibility among the members of the intellectual community may have occasionally been sufficient to restore credit to the public sphere; a new discourse ethics, so to speak, sometimes took root. We may well wonder, when scholarship becomes politicized and entrepreneurialism once again enters the public sphere disguised as activism for a cause, bringing in its wake a relativization of truth and a new skepticism, whether intellectuals in our own time will up to the task.

Notes

Introduction

1. Paul Veyne, *Did the Greeks Believe in Their Myths? An Essay on the Constitutive Imagination*, trans. Paula Wissing (Chicago: University of Chicago Press, 1988).

2. Paul Hazard, *La crise de conscience européenne (1680–1715)*, 3 vols. (Paris: Boivin, 1935). The English translation by J. Lewis May (Cleveland: World Publishing, 1963) omits a rich supply of footnotes.

3. Richard H. Popkin, *The History of Skepticism from Erasmus to Spinoza* (Berkeley: University of California Press, 1979); Alan Charles Kors, *Atheism in France, 1651–1729*, vol. 1, *The Orthodox Sources of Disbelief* (Princeton: Princeton University Press, 1990); Barbara J. Shapiro, *Probability and Certainty in Seventeenth-Century England: A Study of the Relations between Natural Science, Religion, History, Law, and Literature* (Princeton: Princeton University Press, 1983). To these might be added Fabio Todeschi, "'Lector Scepticus': La re-

cezione della tradizione scettica e formazione del pubblico in area tedesca, 1680–1750," Ph.D. diss., European University Institute, Florence, April 1998.

4. Cited authors include Joad Raymond, *The Invention of the Newspaper: English Newsbooks, 1641–1649* (Oxford: Clarendon Press, 1996); C. John Sommerville, *The News Revolution in England: Cultural Dynamics of Daily Information* (Oxford: Oxford University Press, 1996); Arlette Farge, *Subversive Words: Public Opinion in Eighteenth-Century France* (University Park: Pennsylvania State University Press, 1995); Jeffrey K. Sawyer, *Printed Poison: Pamphlet Propaganda, Faction Politics, and the Public Sphere in Early-Seventeenth-Century France* (Berkeley: University of California Press, 1990); Craig Harline, *Pamphlets, Printing, and Political Culture in the Early Dutch Republic* (Boston: Nijhoff, 1987); and Jürgen Habermas, *The Structural Transformation of the Public Sphere,* trans. Thomas Burger (Cambridge: MIT Press, 1989). In addition, see Thomas Schröder, *Die ersten Zeitungen: Textgestaltung und Nachrichtenauswahl* (Tübingen: Gunter Narr Verlag, 1995); *La guerra dels segadors a traves de la premsa de l'epoca,* ed. Henry Ettinghausen, 4 vols. (Barcelona: Curial Edicions Catalanes, 1993); Michel Fogel, *Les cérémonies de l'information dans la France du XVIe au XVIIIe siècle* (Paris: Fayard, 1989); and Ugo Bellocchi, *Storia del giornalismo italiano,* 8 vols. (Bologna: Edison, 1974–84).

5. Donald J. Wilcox, *The Measure of Times Past: Pre-Newtonian Chronologies and the Rhetoric of Relative Time* (Chicago: University of Chicago Press, 1987); Orest Ranum, *Artisans of Glory: Writers and Historical Thought in Seventeenth-Century France* (Chapel Hill: University of North Carolina Press, 1980); Arnaldo Momigliano, *Studies in Historiography* (London: Wiedenfeld and Nicholson, 1966), 1–39.

6. A good discussion of the reception and significance of Hazard's work is in Giuseppe Ricuperati, "Paul Hazard e la storiografia dell'Illuminismo," *Rivista storica italiana* 86 (1974): 372–404. In addition, see Giuseppe Ricuperati, "Le categorie di periodizzazzione e il Settecento: Per un introduzione storiografica," *Studi settecenteschi* 7 (1994): 9–106, esp. 51 ff. I quote from Hazard, *La crise de conscience européenne,* xv.

1 / News Unfit to Print

1. For Italy, still fundamental are Salvatore Bonghi, "Le prime gazzette in Italia," *Nuova antologia,* 1st ser., 11 (1869): 311–46; and René Ancel, "Étude critique sur quelques recueils d'avvisi," *École française de Rome: Mélanges d'archéologie et d'histoire* 28 (1908): 115–39. Enrico Stumpo has published an entire year of a 1588 *avviso:* see *La gazzetta de l'anno 1588* (Florence: Giunti, 1988). The prehistory of the avvisi is the subject of Pierre Sardella, *Nouvelles et speculations à Venise au debut du XVIe siècle,* Cahiers des *Annales* 1 (Paris: A. Colin, 1948); and Federigo Melis, "Intensità e regolarità nella diffusione dell'in-

formazione economica generale nel Mediterranea e in Occidente alla fine del Medioevo," in *Mélanges en l'honneur de Fernand Braudel,* vol. 1, *Histoire économique du monde méditerranéan, 1450–1650* (Toulouse: Privat, 1973), 389–424a, who limit their discussion to the economic sphere. On France, work by François Moureau and others, in *De bonne main: La communication manuscrit au dix-huitième siècle,* ed. F. Moureau (Paris: Universitas, 1993), now supplements the pioneering study of Frantz Funck-Brentano, *Les nouvellistes* (Paris: Hachette, 1905). There are also interesting comments in Henri-Jean Martin, *The History and Power of Writing,* trans. Lydia Cochrane (Paris, 1988; Chicago: University of Chicago Press, 1994), 299–301.

2. For the eighteenth century, see Arlette Farge, *Subversive Words: Public Opinion in Eighteenth-Century France* (Paris, 1992; University Park: Pennsylvania State University Press, 1995).

3. For the diplomatic side, see Garrett Mattingly, *Renaissance Diplomacy* (London: Jonathan Cape, 1955), chaps. 10–11.

4. In general, see John J. McCusker, *The Beginnings of Commercial and Financial Journalism* (Amsterdam: Nederlandsch Economisch-Historisch Archief, 1991); and Viktor Klarwill, *The Fugger News-Letters,* trans. Paulina De Chary and Lionel S. R. Byrne, 2 vols. (New York: Putnam, 1925–26).

5. ASR, Santacroce, busta 116; in addition, see BAV, Barberini latini (Barb. lat.), 5351; and Bob Scribner, *For the Sake of Simple Folk* (Cambridge: Cambridge University Press, 1981), 77–79.

6. On the latter, see ASV, Carpegna, busta 39; and ASV, Segreteria di stato, Particolari, 55, fol. 94v, books found at the house of Pietro Schurffio of Wratislava. In addition, see Adam Fox, "Ballads, Libels, and Popular Ridicule in Jacobean England," *Past and Present* 145 (1994): 47–83.

7. A preliminary study of the Spanish contribution, which, however, does not cover the manuscript production, is Henry Ettinghausen, "The News in Spain: *Relaciones de sucesos* in the Reigns of Philip III and [Philip] IV," *European History Quarterly* 14 (1984): 1–20.

8. See Alexandro Bastiaanse, *Teodoro Ameyden, 1586–1656: Un Neerlandese alla corte di Roma* (The Hague: Staatsdrukkerij, 1968), including an appendix of transcriptions.

9. ASVE, Inquisitori di stato, busta 452, dispatch from Angelo Bon in Milan, May 3, 1679.

10. ASVE, Inquisitori di stato, busta 434, dated August 18, 1648: "per verità sempre maledichi, et . . . rappresentano gli affari della Serenissima Repubblica nella più languente condizione."

11. ASVE, Inquisitori di stato, busta 436, from Paris, by Angelo Correr, dated January 25, 1638/9: "L'informazione degli avvisi che tengono gli Spagnoli, che i genovesi habbino fatto prestito di denaro a questa maestà, ho subito procurato di scoprirne il vero, e con sicuro fondamento riscontro tal imprestito non esser mai

seguito non solo, ma non esser stato mai neanche in piedi la trattazione. Chi di quà somministra in Spagna queste false novelle in una corte sì grande si rende malagevole il sapere."

12. ASV, Segreteria di stato, Venezia, busta 117, fol. 550r, Jacobelli, March 11, 1679.

13. Renata Ago, *Carriere e clientele nella Roma barocca* (Bari: Laterza, 1990), 81.

14. ASVE, Inquisitori di stato, busta 1213, dated December 12, 1615: "Rubava quante lettere poteva, et di notte le copiava nella sua camera, et le mandava la mattina a quel staffiero del Viceré, et pregò il paggio, offrendogli settenta ducati, che rubasse le lettere del Principe e quelle di Savoia e quelle di Inghilterra."

15. ASR, Governatore, Processi, sec. XVII, busta 18, fol. 1v, dated July 23, 1607; and ASVE, Inquisitori di stato, busta 1213, August 19, 1617.

16. ASVE, Inquisitori di stato, busta 472, letter dated August 7, 1649.

17. An example is in BAV, Urbinati latini (Urb. lat.), 1088, fol. 397v, dated July 8, 1620.

18. An example from outside Rome is in ASR, Cartari-Febei, busta 72, 2d bundle, 3d folio, ca. 1670s.

19. ASR, Governatore, Curia Savelli, busta 134, Cardinal Spada to Governor Cardinal Spinola, September 18, 1681.

20. BAV, Barb. lat., 9814, fols. 5r–15v, (1621–23). Common delivery boys as weak links in the communications network are mentioned in ASVE, Inquisitori di stato, busta 453, letter dated from Milan, October 17, 1685.

21. ASR, Governatore, Processi, sec. XVII, busta 28bis, fol. 744v: "Cristianissimo re: Da ministro Barlagli mi è stato inviato un uomo quale dice essere un gentiluomo a propormi modo di far morire Vostra Maestà con la regina per far vedere se ci voleva attendere. Visto questo, si è fatto carcerare in tal luoco. Vostra Maestà sa dove egli è se lo vuole commetter quel che si ha da fare. E qui finisce la lettera. Risposta del re di Francia al duca di Savoia. Monsenieur ho ricevuta una vostra lettera con l'avviso che mi date di quel disgraziato che ha avuto tanto ardire di tentare la vostra volontà et ve ne ringrazio di tutto il cuore."

22. ASVE, Inquisitori di stato, busta 1213, February 29, 1617.

23. ASR, Governatore, Processi, sec. XVII, busta 28bis, fol. 744r, dated October 30, 1603, testimony against "questi altri che vanno a S. Pietro et altri luoghi per sapere le nuove."

24. BAV, Vaticani latini, 13463, fol. 554: "Papa Urbano dalla barba bella, dopo il Giubileo mette la gabella," invented by Theodore Ameyden.

25. ASR, Governatore, Processi, sec. XVII, busta 302, fols. 1249–50, includes the 1635 notes of Roman avviso writer Alfonso Lucci, with the following list of topics:

Proroga di Borgia
Ambasciatore di Malta
Principe di Butiro
Duca di Parma, vendita di Ronciglione
Cardinale siciliano piglia informazione da un astrologo
Presidio di Civitavecchia rinforzato con trecento uomini
Il caso di Torino

Based on these modest mental reminders, he concocted his stories. In the last instance, the original case was, as the newsletter eventually reported (March 24, 1635), that the papal nuncio in Turin had intercepted letters to the duke of Savoy in a portfolio of material addressed to Monsignor Del Verne, bishop of Sicla, who had been the confessor of Prince Filiberto, in Turin on leave granted by the pope through the intercession of the duke of Sarza; the duke had avenged this affront by intercepting the nuncio's letters and reading them in the presence of the nuncio, by demanding the nuncio's expulsion through the Savoy ambassador in Rome, and by having the postmasters thrown into jail.

26. Ibid., busta 28bis, fol. 733r: "Altro è scrivere, altro è fare, come ho detto; et io non li ho fatti li avvisi, ma li ho scritti." Although one could scarcely claim the seventeenth-century newswriters as the first postmoderns, there are stimulating parallels with Michel Foucault, "Qu'est-ce qu'un auteur?" *Bulletin de la Société française de philosophie* 63 (1969): 73–104.

27. Ugo Bellocchi, *Storia del giornalismo italiano,* 8 vols. (Bologna: Edison, 1974–84), 3:85. In addition, see ASR, Governatore, Processi, sec. XVII, busta 660, fol. 816v.

28. ASV, Segreteria di stato, Venezia, busta 117, fol. 507r, Jacobelli to the secretary of state, February 4, 1679.

29. ASR, Governatore, Processi, sec. XVII, busta 302, fols. 1240–48.

30. See Laurie Nussdorfer, *Civic Politics in the Rome of Urban VIII* (Princeton: Princeton University Press, 1992); and Ago, *Carriere e clientele.* Also see Ludwig von Pastor, *History of the Popes,* 40 vols., trans. Ernest Graf, Frederick Ignatius Antrobus, and Ralph Francis Kerr (London, 1891–1953), for the period from Gregory XIII to Benedict XIV, when the newsletters existed; and Jean Delumeau, *La vie économique et sociale de Rome dans la seconde moitié du XVIe siècle,* 2 vols., Bibliothèque des Écoles françaises d'Athène et de Rome, no. 184 (Paris: École française de Rome, 1957–59), p. 33, where he defends the accuracy of newsletters' accounts of the Roman grain supply in January 1585.

31. ASF, Archivio mediceo del principato, 3024, fol. 241, January 30, 1649. Read in the microfilmothèque of the Fondazione Cini, Venice.

32. ASMO, Archivio Segreto, Cancelleria Estense, Ambasciatore a Venezia, busta 109, January 25, 1653, from Ab. Giovanni Pietro Codebò: "Perchè l'A. V. vegga quanto s'ingannano qui i novellisti, vogliono che il Signor Duca Serenis-

simo sia di presente in Venezia: e due ministri hanno mandato per chiarire da me; si che basta che uno inventi che poi vien giudicato per infallibile verità."

33. Ibid., busta 107, from Codbò to the Prince Cardinal, February 20, 1649: "Gli avvisi del P. D. Sciro, che dilettano grandemente, son per lo più pieni di bugie."

34. Girolamo Brusoni, *Delle historie d'Italia, 1625–1678* (Turin: Zappata, 1680), 710: "Pazzia veramente stupenda . . . dei novellisti, che per dar gusto altrui con la pubblicazione di false scritture tirano sovra se stessi delle vere disgrazie."

35. ASVE, Avogaria del Comun, Civile e penale, Civile 233, no. 13, fol. 19: "io con venticinque giulii al mese havevo, nelle note rotture, quello ha l'ambasciatore veneto in Roma, materia pesata, buona e politica, e non zannatte e concetti per cani, che non rilevano un frullo, e si può chiamare piuttosto satire che avvisi."

36. ASMO, Archivio Segreto, Cancelleria Estense, Ambasciatore a Venezia, busta 107, fol. 20: "Io ho fatto scelta del più vecchio e esperienzato menante di questa città, non essendomi contentato così facilmente su le prime della sua dicitura, perchè ho voluto veder il paragone di quei della medesima professione, e ho trovato ch'egli è un oracolo rispetto alle frotte degli altri."

37. BAV, Urb. lat., 1581, fol. 171r.

38. Ibid., fol. 171v.

39. Ibid., fol. 172r.

40. Ibid., fol. 177r.

41. ASVE, Inquisitori di stato, 436, dated October 12, 1638, saying that it might "grandemente alterare le cose, con pregiudizio dell'interesse comune."

42. ASV, Segreteria di stato, Particolari, 21, fol. 290r.

43. Ibid., Nunziatura di Firenze, 25, September 24, 1642.

44. BAV, Urb. lat., 1080, fols. 134r, 156r (1612); ASV, Segreteria di stato, Avvisi, busta 10, fol. 68v (March 16, 1624).

45. ASV, Segreteria di stato, Avvisi, busta 40, fol. 252r (1670).

46. On this issue, there is Laura Antonucci, "L'alfabetismo colpevole: Scrittura criminale esposta a Roma del cinquecento e del Seicento," in *Roma e lo "Studium urbis": Spazio urbano e cultura dal Quattrocento al Seicento,* Atti del convegno, Rome, June 7–10, 1989, ed. Paolo Cherubini (Rome: Quasar, 1989), 277–88; and in general, Laurie Nussdorfer, "Writing and the Power of Speech: Notaries and Artisans in Baroque Rome," in *Culture and Identity in Early Modern Europe, 1500–1800,* ed. Barbara Diefendorf and Carla Hesse (Ann Arbor: University of Michigan Press, 1993), 103–18. Education is explored by Guerrino Pelliccia in *La scuola primaria a Roma dal secolo XVI al secolo XIX* (Rome: Edizioni dell'Ateneo, 1985).

47. ASR, Senatore, Processi, 301.

48. ASR, Governatore, Costituti, busta 9, dated April 1642.

49. See Peter Burke, "Insult and Blasphemy in Early Modern Italy," in *The Historical Anthropology of Early Modern Italy* (Cambridge: Cambridge University Press, 1987).

50. ASR, Governatore, Processi, sec. XVII, busta 22, fols. 429r, 430r (1602). Translations from the Italian reflect the sometimes awkwardly expressed original.

51. The only substantial subscription lists available are not for Rome but for Venice, and they regard the mid-seventeenth-century shop of Giovanni Quorli, with fifty-three entries in all. ASVE, Avogaria del Comun, 233 (1654). In Rome, a short list is in ASR, Governatore, Processi, sec. XVII, busta 660, fols. 812 ff. (1677).

52. Self-styled avviso writers can be found in the parish registers, for instance, in ASVR, SS. Celso e Giuliano, 63a, Stati d'anime, 1614, fols. 34r, 152v. A busy copy shop is described in ASR, Governatore, Processi, sec. XVII, busta 28bis (1603): "M. Pirro . . . fa il menante, et scrivano, che tiene molti giovani che li re-scrive [i.e., the avvisi] insieme con esso come si suole fare."

53. The engraving is reproduced in Delumeau, *Vie économique et sociale de Rome,* after p. 112. The delivery system can be deduced from the depositions of suspects Giovanni Antonio Ballegucci and Giambattista Guidotti, arrested in 1648, in ASR, Governatore, Costituti, busta 772, fols. 130v, 138r. On mail delivery there is Armando Serra, "Corrieri e postieri sull'itinerario Venezia-Roma," in *Le poste dei Tasso: Un'impresa in Europa* (Bergamo: Biblioteca Civica, 1985), 33–50.

54. Quoted in Antonio Bertolotti, *Francesco Cenci e la sua famiglia* (Florence: Gazzetta d'Italia, 1879), 277. The standard source is Corrado Ricci, *Beatrice Cenci,* 2 vols. (Milan: Fratelli Treves, 1923); I found particularly useful the entry "Beatrice Cenci" by Luigi Caiani in *Dizionario biografico degli italiani* 23 (1980): 512–15.

55. Bertolotti, *Francesco Cenci,* 291.

56. Riccardo Bassani and Fiora Bellini, *Caravaggio assassino: La carriera di un "valenthuomo" fazioso nella Roma della Controriforma* (Rome: Donzelli, 1994), 86.

57. Ibid., chap. 5. A bibliography of the manuscripts may be found in Ricci, *Beatrice Cenci.*

58. Albano Biondi, "La giustificazione della simulazione nel cinquecento," in *Eresia e riforma nell'Italia del cinquecento* (Florence: Sansoni, 1974). Lipsius's work is *Politicorum sive civilis doctrinae libri sex* (Antwerp: Plantin, 1589), where the topic is discussed in bk. 4, chap. 14, pp. 206–24.

59. Botero's discussion of course had medieval roots; see, for instance, Ernest H. Kantorowicz, "Mysteries of State: An Absolutist Concept and Its Late Medieval Origins," *Harvard Theological Review* 47 (1955): 65–92. The notion that some knowledge reserved for the elites should be shut off from the rest of the

population is explored by Carlo Ginzburg in "High and Low: The Theme of Forbidden Knowledge in the Sixteenth and Seventeenth Centuries," *Past and Present* (1976): 28–41.

60. Giovanni Botero, *Della ragion di stato,* ed. Luigi Firpo (Turin: UTET, 1948), 68. The present rather crude and imprecise exposition of a few elements of Botero's thought, necessary to this argument, is not intended as a substitute for a more complete analysis of his work, for which I refer the reader to Maurizio Viroli, *From Politics to Reason of State: The Acquisition and Transformation of the Language of Politics, 1250–1600* (Cambridge: Cambridge University Press, 1992), chap. 6, the only up-to-date study in spite of partial analyses by Robert Bireley, John Elliott, and others.

61. Botero, *Della ragion di stato,* 124. The issue of secrecy in Botero is explored in Gianfranco Borrelli, *Ragion di stato e leviatano: Conservazione e scambio alle origini della modernità politica* (Bologna: Il Mulino, 1993), 63–94, but mainly in the context of dissimulation.

62. Girolamo Frachetta, *Il principe* (Rome: ad istanza di B. Beccari, 1597), chap. 2. Frachetta's career is the subject of A. Enzo Baldini's *Puntigli spagnoleschi e intrighi politici nella Roma di Clemente VIII: Girolamo Frachetta e la sua relazione del 1603 sui cardinali* (Milan: Angeli, 1981).

63. Federico Bonaventura, *Della ragion di stato e della prudenza politica* (ca. 1601) (Urbino: Corvini, 1623), 360. The only detailed account of Bonaventura's role is in Friedrich Meinecke, *Die Idee der Staatsräson in der neueren Geschichte* (Munich: Oldenbourg, 1924), bk. 1, chap. 5. The purpose of the present discussion is merely to outline one feature of Bonaventura's thought, not to do complete justice to him as a political thinker, a task that has yet to be done.

64. Prospero Farinacci, *Praxis et theoricae criminalis,* vol. 4, (Venice: Giunti, 1609), bk. 3, chaps. 10–11; vol. 5 (Venice: Giunti, 1612), bk. 4, question 112.

65. The 1602 decree is in ASV, Miscellanea armadio, IV–V, vol. 66.

66. Onorato Pastine, *La repubblica di Genova e le gazzette* (Genoa: Waser, 1923), 9.

67. BAV, Urb. lat., 1074, fol. 126. The entire controversy is carefully analyzed by William J. Bouwsma in *Venice and the Defense of Republican Liberty* (Berkeley: University of California Press, 1968).

68. BAV, Urb. lat., 1074, fol. 141 (March 8, 1606).

69. Ibid., fol. 144 (March 11, 1606).

70. ASV, Segreteria di stato, Avvisi, busta 2, fol. 42, Roma, February 15, 1606: "Le ragioni che generalmente si vanno adducendo per la parte de' Signori Veneziani per corroboratione et giusto titolo del loro decreto fatto (come si dice) contro la libertà ecclesiastica, tutte sono fondate sopra le ragioni di stato, et hanno qualche apparente ragione; tuttavia vengono convinte da coloro che giudicano le cose senza passione; et in compendio sono queste."

71. BAV, Urb. lat., 1080, fol. 46v (January 21, 1612).

72. Ibid., fols. 729r, 829r (1620).

73. Ibid., 1075, fol. 16 (January 13, 1607). See also Bassani and Bellini, *Caravaggio assassino*, 127 ff.

74. ASR, Governatore, Processi, sec. XVII, busta 28bis, fols. 758r ("Crucifigete") and 377r ("Cries of Whores").

75. Ibid., busta 304, fol. 218r (1635).

76. Ibid., busta 251, fol. 144r (1630).

77. BAV, Urb. lat., 1074, fol. 232r (May 3, 1606): "Non sarà fuor di proposito contar una delle pasquinate, che hanno fatto: una pittura rappresentante l'immagine del papa, in habito pontificio, con la torcia e la scomunica, et il re di Spagna gli è dietro con il fucile, et l'esca accendendo fuoco, et dall'altra banda il re di Francia a cavallo minaccioso et in habito da guerra, et il doge Veneto gli sta con buste di scudi d'oro aperte contando gli danari, e così si burlano."

78. Still indispensable on late humanism, astrology, and modern science's connection is Eugenio Garin, *Astrology in the Renaissance: The Zodiac of Life,* tr. Carolyn Jackson and June Allen (Bari, 1976; London: Routledge and Kegan Paul, 1983). See also Paolo Galluzzi, "Motivi paracelsiani nella Toscana di Cosimo II e di Don Antonio de' Medici: Alchimia, medicina 'chimica,' e riforma del sapere," in *Scienze, credenze occulte, livelli di cultura,* Convegno internazionale di studi, Florence, June 26–30, 1980 (Florence: Olschki, 1982), 31–61.

79. ASR, Governatore, Processi, sec. XVII, busta 251, fol. 506r. But the main study is D. P. Walker, *Spiritual and Demonic Magic from Ficino to Campanella* (London: Warburg Institute, 1958). Also see John M. Headley, *Tommaso Campanella and the Transformation of the World* (Princeton: Princeton University Press, 1997), chap. 3.

80. ASR, Governatore, Processi, sec. XVII, busta 251, fol. 480v. Biographical details are in Germana Ernst, "Scienza, astrologia, e politica nella Roma barocca: La biblioteca di Don Orazio Morandi," in *Bibliothecae selectae da Cusano a Leopardi,* ed. Eugenio Canone (Florence: Olschki, 1993), 218–52. On his early career, there is Begnino Bracciolini, *Oratio . . . de laudibus . . . Horatii Morandi romani* (Rome: Francesco Corbelletti, 1626). In general, see my forthcoming *The Last Prophecy of Morandi: Politics and the Occult in Baroque Rome* (Princeton: Princeton University Press). The libertine culture of the reign of Urban VIII is explored in René Pintard, *Le libertinage érudit dans la première moitié du XVIIe siècle* (Paris: Boivin, 1943), 1:209–70. Compare Luigi Fiorani, "Astrologi, superstiziosi, e devoti nella società romana del Seicento," *Ricerche per la storia religiosa di Roma* 2 (1978): 97–162.

81. ASR, Governatore, Processi, sec. XVII, busta 251, fol. 230r. The document is transcribed fairly accurately in Antonio Bertolotti, "Giornalisti, astrologi, e negromanti in Roma nel secolo XVII," *Rivista europea* 5 (1878): 466–514, but it is interpolated into another document where it does not belong.

82. ASR, Governatore, Processi, sec. XVII, busta 251, fol. 479r. I found use-

ful technical information in J. D. North, *Horoscopes and History,* Warburg Institute Surveys and Texts, no. 13 (London: Warburg Institute, 1986). The type of geniture in circulation in Rome corresponds to North's fig. 1e.

83. ASR, Governatore, Processi, sec. XVII, busta 251, fol. 451v.

84. Galileo Galilei, *Edizione nazionale delle opere di Galileo Galilei,* ed. Antonio Favaro (repr. Florence: Giunti Barbera, 1967), 14:103, avviso dated May 18, 1630. Galileo's modest astrological interests are the subject of Germana Ernst, "Astrologia e profezia in Galileo e Campanella," in *Novità celesti e crisi del sapere: Convegno internazionale di studi galileiani,* ed. Paolo Galluzzi (Florence: Giunti Barbera, 1984), 255–66, now in her *Religione, ragione, e natura: Ricerche su Tommaso Campanella e il tardo Rinascimento* (Milan: F. Angeli, 1991), chap. 10.

85. Walker, *Spiritual and Demonic Magic,* 205–7.

86. ASR, Governatore, Processi, sec. XVII, busta 251, fols. i–xviii.

87. Zeno's *Relazione* is published in *Relazioni degli stati europei letti al senato dagli ambasciatori veneti,* ed. Nicolo Barozzi and Guglielmo Berchet, ser. 3, *Italia: Relazioni di Roma* (Venice: P. Naratovich, 1877), 1:137–94. Among the many extant manuscripts of it in Rome there is BAV, Urb. lat., 966. Possible editions of other works (not clearly indicated in the document) may be Desiderius Erasmus, *Moriae encomium* (Strasburg: Schurer, 1511); Johannes Trithemius, *Steganographia, hoc est: Ars per occultam scripturam animi sui voluntatem absentibus aperiendi certa* (Frankfurt: Becker, 1606) (analyzed in Lynn Thorndike, *A History of Magic and Experimental Science* [New York: Macmillan, 1923–58], 5:438–40); and John Barclay, *Euphormionis lusinini satyricon* (Paris: Huby, 1605). Niccolò Machiavelli is harder to pin down, referred to in Morandi's library list by the symbol "N. M." In general, see Sergio Bertelli and Piero Innocenti, *Bibliografia machiavelliana* (Verona: Valdonega, 1979). No doubt *The Prince* is mainly intended; and possibilities include *Il principe* (Florence: Giunti, 1532); *De principe libellus,* trans. Silvestro Tellio (Basel: Perra, 1560); and *Tutte le opere* (n.p., 1550) (the so-called "Testina" edition, actually published in the first years of the seventeenth century). In addition, Jacques-Auguste de Thou, *Historiarum sui temporis,* 5 vols. (Frankfurt: Typis Egenolphi Emmelij, 1614–21), to which Jean de Machault replied in *I. A. Thuani Historiarum libros notationes* (Ingolstadt: Ederianis, 1614).

88. ASR, Governatore, Processi, sec. XVII, busta 403, fol. 1799r (February 2, 1647).

89. Ibid., busta 309, fol. 5r (October 11, 1635).

90. Paolo Sarpi, *Scritti giurisdizionalistici,* ed. Giovanni Gambarin (Bari: Laterza, 1958), 221.

91. Ibid., 230.

92. *Il governatore politico e cristiano* (1617; Fabriano: Cesare Scaccioppa, per Mauritio Bona, 1628), 75. On Carbonario, there is an entry by Gino Benzoni in *Dizionario biografico degli italiani* 19 (1976): 683–84.

93. Evangelista Sartonio, *Essercitio politico de' grandi ecclesiastici e secolari* (Bologna: Ferroni, 1628), 32.

94. Ibid.

95. The only biography of Castelli is by Guiseppe Gangemi in the *Dizionario biografico degli italiani* 21 (1978): 741–42. In addition, see Valerio Castronovo, "I primi sviluppi della stampa periodica fra cinque e Seicento," in *La stampa italiana dal cinquecento all'ottocento,* ed. V. Castronovo and Nicola Tranfaglia (Bari: Laterza, 1976), 26. For what follows, there is valuable bibliographical information in Bellocchi, *Storia del giornalismo italiano*, vol. 3. The authority on Germany is now Thomas Schröder, *Die ersten Zeitungen: Textgestaltung und Nachrichtenauswahl* (Tübingen: Gunter Narr Verlag, 1995).

96. ASV, Segreteria di stato, Avvisi, 134: "Monsignor Ravizza partito dalla corte se n'è andato ad Orvieto et ha disseminato andare all'aria nativa per guarire dalla sua terzana, ma però la comune opinione è che la sua partenza sia stata forzosa, anzi, dicesi che oltre allo sfratto datogli, *de mandato sanctissimi*, gli abbia imposto rinunciare al canonicato di San Pietro, dandogli però la facolta di imporvi qualche persona à suo favore."

97. Ibid.: "Mons. Ravizza secretario della Consulta è andato ad Orvieto, sua patria, à godere per qualche settimana dell'aria nativa stante la sua indisposizione di ritentione d'orina."

98. Quoted in Luigi Firpo, "In margine al processo di Giordano Bruno: Francesco Maria Vialardi," *Rivista storica italiana* 68 (1956): 341. Those who desired more "secret" avvisi had to shop around. See, for instance, ASR, Governatore, Processi, sec. XVII, busta 514, fol. 466r (August 16, 1659).

99. Both are represented in BAV, Urb. lat.; and the latter also in BAV, Barb. lat., 6351. A letter from Dardano requesting leave to seek "better fortunes" is published in Antonio Bertolotti, "Uno scrittore di avvisi da Roma," *Il bibliofilo* 9 (1888): 183.

100. Quoted in Achille Neri, "Curiose avventure di Luca Assarino, genovese: Storico romanziere e giornalista del secolo XVII, II," *Giornale ligustico di archeologia, storia, e belle arti* 2 (1875): 14.

101. Examples of this dependence abound. See, for instance, ASVE, Inquisitori di stato, busta 506, December 28, 1652; and ASV, Segreteria di stato, Avvisi, buste 19, 96. The Bologna paper and the Venetian avviso sheet are both in BAV, Ottoboniani latini, 2450, passim.

102. Information kindly supplied to me by Paul Arblaster at Oxford University.

103. Quoted in A. Van Houtte, "Un journal manuscrit interessant, 1554–1648: Les avvisi du fonds Urbinati et d'autres fonds de la Bibliothèque vaticain," *Bulletin de la Commission royale d'histoire, Belgique* 89 (1925): 361.

104. Quoted in Bonghi, "Le prime gazzette in Italia," 322.

105. An example occurred during the War of Castro, when information about papal troop movements occasioned a surprise attack by the Tuscan grand duke against the pope's enemy, the duke of Parma; see ASV, Segreteria di stato, Nunziatura di Firenze, busta 25, missive dated September 24. For the use of avvisi in the family politics of the ruling elite, see Ago, *Carriere e clientele*, 94, and elsewhere. This work is also helpful for understanding the patronage structure.

106. Bruno Caizzi, *Dalla posta dei re alla posta di tutti: Territorio e comunicazioni in Italia dal XVI secolo all'Unità* (Milan: Franco Angeli, 1993), chap. 1.

107. ASV, Segreteria di stato, Particolari, 21B.

108. Sergio Rotta, "Francesco Giuseppe Borri," *Dizionario biografico degli italiani* 13 (1971): 4–13.

109. Giorgio Spini, "In margine al processo di Giordano Bruno," *Rivista storica italiana* 68 (1956): 325.

110. Bellocchi, *Storia del giornalismo,* 3:54.

111. ASVE, Inquisitori di stato, busta 452.

112. On Castiglione, see the entry by Agostino Borromeo, *Dizionario biografico degli italiani* 22 (1979): 171–72.

113. Bastiaanse, *Teodoro Ameyden*, chap. 3.

114. Irene Polverini Fosi, "Signori e tribunali: Criminalità nobiliare e giustizia pontificia nella Roma del Cinquecento," in *Signori, patrizi, cavalieri nell'età moderna*, ed. Maria Antonietta Visceglia (Bari: Laterza, 1992), 214–30.

115. Grotius's work was *De jure belli ac pacis* (1625). Its role in the immunity question is discussed in Mattingly, *Renaissance Diplomacy,* chap. 27. The case of Rome is discussed in Nussdorfer, *Civic Politics,* 40.

116. ASR, Santacroce, busta 57, fol. 23v, [Marcello Santacroce], Diario dell'anno 1650, entry dated August 6, 1650, concerning an anonymous poster claiming that more than eight hundred youths had been impressed into Spanish service.

117. ASVR, SS. Celso e Giuliano, 63a, Stati d'anime, 1614, fols. 45v–46v, lists the inhabitants of the offices of Loreto Persico and Celso Cusano, both notaries of the Apostolic Chamber.

118. ASR, Governatore, Processi, sec. XVII, busta 606, fol. 816v (January 23, 1677). Antonetti's notarial activity is recorded in ASR, 30 Notai Capitolini, ufficio 1, vols. 179–336.

119. ASR, Governatore, Costituti, busta 772, fol. 123 (September 11, 1648). Records of Simoncelli's official activities are in ASR, Notai del Tribunale dell'Auditor Camerae 3, ufficio 3, buste 6595–6671.

120. ASR, Governatore, Processi, sec. XVII, busta 304, fol. 137r (June 13, 1635).

121. Antonio Bertolotti, "Un correttore di libri tedesco in Venezia giornalista," *Il bibliofilo* 10 (1888): 147.

122. ASVE, Inquisitori di stato, busta 472, dated November 10, 1629. On

Vrlstorff and Galata, see Antonio Bertolotti, "Scrittori d'avvisi antesignani del giornalismo," *Il bibliofilo* 11 (1890): 150–53; on Lucci, see ASR, Governatore, Processi, sec. XVII, busta 302, fol. 1234r (March 18, 1635).

123. ASVE, Inquisitori di stato, busta 473, dated October 29, 1650.

124. ASR, Governatore, Processi, sec. XVII, busta 403, fols. 1805 ff. (February 2, 1647).

125. On Regii, see ibid., busta 251, fol. 144r (July 27, 1630); on Canatella, see ibid., busta 403, fol. 1799r (February 2, 1647).

126. BAV, Archivio Chigi, busta 32 (Carteggi), fol. 427r (September 22, 1674); ASR, Governatore, Processi, sec. XVII, busta 251, fol. 564.

127. ASR, Governatore, Processi, sec. XVII, busta 304, fol. 153 (June 14, 1635). Amadeo was tortured and executed, but his avvisi writing was merely used as a pretext for convicting him on murder and extortion charges that failed to stick. So said Governor Giambattista Spada, in his memoirs, BAR, ms. 1590, fol. 14v.

128. ASR, Governatore, Processi, sec. XVII, busta 484, fol. 235v (July 10, 1657, trial of Alfonso Lucci).

129. ASR, Camerale II, 58.

130. See, for instance, ASVR, Santa Cecilia in Monte Giordano, *Stati delle anime, anni 1620–22*, fol. 8v, lists inhabitants of the house of Jacopo Filippo, copyist; in the volume for 1595–1616, fol. 41v, is the house of Bartolomeo Ruscone. Other examples abound.

131. For the case of Nicolo Mancini, who was molested, see ASR, Governatore, Processi, sec. XVI, busta 303 (1597).

132. ASR, Governatore, Processi, sec. XVII, busta 403, fol. 1799r (February 2, 1647).

133. BCR, ms. 1545, contains the 1561 statute and the 1562 modifications. ASR, Camerale 2, Arti e mestieri, facs. 74, contains the 1662 statute. See also Émile Rodocanachi, *Les corporations ouvrières à Rome depuis la chute de l'empire romain* (Paris: Picard, 1894), 1:li–xci, 353; and Richard MacKenney, *Tradesmen and Traders: The World of the Guilds in Venice and Europe, 1250–1650* (London: Croom Helm, 1987).

134. ASR, Governatore, Costituti, 772B.

135. Ibid., Processi, sec. XVII, busta 251, fol. 144r.

136. Ibid., Relazioni sbirri, busta 3, fol. 1595.

137. Ibid., Processi, sec. XVII, busta 660, fol. 812r (January 23, 1677).

138. Amadeo Quondam, "Le accademie," in *La letteratura italiana*, ed. Alberto Asor Rosa, vol. 1: *Il letterato e le istituzioni* (Turin: Einaudi, 1982), 890–98.

139. ASVE, Avogaria del Comun, 233, fol. 8.

2 / Politics' New Clothes

1. Ahasver Fritsch's comments are in his *De novellarum, quae vocant Neue Zeitungen, hodierno usu et abusu* (Jena: Bielckianis, 1676), n.p. Quantitative data are in Sandro Bulgarelli, *Il giornalismo a Roma nel Seicento: Avvisi a stampa e periodici italiane conservati nelle biblioteche romane* (Rome: Bulzoni, 1988), vi; Thomas Schröder, *Die ersten Zeitungen: Textgestaltung und Nachrichtenauswahl* (Tübingen: Gunter Narr Verlag, 1995), 1; and G. A. Cranfield, *The Press and Society: From Caxton to Northcliffe* (New York: Longman, 1978), 19. Compare David L. Paisey, "Literatur die nicht in den Messkatalogen steht," in *Bücher und Bibliotheken im 17 Jahrhundert in Deutschland,* ed. Paul Raabe, Wolfenbüttler Arbeitskreise für Geschichte des Buchwesens, 4 Jahrestreffen (Hamburg: Hauswedell, 1979), 124.

2. Quoted from *Istoria graziosa e piacevole: La quale contiene un bellissimo contrasto, che fà la città di Napoli con la città di Venezia, dove si vede la grandezza e la magnificenza di queste due gran città d'Italia* (Padua: Penada, n.d.), datable from internal references to the late seventeenth century. My quote is from the first unnumbered page. An excellent repertory of basic information about Italian newspapers is Ugo Bellocchi, *Storia del giornalismo italiano* (Bologna: Edison, 1974–76), vol. 3.

3. Jeffrey K. Sawyer, *Printed Poison: Pamphlet Propaganda, Faction Politics, and the Public Sphere in Early-Seventeenth-Century France* (Berkeley: University of California, 1990); Sarah Hanley, "Social Sites of Political Practice in France: Lawsuits, Civil Rights, and the Separation of Powers in Domestic and State Government, 1500–1700," *American Historical Review* 102 (1997): 27–52; Craig Harline, *Pamphlets, Printing, and Political Culture in the Early Dutch Republic* (Boston: Nijhoff, 1987); C. John Sommerville, *The News Revolution in England: Cultural Dynamics of Daily Information* (Oxford: Oxford University Press, 1996); Schröder, *Die ersten Zeitungen.*

4. The concept is modified from Jürgen Habermas, *The Structural Transformation of the Public Sphere,* trans. Thomas Burger (Cambridge: MIT Press, 1989) (originally *Strukturwandel der Öffentlichkeit* [Neuwied: H. Luchterhand, 1962]). Habermas later provided a summary of his argument in "The Public Sphere: An Encyclopedia Article," *New German Critique* 3 (1974): 49–55.

5. Concerning these problems, interesting perspectives are offered by the papers collected from the conferences at Göttingen (1990) and Paris (1993) in, respectively, *Histoires du livre: Nouvelles orientations,* Hans Erich Bödeker (Paris: Éditions de la Maison des sciences de l'homme, 1995); and *Histoires de la lecture: Un bilan des recherches,* ed. Roger Chartier (Paris: Éditions de la Maison des sciences de l'homme, 1995).

6. See *Colonia,* March 30, 1659, BAV, Stampati Barberini Q II 45. The *Riminio*'s report of a rain of blood is noted in Nevio Matteini, *Il "Riminio," una delle*

prime gazzette d'Italia: Saggio storico sui primordi della stampa (Bologna: Cappelli, 1967), 42.

7. Instances occur in ASVE, Inquisitori di stato, 436, letter dated October 12, 1638; and 472, August 11, 1635.

8. ASR, Cartari-Febei, 72, 2d bundle, account beginning "Monsignor Riva"; 3d bundle, entry dated 17 November, 1676.

9. ASV, Segreteria di stato, Nunziatura di Firenze, busta 25, letter dated May 28, 1642.

10. The work in question was Gneo Falcidio Donaloro [Giovanni Francesco Loredano], *Ribellione e morte del Volestain: Generale della maestà Cesarea* (Venice: Sarzina, 1634). The reprimand is in ASVE, Inquisitori di stato, busta 522, dated July 29, 1634.

11. Onorato Pastine, *La repubblica di Genova e le gazzette* (Genoa: Waser, 1923), 7.

12. A particularly revealing example is in BNC, Codici Magliabechiani, 1053, letter dated January 29, 1703.

13. ASVE, Inquisitori di stato, 474, included with letter dated February 22, 1670.

14. For example, ASR, Cartari-Febei, 72, 2d bundle, fascicle beginning "Avvocati concistoriali," dated 1684.

15. Paolo Sarpi, *Scritti giurisdizionalistici*, ed. Giovanni Gambarin (Bari: Laterza, 1958), 213–20.

16. ASVE, Consultori in jure, busta 310, fol. 117, dated December 4, 1624.

17. For a few dozen more examples of such testimonies, see my "Printing and Entrepreneurialism in Seventeenth-Century Italy," *Journal of European Economic History* (1996): 569–97. I provide a selection from Pallavicino in my *Italy in the Baroque: Selected Readings* (New York: Garland, 1995), 337–41.

18. Silvia Sbordone, *Editori e tipografi a Napoli nel Seicento,* Quaderni dell'Accademia pontaniana, no. 12 (Naples: Accademia Pontaniana, 1990), 8. Concerning the whole issue of censorship, the best account is now Mario Infelise, *I libri prohibiti da Gutenberg à l'"Encyclopédie"* (Bari: Laterza, 1999).

19. ASR, Santacroce, 57, fol. 29, October 1650. The Galileo case was based on the same principle.

20. Mario Infelise, "La censura dans les pays méditerranéens (1600–1750)," in *Commercium litterarium: La communication dans la république des lettres*, ed. Hans Bots and Françoise Waquet (Amsterdam: APA-Holland University Press, 1994), 277–79.

21. The Degni case is recorded in Giorgio Montecchi, "La censura di stato nel ducato estense dalle origini alla fine del 700," in *Formazione e controllo dell'opinione pubblica a Modena nel Settecento,* ed. Albano Biondi (Modena: Mucchi, 1986), 27.

22. The case of the Venetian Jews is recorded in Benjamin S. P. Shen, "Social Purpose of Copyright Legislation," in *The Communication of Scientific Information*, ed. Stacey B. Day (Basel: Karger, 1975), 108.

23. ASR, Cartari-Febei, 75, contains an example, the *Vittoria ottenuta dalle armi felicissime della Serenissima Repubblica Veneta nell'impresa dell'inespugnabile fortezza di Clissa* (Rome: Grignani, 1648; originally printed in Venice by Leni). The number of others is remarkable.

24. *Nuova e vera relazione del combattimento nuovamente seguito in Candia* (Venice: Giulio Bulzoni Giglio, 1669).

25. ASR, Governatore, Processi, sec. XVII, busta 228, fol. 184v.

26. Franca Petrucci Nardelli, "Torchi, famiglie, libri, nella Roma del Seicento," *La bibliofilia* 86 (1984): 166.

27. Bellocchi, *Storia del giornalismo*, 3:22; Mario Infelise, "La guerra, le nuove, i curiosi: I giornali militari negli anni della Lega contro il Turco," in *I Farnese: Corti, guerra, e nobiltà in antico regime*, ed. Antonella Bilotto, Piero Del Negro, and Cesare Mozzarelli (Rome: Bulzoni, 1997), 321–48.

28. ASR, Cartari-Febei, 73, fol. 116.

29. Bellocchi, *Storia del giornalismo*, 3:22.

30. *Il "Syntagma de arte typographica" di Juan Caramuel ed altri testi secenteschi sulla tipografia e l'edizione*, ed. Valentino Romani (Manziana: Vecchiarelli, 1988), 45.

31. Giorgio Montecchi, "Botteghe tipografiche, libri, e stampe a Modena dal 15 al 17 secolo," in *Aziende tipografiche, stampatori, e librai a Modena dal quattrocento al Settecento* (Modena: Mucchi, 1988), 16.

32. Francesco Barberi, *Il libro italiano del Seicento* (Rome: Editrice Gela Reprints, 1985), 4.

33. Renzo Sabbatini, *Tra passato e futuro: L'industria cartaria a Lucca* (Lucca: Maria Pacini Fazzi, 1990), chaps. 1–3; Ivo Mattozzi, *Produzione e commercio della carta nello stato veneziano settecentesco* (Bologna: Università, 1975), chap. 1.

34. Montecchi, "Botteghe tipografiche," 23.

35. Annibale Alberti and Roberto Cessi, *La politica mineraria della repubblica veneta* (Rome: Provveditorato Generale dello Stato, Libreria, 1927).

36. Clementina Rotondi, "Il diritto di stampa in Toscana," *La bibliofilia* 82 (1980): 137; Caterina Santoro, "Una controversa disposizione sulle copie d'obbligo nel secolo diciassettesimo," in *Studi bibliografici*, Atti del convegno storico sul libro italiano (Florence: Olschki, 1967), 169–74; Henri-Jean Martin, *Livre, pouvoirs, et société à Paris au dix-septième siècle (1598–1701)*, 2 vols. (Geneva: Droz, 1969) (in English, *Print, Power, and People in Seventeenth-Century France*, trans. David Gerard [Metuchen, N.J.: Scarecrow Press, 1993]).

37. Quoted in Maria Augusta Timpanaro Morelli, *Delle prime gazzette fiorentine* (Florence: STIAV, 1963), 6.

38. On Messina, see Giuseppe Lipari, "Committenza messinese per i tipografi calabresi del Seicento," in *Messina e la Calabria: Nelle rispettive fonti documentarie dal basso Medioevo all'età contemporanea,* Atti del colloquio calabro-siculo (Messina: Biblioteca dell'Archivio Storico Messinese, 1988), 389–403. On Venice, the best information is from a 1765 report by Gasparo Gozzi to the local magistrates, reproduced in Horatio F. Brown, *The Venetian Printing Press* (London: J. C. Nimmo, 1891), 347, pointing out that the practice was allowed on an experimental basis between 1671 and 1681. On Naples, in general, there is Pasquale Lopez, "Stampa e censura a Napoli nel Seicento," *Atti dell'Accademia di scienze morali e politiche della Società nazionale di scienze, lettere, ed arti di Napoli* 76 (1965): 93–136.

39. On handbills, Bellocchi, *Storia del giornalismo,* vol. 3, facs. 4, reproduces the *Gazzetta di Genova,* April 25, 1640, during the siege of Turin. An actual example of such a print exists in ASV, Segreteria di stato, Particolari, 21, fol. 383. On the Milanese government in Cremona during Duke Francesco I of Modena's 1648 siege attempt with the French, see ASV, Segreteria di stato, Particolari, 23, fol. 528.

40. ASR, Cartari-Febei, 72, 1st bundle, notes dated August 5, 1672.

41. Quoted in Andrew Mousley, "Self, State, and Seventeenth-Century News," *Seventeenth Century* 6 (1991): 149–68, 159.

42. Gregorio Leti, *Dialoghi politici, ovvero La politica che usano in questo tempo i principi e repubbliche italiani per conservare i loro stati e signorie* (Geneva: Chouet, 1666), i, 258.

43. Enrico Jovane, *Il primo giornalismo torinese* (Turin: Di Modica, 1938), 61; Bellocchi, *Storia del giornalismo italiano,* 3:39–43. In addition, see Howard M. Solomon, *Public Welfare, Science, and Propaganda in Seventeenth-Century France: The Innovations of Théophraste Renaudot* (Princeton: Princeton University Press, 1972), 149.

44. Bellocchi, *Storia del giornalismo,* 3:75.

45. Timpanaro Morelli, *Delle prime gazzette fiorentine,* 10.

46. The work in question was perhaps Matteo Castello, *Il trofeo furia di Marte sopra l'assedio di Verrua* (Nizza, 1626). Morandi's lending list is in ASR, Governatore, Processi, sec. XVII, busta 251, fols. i–xviii.

47. Perhaps Herman Hugo, *Obsidio Bredana armis Philippi IV . . . ductu Ambr. Spinolae* (Antwerp: Plantin, 1626), published also in French by the same press.

48. A parish priest named Marcello Crivelli listed the peace treaty of the Pyrenees of 1659, printed by Nicholaes Kork, 1663 (ASVE, Petizion, Inventari, 396.61.41, 1684). Compare Luciano Allegra, *Ricerche sulla cultura del clero in Piemonte: Le biblioteche parrocchiali nell'Archidiocesi di Torino, secoli XVII–XVIII,* Deputazione subalpina di storia patria, vol. 17 (Turin: Deputazione Subalpina di Storia Patria, 1978).

49. On Gritti, see ASVE, Petizion, Inventari, 390.55.27, February 12, 1690–91; and on Calergi, ibid., 372.26, May 1664.

50. On Bavella, see ASVE, Petizion, Inventari, 390.55.32, 1689; and on Farolfo, ibid., 367.32.33, August 15, 1658.

51. Ibid., 366.30.90, from the 1680s.

52. Ibid., 388.53.29bis., January 17, 1687.

53. A. K. Liebreich, "Piarist Education in the Seventeenth Century, II," *Studi secenteschi* 27 (1986): 57–88. Jesuit education has been examined by Gian Paolo Brizzi, *La formazione della classe dirigente nel Sei-Settecento* (Bologna: Il Mulino, 1976).

54. Paul Grendler, *Schooling in Renaissance Italy: Literacy and Learning, 1300–1600* (Baltimore: Johns Hopkins University Press, 1989), 106.

55. Jean-Michel Sallmann, "Alphabetisme et hierarchie sociale à Naples à la fin du XVIe siècle et au début du XVIIe siècle," in *Sulle vie della scrittura: Alfabetismo, cultura scritta, e istituzioni in età moderna,* Atti del convegno, Salerno, 1987, ed. Maria Rosaria Pelizzari (Naples: Edizioni scientifiche, 1989), 79–98.

56. ASVE, Inquisitori di stato, busta 1213, dated February 29, 1617–18.

57. Guerrino Pelliccia, *La scuola primaria a Roma dal secolo XVI al secolo XIX* (Rome: Edizioni dell'Ateneo, 1985).

58. Palluzzi's autobiography is in *Caterina Palluzzi e la sua autobiografia,* ed. Giovanni Antonazzi, Archivio italiano per la storia della Pietà, no. 8 (Rome: Edizioni di Storia e Letteratura, 1980), 167–192, 200–205, 218–43.

59. Jovane, *Il primo giornalismo torinese,* 47.

60. *Macerata,* September 18, 1664 (BAV, Stampati Barberini, Q II 43).

61. ASV, Segreteria di stato, Particolari, 27, fol. 424r.

62. A recent attempt to analyze a cross section of attitudes based on the circulation of information is Arlette Farge, *Subversive Words: Public Opinion in Eighteenth-Century France,* (University Park: Pennsylvania State Press, 1995), trans. Rosemary Morris.

63. BAV, Urbinati latini (Urb. lat.), 1075, fol. 16 (January 13, 1607). In addition, see Riccardo Bassani and Fiora Bellini, *Caravaggio assassino: La carriera di un "valenthuomo" fazioso nella Roma della Controriforma* (Rome: Donzelli, 1994), 127 ff.

64. Entitled "Il venditore di stampe e d'avvisi," the engraving is reproduced in Francesco Novati, "La storia e la stampa nella produzione popolare italiana," *Emporium* 24, no. 141 (1906): 181–209.

65. Marc Huguetan, *Voyage en Italie* (Lyons: Amaulry, 1681), 20.

66. BAV, Codici Capponiani, V, 3, inserts 1 and 2.

67. Achille Neri, "Curiose avventure di Luca Assarino, genovese: Storico romanziere e giornalista del secolo XVII, I" *Giornale ligustico di archeologia, storia, e belle arti* 1 (1874): 462–73.

68. Gaspare Squarciafico, *Le politiche malattie della repubblica di Genova e loro medicine* ("Amburgo" [Genoa?], 1676), chap. 8.

69. Alessandro Giraffi, prologue to *Ragguaglio del tumulto di Napoli* (Venice: Baba, 1647), translated in Dooley, *Italy in the Baroque*, 242 ff.

70. Giuseppe Giarrizzo, "La Sicilia dal viceregno al regno," in *Storia della Sicilia*, ed. Rosario Romeo (Naples: Società Editrice Storia di Napoli e della Sicilia, 1977–78), vol. 6 (1978), chap. 4; Giuseppe Bonaffini, *Le rivolte di Palermo del 1647: Note storiografiche* (Palermo: Renzo Mazzone, 1975), 29.

71. Instances occur in Scipione Guerra, *Diurnali,* Società Napoletana di Storia Patria, Monumenti Storici, vol. 1, ed. Giuseppe de Montemayor (Naples: Francesco Gianni e Figli, 1891), 149–68.

72. The works in question are Bentivoglio, *Relationi, pubblicate da Erycio Puteano [Henry du Puy]* ("Colonia", 1629), or, more likely, his *Della guerra di Fiandra* ("Colonia" [possibly Leyden: Elzevier], 1632–36, possibly in the edition of Venice: Baba, 1640; and Strada, *De bello belgico* (Rome: Corbelletti, 1632), probably known in the Italian translation by Carlo Papini (Rome: Facciotti, 1638).

73. Pier Luigi Rovito, "La rivolta costituzionale di Napoli, 1647–1648," *Rivista storica italiana* 98 (1986): 367–462; Salvo Mastellone, "Holland as a Political Model in Italy in the Seventeenth Century," *Bijdragen en Mededelingen betreffende de Geschiednis der Nederlanden* 98 (1983): 568–82.

74. Some are reproduced in Vittorio Conti, *Le leggi di una rivoluzione: I bandi della repubblica napoletana dall'ottobre 1647 all'aprile 1648* (Naples: Jovene, 1983).

75. Note that the pamphlet by Alejandro del Ros, *Catalogna disingannato: Discorsi politici* (Naples: Egidio Longo, 1647), was published in Naples in both Italian and in Spanish. The pamphlet entitled *Il cittadino fedele: Discorso breve della giusta generosa e prudente risolutione del valoroso e fedelissimo popolo di Napoli, per liberarsi dall'insoportabili gravezze impostegli da spagnuoli* (Naples, 1647), is in *Per il re o per la patria: La fedeltà nel Seicento,* ed. Rosario Villari (Bari: Laterza, 1994), 41–58. In addition, there was Don John's brief but controversial pardon, declaring that the people could hold their own fort but neglecting most of their other demands.

76. *Gazzetta di Messina,* ed. Antonio Saitta, facsimile ed. (Milan: Feltrinelli, 1967), April 24, 1677. Also see October 29, 1675, and December 1, 1675.

77. ASR, Governatore, Processi, sec. XVII, busta 55, fols. 75r, 77r.

78. *Relazione di quanto è successo fra l'arme della lega toscana e quelle dei Barberini dal 23 passato al 10 corrente* (Venice, n.d. [1643]; *Relazione della seguita quiete in Napoli il dì di 5 aprile 1648, giorno solenne delle palme* (Venice: Giuseppe Leni, 1648); Il commendatore d'Icaria, *Descrizione idrografica della meravigliosa e stupenda opera del Gran Canal Reale nella provincia di Lin-*

guadocca, per la communicazione delle mari Oceano e Mediterraneo, fatta dalla potente mano dell'augusto Monarca Luigi XIV, re di Francia, e di Navarra (Venice: Miloco, 1685); *Editto del re cristianissimo prohibendo ogni sorte di esercizio pubblico della religione pretesa riformata nel suo regno, 2 marzo 1686* ("Parigi e Venezia": "Prodocimo," 1686).

79. G. B. Chiarello and Giovanni Domenico Rossi, *Informazione della guerra corrente, forze, e uomini dei principi cristiani, e qualità della militia turchesca . . .* (Venice: Stefano Curti, 1684), Lo stampatore a chi legge.

80. ASR, Governatore, Processi, sec. XVII, busta 251, fol. 223v.

81. Ibid., busta 408, fols. 18r–19r.

82. Cost of paper is discussed in Renzo Sabbattini, "La cartiera Bonvisi di Villa Basilicata, sec. XVI–XIX," *Archivio storico italiano* 140, no. 513, pt. 2 (1982): 263–308.

83. For instance, the *Proseguimento delle notizie delle moti della Turchia*, in two pages, existed in some 925 copies in Antonio Bosio's bookshop in Venice at his death in 1694. ASVE, Petizion Inventari, 393.58.

84. This is what Antonio Montecatini supposed when he decided to take his genealogies to Venice and, in his words, earn "more than two thousand scudi" in 1684. ASR, Cartari-Febei, 72, fascicle in pen, beginning "Avvocati concistoriali."

85. Agostino Zanelli, "Debiti e crediti di un libraio bresciano del secolo sedecesimo," *La bibliofilia* 4 (1902): 99.

86. Adolf Dresler, *Über die Anfänge der Römischer Zeitungspresse* (Munich: Südost Verlag Adolf Dresler, 1930), 17–21; Sandro Bulgarelli and Tullio Bulgarelli, *Il giornalismo a Roma nel Seicento: Avvisi a stampa e periodici italiane conservati nelle biblioteche romane* (Rome: Bulzoni, 1988), passim. Copies of many of these publications are scattered throughout ASR, Cartari-Febei, 74.

87. Thomas Ashby, "Un incisore antiquario del Seicento: Note intorno alla vita ed opere di Giacomo Lauro," *La bibliofilia* 28 (1926): 361–73, 453–56; 29 (1927): 356–69; 31 (1929): 105–22.

88. Albrizzi, *L'origine del Danubio, con li nomi antichi e moderni di tutti i fiumi ed acque* (Venice: All'insegna del nome di Dio, 1685). On Albrizzi and his family, there is a brief entry by Giorgio E. Ferrari in *Dizionario biografico degli italiani* 2 (1960): 58–59; see also Maddalena Lanaro, "Accademie ed editoria: L'attività degli Albrizzi a Venezia," in *Accademie e cultura: Aspetti storici tra sei e Settecento* (Florence: Olschki, 1979), 227–72; and Infelise, "La guerra, le nuove, i curiosi," 336–37.

89. Albrizzi's invitation appears in *Protogiornale veneto*, 18 (1692): 192. He later published the news book series as *Veridica raccolta de' giornali di Buda sino alla presa di essa* (Venice: Albrizzi, 1686). In addition, see *Esatta notizia del Peloponneso* (Venice: Albrizzi, 1687).

90. On Coronelli's publishing activity, there is Teresa Colletta, "Vincenzo Coronelli: Cosmografo della repubblica veneta e gli *Atlanti di città* tra il XVII e

il XVIII secolo," in *Libro e incisione a Venezia e nel Veneto nei secoli XVII e XVIII,* vol. 1, T. Colletta, Adriano Marinz, Margherita Azzi Visentini, Elena Bassi, Vincenzo Fontana, Mario Infelise, and Neri Pozza (Venice: Università Internazionale dell'Arte, 1988); and Denis E. Rhodes, "Some Notes on Vincenzo Coronelli and His Publishers," *Imago Mundi: Journal of the International Society for the History of Cartography* 39 (1987): 77–79. Coronelli's other contributions are outlined in Antonella Barzazi, "Enciclopedismo e ordini religiosi tra sei e Settecento: La *Biblioteca universale* di Vincenzo Coronelli," *Studi settecenteschi* 16 (1996): 61–83.

91. *Isola di Rodi: Geografica-storica, antica e moderna,* 2 vols. (Venice: Libreria della Geografia sopra il Ponte del Rialto, 1688), 1:2.

92. On this point, I agree with Christian Wagenknecht, "Einführendes Referat zum Rahmenthema Buchwesen und Literatur im 17 Jahrhundert," in *Stadt, Schule, Universität, Buchwesen, und die deutsche Literatur im 17 Jahrhundert: Vorlegen und Diskussionen eines Barock-Symposions der Deutscher Forschungsgemeinschaft 1974 in Wolfenbüttel,* ed. Albrecht Schöne (Munich: C. H. Beck, 1976), 468.

93. Bellocchi, *Storia del giornalismo,* 3:75.

94. Ibid.

95. See the Castelli entry, by G. Gangemi, in *Dizionario biografico degli italiani* 21 (1978): 740–72. In addition, see Pastine, *La repubblica di Genova e le gazzette,* 12–13; and Achille Neri, "Michele Castelli e le prime gazzette a Genova," *Rivista d'Italia* 26, pt. 2 (1913): 300–309.

96. *Discorso fatto in lode di Genova in occasione delle nuove mura* (Genoa: Pavoni, 1631). Concerning Assarino there is an entry by Alberto Asor Rosa in *Dizionario biografico degli italiani* 4 (1962): 430–33; also see Ivo Da Col, *Un romanzo del Seicento: "La stratonica" di Luca Assarino* (Florence: Olschki, 1981), 1–31; Achille Neri, "Curiose avventure di Luca Assarino, Genovese: Storico romanziere e giornalista del secolo XVII," *Giornale ligustico di archeologia, storia, e belle arti* 1 (1874): 462–73, and 2 (1875): 10–37; as well as his letters, self-published as *Lettere da lui medesimo in quest'ultima impressione, corrette et emendate* (Milan: Francesco Mognaga, 1650).

97. Ulisse Proto-Giurleo, *I teatri di Napoli nel Seicento* (Naples: Fausto Fiorentino, 1962), 251.

98. Nino Cortese, *Cultura e politica a Napoli dal Cinque al Settecento* (Naples: Edizioni Scientifiche, 1965), 163–84.

99. See, especially, *Teatro eroico e politico dei governi dei viceré di Napoli* (Naples: Parrino, 1692); and G. B. Pacichelli, *Lettere* (Naples: Parrino, 1695). On all this, see Francesco A. Soria, *Memorie storico-critiche degli storici napoletani* (Naples, Simoniana, 1782), 2:265; Proto-Giurleo, *I teatri di Napoli,* 264–65, and Bellocchi, *Storia del giornalismo,* 3:89.

100. Bellocchi, *Storia del giornalismo,* 3:75.

101. Luigi Servolini, "Un tipografo del Seicento: Amadore Massi," *Accademie e biblioteche d'Italia* 19 (1951): 206–26.

102. Antonio Mambelli, "Giovanni Pellegrino Dandi: Giornalista forlivese del Settecento," *Atti e memorie della Deputazione di storia patria per l'Emilia e la Romagna* 2 (1937): 135–45; Pierangelo Bellettini, "Gli anni ravennati della stamperia Dandi, 1694–1698," *Studi secenteschi* 23 (1991): 269–313; and Martino Capucci, "Gran giornale de' letterati," in *La biblioteca periodica: Repertorio dei giornali letterari del sei-Settecento in Emilia e in Romagna*, ed. Martino Capucci, Renzo Cremante, and Giovanna Gronda, vol. 1, *1668–1726* (Bologna: Il Mulino, 1985), 341–49.

103. *Milano,* January 2, 1641 (ASMO, Giornali, fogli di Milano, facs. 1).

104. *Anversa* (Florence), January 4, 1641 (ASV, Segretaria di stato, Avvisi, 19).

105. Quoted in Nevio Matteini, *Il "Riminio,"* 45. The previous quote is ibid., facs. figs. 9–12, October 7, 1660.

106. *Genova,* September 17, 1644 (ASV, Segreteria di stato, Avvisi, 19).

107. *Bologna,* January 15, 1648, (BAV, Ottoboniani latini [Ottob. lat.], 2450).

108. *Bologna,* January 1, 1648, ibid.

109. *Bologna,* January 22, 1648, ibid.

110. *Milano,* January 12, 1650, (ASMO, Giornali, fogli di Milano, facs. 1).

111. *Macerata,* 16 October, 1664, (BAV, Stampati Barberini, Q II 43).

112. *Colonia,* May 2, 1659 (BAV, Stampati Barberini, Q II 45).

113. *Napoli,* June 3, 1681 (BNN, SQ xxiv l 23).

114. Report dated Paris, February 18, *Mantova,* March 10–11, 1689 (Biblioteca Civica di Mantova).

115. *Copia della supplica presentata in Venezia all'Ecc.mo Collegio dall'Ill.mo et Ecc.mo Sig. Antonio Marino Cappello, ai 12 settembre 1651* (Siena: Bonetti, 1651). The other works in question are *Copia di lettera scritta da N. N. dalla nave venetiana La Capitana delle navi armate, sotto la direzione e commando dell'Ill.mo et Ecc.mo Sig. Iseppo Dolfino, 27 maggio 1654* (Venice: Pinelli, 1654); *Vittoria ottenuta dalle armi felicissime della Serenissima Repubblica Veneta nell'impresa dell'inespugnabile fortezza di Clissa* (Venice: Leni, 1648); and *Riacquisto di S. Teodoro dalle mani di Turchi: Seguito sotto il comando dell' Ill.mo e Ecc.mo Sig. Alvize Mocenigo II, Provedditore dell'Armata* (Venice: Pinelli, 1650).

116. ASR, Governatore, Processi, sec. XVII, busta 408, fol. 19, December 18, 1647.

117. BAV, Ottob. lat., 2450, contains closely related gazettes and newsletters sent from the same source in Bologna. *Bologna,* January 22, 1648 (BAV, Ottob. lat., 2450, fol. 26r): "Le lettere di Anversa delli 3 stante aggiungono che . . . i Francesi si affati[cano] appresso di quelli Stati per far ritardare la pubblicazione

della pace tra essi, e la Spagna contin[ua] più che mai le loro levate." Compare newsletter of Antwerp, January 3, 1648 (ibid., fol. 30r): "Di Bruxelles si ha che tutte le genti regie si trovassero a quartiere in quelle provincie, havendo il Serenissimo Arciduca resoluto di far altri rifornimenti di sei regimenti di cavalli e quattro di fanti, con sette compagnie ordinarie di cavalleria. . . . In quanto alla pace d'Olanda non si puol dire ancor di certo il tempo della pubblicazione . . . poichè Francesi trovano ogni giorno nove inventioni et difficoltà per tirar il negotio in lungo sino d'aver ridotte le sue cose a maggior vantaggio."

118. *Bologna,* March 4, 1648 (BAV, Ottob. lat., 2450, fol. 92r): S'intende di Dalmazia come il generale Foscolo fosse marchiato con tutta la soldatesca alla volta di Sebenico ove si doverà risolvere quello havesse a tentare; e havesse prima rotto in campagna un nervo di soldatesca mandata dal Bassà della Bossina, che voleva castigar quei di Bernissa, per haver trattato con li Morlacchi, andati alla divozione della Repubblica e per voler anch'essi passar con il detto luogo sotto la protezione della medesima Repubblica nel quale incontro erano restati morti da settanta Turchi et ottanta altri fatti prigioni. A Spalatro si tiravano avanti quelle fortificazioni con grande premura, e vi lavoravano di continuo anco le feste, da cinquecento persone.

Compare newsletter of Venice, March 1, 1648 (BAV, Ottob. lat., 2450, fol. 89r): Dalle lettere venute la presente settimana da Dalmazia s'intende come il Generale Foscolo si fosse inviato con la marchia di tutta la soldatesca tanto fanteria quanto cavalleria alla volta di Sebenico per far ivi sino alla risoluzione di quello debba tentar. . . . Che avendosi penetrato dal Bassà della Bossina che quelli di Beorniza trattassero con li Morlacchi venuti alla divozione della Serenissima Repubblica per darsi ancora essi con il luogo insieme anzi per sicurezza all'evento havessero inviato li ostaggi a Foscolo, havesse mandato a quella volta gran nervo di gente, il che risaputosi dal generale e mandatoli uno sforzo di cavalleria per opporsi loro questi si incontrasse con la nemica delle proprie campagne di Beorniza, e la rompesse totalmente tagliandone a pezzi e ottanta facendone prigioni. Che a Spalatro si tirassero avanti le fortificazioni con grande premura, onde vi lavorassero intensamente anco le feste circa cinquecento persone.

119. The two issues dated May 26, 1677, printed in the shops of Francesco Serafini and G. B. Salvioni, are in ASV, Segreteria di stato, Avvisi, 42, fol. 8r.

120. Ibid., 24, fols. 359r and 367r.

121. Ibid., 101, November 5, 1650: General Spereiter had received "insults from general Mocenigo while he was doing more than his share at Candia" and hoped to "show the Senate the bad treatment he received." Girolamo Foscarini, general of the force in Dalmatia, had his career sabotaged by trumped-up charges against his uncle; ibid., November 17, 1650: "From Candia in particular they say success is impeded by the lack of agreement between the leaders."

122. Ibid., 19, June 11 and 18, 1644.

123. *Bologna*, March 11, 1648 (BAV, Ottob. lat., 2450, fol. 101v): "S'intende di Venezia che dopo lo scritto successo nella campagna di Bernissa, havessero i Turchi nella Terra di S. Cassiano nel Dominio Veneto ucciso cinque persone, che erano malate, con haverne fatto da cinquanta altri prigioni, e condotti via da venti bovi. . . . Per essere il luogo di qualche considerazione rispetto al sito, poichè sta posto sopra una collinetta in mezzo due fiumi, si credeva che fossero ivi per fortificarsi i Veneti, havendovi trovato cinque pezzi di ferro." Compare newsletter of Venice, March 7, 1648 (BAV, Ottob. lat., 2450, fol. 97r):

> Giunse sin da Borenica Caiccho partito da Scardona con avviso che dopo il successo seguito nella campagna di Bernizza nella forma che fu scritto la passata si fossero portati alcuni Turchi ad una serra di questi signori quivi vicina a detta di Cassiano, e ci havessero uccisi cinque persone malate e fattane prigioni da cinquanta altre tra putti e donne, et altra gente e condottivi circa da venticinque bovi. . . . S'avvisava ancora che il scritto luogo non fosse tanto facile, poichè sta posto sopra d'una collinetta, la quale viene fatta forse da due fiumi, che la circondano, Crinia l'uno e l'altro Tinio, e che vi fosser dentro cinque pezzi di ferro.

Other examples are in ASV, Segreteria di stato, Avvisi, 19, comparing fol. 98r with fol. 101r; and comparing Avvisi, 96, fols. 241r and 262v, with Avvisi, 19, Genoese gazettes dated September 17 and October 1, 1644. Also see BAV, Ottob. lat., 2450, of which I would compare fol. 26, *Bologna*, January 22, 1648, with fol. 30, newsletter of Antwerp dated January 3, 1648; and fol. 48, newsletter of Antwerp dated January 17, 1648, with fol. 53, *Bologna*, February 5, 1648.

124. Compare *Bologna*, February 12, 1648 (BAV, Ottob. lat., 2450, fol. 62r): "Scrivono di Milano li 5 stante essersi ritirato da quello stato il signor Principe Tommaso, senza haver invaso il Novarese," with newsletter of Venice, February 15, 1648 (BAV, Ottob. lat., 2450, fol. 64r): "Scrivono di Milano li 5 stante la confermazione che il Principe Tommaso sia ritirato dal Novarese."

125. *Bologna*, January 28, 1648 (BAV, Ottob. lat., 2450, fol. 44r): "Alli 3, l'armata veneta, dalla quale sarebbe sbarcata buona quantità di soldatesca per rinforzo di detta città, et unito il detto sbarco alle militie, si sarebbe formato un corpo di armata di tremila uomini." Compare newsletter of Venice, January 24, 1648 (BAV, Ottob. lat., 2450, fol. 47r): "Asspettammo d'armata l'arrivo di sette vascelli francesi privatici da Tolone un mese fa con 1500 combattenti della condotta del conte di Toe; et il duca della Valletta, arrivato alla corte di Francia, sollecitarà indifessamente le levate promosse alla Serenissima Repubblica, che deono esser tremila combattenti, havendo Sua Eccellenza inviato buona parte di suoi officiali à luoghi stabiliti dalle leve per accelerarle la spedizione quanto più presto potrà."

126. My copy was among other short Venetian publications in BNM, Misc. 1226. In general, concerning Italian views of these events, there is Pietro Messina,

"La rivoluzione inglese e la storiografia italiana del Seicento," *Studi storici* 25 (1984): 725–46. For the original, see J. G. Muddiman, *Trial of Charles I* (Edinburgh: Wm. Hodge, 1928), 260–65.

127. Reproduced in full in Bellocchi, *Storia del giornalismo,* vol. 3, facs. 44.

128. Jovane, *Il primo giornalismo torinese,* 89.

129. *Relation veritable de la mort barbare et cruelle du roy d'Angleterre: Arrivé à Londres le 8me février 1649* (Paris: Robert Feugé prez le Puits-Certain, 1649).

130. *Il sincero,* February 9, 1649 (reproduced in Jovane, *Il primo giornalismo Torinese,* 88).

131. James Sutherland, *The Restoration Newspaper and Its Development* (Cambridge: Cambridge University Press, 1986), 48.

132. Girolamo Brusoni, *Historia dell'ultima guerra tra Veneziani e Turchi* (Bologna: Giovanni Recaldini, 1674), 2:13.

133. ASR, Cartari-Febei, 72, note dated November 17, 1676. In addition, see ASVE, Inquisitori di stato, 507, dated February 2, 1680, including a document, "Breve relatione dell'armi imperiali unite con quelle di S. M. Polacca."

134. Sutherland, *Restoration Newspaper,* 54. In addition, Giacinto Gigli's comment is in *Diario romano, 1608–1670,* ed. Giuseppe Ricciotti (Rome: Tuminelli, 1958), 263.

135. I consulted this newspaper in the facsimiles presented by Nevio Matteini, *Il "Riminio," una delle prime gazzette d'Italia: Saggio storico sui primordi della stampa* (Bologna: Cappelli, 1967). The quote is from p. 19, the number for April 5, 1661.

136. Ugo Silvagni, *Mazzarino* (Turin: Bocca, 1928), 529–30.

137. BAV, *Stamp. Barberini,* Q II 45, January 1, 1657.

138. See Ludwik Kubala, "Proces Radziejowskiego," *Przewodnik naukowy i literacki* 1, no. 3 (1875): 19–32, 113–129, 246–55, 364–75.

139. Girolamo Brusoni's comment is in *Delle historie memorabili* (Venice: Turrini, 1656), 656.

140. Nicolo Vellaio, *La guerra cretense tra la Serenissima Repubblica di Venezia e Soltano Hibraim, Imperator de' Turchi* (Bologna: Carlo Zenero, 1647).

141. *Nuova e vera relazione del combattimento nuovamente seguito in Candia.* See note 2A.

142. Giovanni Carlo Serpentino, *Lettera di ragguaglio della vittoria navale conseguita dall'armata della Serenissima Repubblica di Venezia sotto il commando del Procuratore Cap. Gen. da Mar Mocenigo contro Turchi nel Archipelago* (Venice: Pinelli, 1651).

143. Quoted in Howard M. Solomon, *Public Welfare, Science, and Propaganda in Seventeenth-Century France: The Innovations of Théophraste Renaudot* (Princeton: Princeton University Press, 1972), 160.

144. Text in Bellocchi, *Storia del giornalismo,* vol. 3, facs. 6. Another exam-

ple is in the newspaper *Modena,* dated July 6, 1658 (ASMO, Giornali, fogli di Modena, facs. 1).

145. BAV, Ottob. lat., 2450, fol. 2v, dated January 1, 1648.

146. Ibid., fol. 26, January 22, 1648.

147. Ibid., fol. 2v, dated January 1, 1648.

148. The examples are from Sutherland, *Restoration Newspaper,* 61, 152.

149. *Gazzetta di Genova,* September 22, 1657 (BAV, Stampati Barberini, Q II 45).

150. BAV, Ottob. lat., 2450, fol. 63r.

151. Ibid., fol. 56r.

152. BNM, Codici italiani, VI, 461 (12105), fol. 235r.

153. *Bologna,* dated January 5, 1678 (BAB, 17D, no. 1).

154. *Napoli,* no. 6 (June 26, 1685) (BNN, SQ XXIV I 22).

155. *Diario de' fatti d'arme successi in Dalmazia tra la Serenissima Repubblica di Venezia e il barbaro Ottomano, l'anno 1648* (Venezia: Miloco, 1648), n.p.; *Diario de' successi delle armi cesaree nell'Ungheria dopo la presa di Strigonia nelle due campagne 1684 e 1685* (Venice: Combi e Lanou, 1685), 13.

156. G. B. Chiarello and Giovanni Domenico Rossi, *Informazione della guerra corrente, forze, e uomini dei principi cristiani, e qualità della militia turchesca. . .* (Venice: Stefano Curti, 1684), n.p.

157. ASV, Segreteria di stato, Avvisi, 40, fol. 384.

158. *Firenze,* October 31, 1643 (ASV, Segretaria di stato, Avvisi, 90).

159. Text in Bellocchi, *Storia del giornalismo,* vol. 3, facs. 22, dated February 1, 1645.

160. Valerio Castronovo, "I primi sviluppi della stampa periodica fra cinque e Seicento," in *La stampa italiana dal cinquecento all'ottocento,* ed. V. Castronovo and Nicola Tranfaglia (Bari: Laterza, 1976), 26.

161. Gregorio Leti, *Dialoghi politici, ovvero La politica che usano in questo tempo i principi e repubbliche italiane per conservare i loro stati e signorie* (Geneva: Chouet, 1666), 1:251.

162. Solomon, *Public Welfare, Science, and Propaganda,* 149.

163. *Milano,* dated May 24, 1651 (ASMO, Giornali, fogli di Milano, fascicle 1). The case of a newsletter influenced by the duke of Modena is evidenced in ASMA, Segreteria di stato, Venezia, 117, letter dated March 11, 1679.

164. BAV, Stamp. Barberini, Q II 45, *Genova,* includes broadsheet, "Copia della lettera del sig fisico Angelo Homoboni," dated Lecco 11 Aprile 1666.

165. Jovane, *Il primo giornalismo torinese,* 81.

166. Neri, "Michele Castelli," 307.

167. The episode is recounted in Luigi Amabile, *Il santo officio della inquisizione in Napoli: Narrazione con molti documenti inediti* (Città di Castello: S. Lapi, 1892), 2:63. Evidence of official discussions of the matter is in ASN, Consiglio collaterale, Notamenti, 83, fol. 37, dated February 18, 1693. The "atheist

trials" are analyzed in detail by Luciano Osbat, *L'inquisizione a Napoli: Il processo agli ateisti, 1688–1697* (Rome: Edizioni di storia e letteratura, 1974).

168. Bayle, *Dictionnaire historique et critique* (Amsterdam: Brunel, 1740), 2:634. Further examples are in 3:274.

169. Ibid., 2:8.

170. Ibid., 4:582.

171. Samuel Butler, *Characters and Passages from Notebooks,* ed. A. R. Waller (Cambridge: Cambridge University Press, 1908), 127.

172. Ibid., 293.

173. Quoted in *The Rochester-Savile Letters, 1671–1680,* ed. John Harold Wilson (Columbus: Ohio State University Press, 1941), 40.

174. Ibid., 73.

175. Thomas Hobbes, *Elements of Law,* ed. Ferdinand Tönnies (Cambridge: Cambridge University Press, 1928), 48; compare *Les Pensées de Blaise Pascal,* ed. Léon Brunschvigg (Paris: Hachette, 1904), 2:10, pensée 82, more commonly known as no. 235. These and other references are in Paul A. Palmer, "The Concept of Public Opinion in Political Theory," in *Essays in History and Political Theory in Honor of Charles Howard McIlwain* (Cambridge: Harvard University Press, 1936), 234.

176. Vittorio Siri, *Mercurii* (Casale: Giorgio del Monte, 1667), 7:382.

177. Leti, *Dialoghi politici,* 1:250.

178. De Luca, *Il dottor volgare* (Rome, 1673; Venice: Modesto Fenzo, 1740), preface to chap. 1. The importance of this work is noted by Piero Fiorelli, "La lingua giuridica dal De Luca al Bonaparte," in *Teorie e pratiche linguistiche nell'Italia del Settecento,* Annali della Società italiana di studi sul secolo diciottesimo, ed. Lia Formigari (Bologna: Il Mulino, 1984), 127–54. The most extensive monograph on De Luca, which, however, does not cover this aspect of his work, is Andrea Zanotti, *Cultura giuridica del Seicento e jus publicum ecclesiasticum nell'opera del cardinal Giambattista De Luca* (Milan: Giuffré, 1983).

179. On England, see Barbara J. Shapiro, *Probability and Certainty in Seventeenth-Century England: A Study of the Relations between Natural Science, Religion, History, Law, and Literature* (Princeton: Princeton University Press, 1983), chap. 6.

180. Giulio Dal Pozzo, *Le istituzioni della prudenza civile, fondate sulle leggi romane e conformate alle leggi venete, nel quale si stabilisce il jus universale delle genti con l'autorità dei giurisconsulti, con le massime dei politici, e con riscontri degli storici: Opera postuma* (Venice: Albrizzi, 1697); compare De Luca, *Il dottor volgare,* 1:13. Among the first historians to notice Dal Pozzo was Gaetano Cozzi, *Repubblica di Venezia e stati italiani: Politica e giustizia dal secolo XVI al secolo XVIII* (Turin: Einaudi, 1982), 324.

181. Dal Pozzo, *Le istituzioni,* 46.

182. Ibid., 45.

183. Gabriele Tontoli, *Il Masaniello, ovvero Discorsi narrativi la sollevazione di Napoli* (Naples: Mollo, 1648), L'autore a chi legge.

184. ASR, Cartari-Febei, 73, fol. 187 ff., *Descrizione delle cerimonie fatte dentro e fuori del conclave avanti e dopo la creazione del Sommo Pontefice Innocenzo X* (Rome: Marcioni, 1644).

185. Leti, *Dialoghi politici*, 1:255.

3 / Snatching Victory from the Jaws of Defeat

1. Pietro Gazzotti, *Historia delle guerre d'Europa: Arrivate dall'anno 1643 sino al 1680* (Venice: Pezzana, 1681), vol. 2, *Ai lettori*. The present chapter intends to update the accounts of Sergio Bertelli, *Ribelli, libertini, ed ortodossi nella storiografia barocca* (Florence: Sansoni, 1973), chap. 8; and Eric Cochrane, "The Transition from Renaissance to Baroque: The Case of Italian Historiography," *History and Theory* 19 (1980): 21–38. The Italian scene could be compared to the French one described by Orest Ranum, *Artisans of Glory: Writers and Historical Thought in Seventeenth-Century France* (Chapel Hill: University of North Carolina Press, 1980).

2. Agostino Mascardi, *Dell'arte istorica* (Rome, 1636; Florence: Le Monnier, 1859), 3d treatise, 160.

3. Gaetano Cozzi, "Cultura politica e religione nella 'pubblica storiografia' veneziana del cinquecento," *Bollettino dell'Istituto di storia della Società e dello stato veneziano* 5–6 (1963–64): 215–94.

4. Eric Cochrane, *Historians and Historiography in the Italian Renaissance* (Chicago: University of Chicago Press, 1981), 479; Bertelli, *Ribelli, libertini, ed ortodossi*, 3–24. Compare Gary Ianziti, *Humanistic Historiography under the Sforzas: Politics and Propaganda in Fifteenth-Century Milan* (Oxford: Oxford University Press, 1988).

5. Scipione Ammirato, *Istorie fiorentine*, ed. Ferdinando Ranalli (Florence: V. Batelli, 1846–49), vol. 1, preface, 15.

6. Emilio Teza, "Correzioni alla *Istoria veneziana* di Pietro Bembo proposte dal Consiglio dei Dieci nel 1548," *Annali delle università toscane* 18 (1888): 75–93.

7. Traiano Boccalini, *Ragguagli di Parnaso*, vol. 1, ed. Giuseppe Rua (Bari: Laterza, 1910), Ragguaglio 54, p. 198.

8. ASVE, Consultori in jure, 43, dated September 7, 1629. Micanzio's consultations are helpfully introduced and indexed in Antonella Barzazi, *I consulti di Fulgenzio Micanzio* (Pisa: Giardini, 1986).

9. The pamphlet in question was *Istruzione secretissima data a Federico V conte palatino*, printed in several languages in 1620. A manuscript of the work is in MCV, Misc. Correr 1099, fols. 21 ff. This period in Sarpi's life is analyzed by Gaetano Cozzi, "Nota introduttiva," in Paolo Sarpi, *Opere*, ed. G. Cozzi and Luisa Cozzi (Milan: Ricciardi, 1969), 3–37.

10. Paolo Sarpi, *Scritti giurisdizionalistici,* ed. Giovanni Gambarin (Bari: Laterza, 1958), 221, 227.

11. Ibid., 222.

12. Peter Burke, *The Fabrication of Louis XIV* (New Haven: Yale University Press, 1992), 153.

13. Denys Hay, "The Historiographer Royal in England and Scotland," *Scottish Historical Review* 30 (1951): 15–29; and Royce Macgillivray, *Restoration Historians and the English Civil War* (The Hague: Nijhoff, 1974).

14. The report of counselors Scipione Ferramosca and Baitelli is recorded in Emmanuele Cicogna, *Delle iscrizioni veneziane* (Venice: Presso Giuseppe Orlandelli, 1824–53), vol. 3 (1830), 289. The affair is analyzed in Gaetano Cozzi, *Il doge Nicolò Contarini* (Venice: Istituto per la collaborazione culturale, 1958), 197 ff; and Tiziano Zanato, "Per l'edizione critica delle *Historie veneziane* di Nicolò Contarini," *Studi veneziani,* n.s., 4 (1980): 129–98.

15. Sarpi, *Scritti giurisdizionalistici,* 227.

16. ASVE, Consultori in jure, 43, dated September 7, 1629, 247v. The work in question was *Historia motorum et bellorum postremus hisce annis in Rhaetia excitatorum et gestorum* (Geneva: Chouet, 1629).

17. ASVE, Consultori in jure, 43, dated September 7, 1629.

18. Quoted in Burke, *Fabrication of Louis XIV,* 53.

19. Spini, *Barocco e Puritani: Studi di storia del Seicento in Italia, Spagna, e New England* (Florence: Vallecchi, 1991), 135; and entry by Elvira Gencarelli in *Dizionario biografico degli italiani* 4 (1962): 2–4.

20. Biographical and bibliographical details on Leti are in Franco Barcia, *Un politico dell'età barocca: Gregorio Leti* (Milan: Angeli, 1983), *Bibliografia delle opere di Gregorio Leti* (Milan: Angeli, 1981), and *Gregorio Leti: Informatore politico di principi italiani* (Milan: Angeli, 1987).

21. *Delle rivoluzioni di Catalogna,* 4 vols. (Genoa: Farroni, 1644–47).

22. *Delle guerre successe d'Italia* (Turin: Zavatta, 1665).

23. Alberto Asor-Rosa, entry in *Dizionario biografico degli italiani* 4 (1962): 432.

24. ASV, Archivio Chigi, Carteggi, busta 2.

25. ASVE, Inquisitori di stato, busta 437, letters dated September 20, 1670, and March 14, 1671.

26. The reply is contained in ASVE, Inquisitori di stato, busta 437, in a letter of Giovanni Morosini, dated February 18, 1670.

27. Quoted in Bertelli, *Ribelli, libertini, ed ortodossi,* 173, dated November 12, 1627.

28. Ibid., 176.

29. ASFI, Archivio mediceo del principato, busta 1481, fol. 9r, October 20, 1646; 14r, October 6, 1646; 27r, June 30, 1646. Siri's career and work are analyzed in Marcello Turchi, "L'attività storiografica di Vittorio Siri e il suo gusto per

la decifrazione degli enigmi politici dell'età barocca," *La rassegna* 84, no. 3 (1980): 458–72.

30. Fulvio Testi, *Lettere,* ed. Maria Luisa Doglio (Bari: Laterza, 1967), 3:304, letter dated September 8, 1642.

31. The first works were *Istoria della disunione del regno di Portogallo dalla corona di Castiglia* (Lyons, 1643) and *Mercurio veridico* (Venice: Leni, 1643); next came *Sollevazioni di stato de' nostri tempi* (Venice: Turrini, 1653), and *Turbolenze d'Europa* (Venice: Ginami, 1654). Of some use is the entry by Valerio Castronovo in *Dizionario biografico degli italiani* 10 (1968): 620–24.

32. ASFI, Archivio mediceo del principato, busta 3024, fol. 290r, March 13, 1649, the Florentine ambassador in Venice to the secretary of state. See also ibid., fol. 410r, March 27, 1649.

33. Gazzotti, *Historia,* 506–7.

34. Ibid., 239.

35. Ibid., chap. 2.

36. Girolamo Tiraboschi, *Biblioteca modenese* (Modena: Società tipografica 1782), 2:280.

37. *Historia sopra i movimenti d'arme successi in Italia dall'anno di N. S. 1613 fino al 1618* (Genoa: Pavoni, 1625).

38. Mirella Giansante, entry in *Dizionario biografico degli italiani* 19 (1976): 106, quoting from *Lettere del card. G. Mazzarino a G. Giustiniani,* ed. Vincenzo Ricci (Turin, 1863), 4:116.

39. Quoted in Pier Luigi Rovito, "La rivolta costituzionale di Napoli, 1647–1648," *Rivista storica italiana* 98 (1986): 367–462, 369.

40. ASVE, Inquisitori di stato, busta 451, memoir included in letter dated December 29, 1638, from Valerio Antolini in Milan.

41. Giuliana Toso Rodinis, *Galeazzo Gualdo Priorato: Un moralista veneto alla corte di Luigi XIV* (Florence: Olschki, 1968). The work on Christina was *Historia della Sacra Real Maestà di Christina Alessandra Regina di Svezia* (Venice: Baba, 1656). Perhaps his best-selling work was *Historia della vita di Alberto Valestain* (Lyons: Jean-Ayme Candy, 1643).

42. Maiolino Bisaccioni, *Historia delle guerre civili di questi ultimi tempi* (Venice: Francesco Storti, 1653), 1. Biographical details are in the entry by Valerio Castronovo in *Dizionario biografico degli italiani* 10 (1968): 639–43.

43. Paolo Preto, *I servizi segreti di Venezia, spionaggio e controspionaggio: Cifrari, intercettazioni, delazioni, tra mito, e realtà* (Milan: Il Saggiatore, 1994), 134. In addition, see Gino Luzzatto, "Cenni intorno alla vita e alle opere storiche di Girolamo Brusoni," *Ateneo veneto* 21 (1898): 272–306, and 22 (1899): 6–26 and 226–44; the entry by Gaspare De Caro in *Dizionario biografico degli italiani* 14 (1972): 713–20; and Francesco Piero Franchi, "Bibliografia degli scritti di Girolamo Brusoni," *Studi secenteschi* 29 (1988): 266–310.

44. Assarino, preface to *Delle guerre successe d'Italia.*

45. *Historia dell'ultima guerra tra Veneziani e Turchi,* 2 vols. (Bologna: Giovanni Recaldini, 1674); documents are included in 2:70 and 2:323. His methodological comments are in 1:21.

46. Works mentioned include Ottavio Ferrari, *Analecta de re vestiaria,* 2 vols. in 1 (Padua: M. Frambotti, 1670); and Fortunio Liceti, *De anulis antiquis librum singularum* (Udine: Nicolo Schiratti, 1645). The tradition is analyzed in Arnaldo Momigliano, "Ancient History and the Antiquarian," in *Studies in Historiography* (London: Weidenfeld and Nicholson, 1966), 1–39.

47. Capriata, *Dell'Historia, libri XII* (Genoa: Calenzano, 1638), 680–81.

48. Sforza Pallavicino, *Trattato dello stile e del dialogo* (Rome: Mascardi, 1662), 39–41.

49. His novels include *L'Astarlida, La Clorida, L'Absolone, L'onestà vilipesa,* and *Il tiranno d'Italia.* His career is examined by Giovanni Battista Passano, *I novellieri italiani in prosa* (Turin: G. B. Paravia, 1878), 2:214.

50. Eric Cochrane makes this point in *Historians and Historiography,* 265.

51. Mascardi, *Dell'arte istorica,* 2d treatise, chap. 4, p. 115.

52. Bisaccioni, *Demetrio moscovita* (Rome: Moneta, 1643). Peter Burke makes the point in "Some Seventeenth-Century Anatomists of Revolution," *Storia della storiografia* 22 (1992): 29.

53. Gian Carlo Roscioni, *Sulle tracce dell'"Esploratore turco"* (Milan: Rizzoli, 1992), 101–2.

54. Bisaccioni, *Historia delle guerre civili,* 104.

55. Gabriele Tontoli, preface to *Il Masaniello, ovvero Discorsi narrativi la sollevazione di Napoli* (Naples: Mollo, 1648).

56. Preface to *Successi historici degli acquisti della Serenissima Repubblica di Venezia in Levante* (Venice: Parè, 1688).

57. The novel was first published as no. 10 in a collection whose title, *Il porto: Novelle più vere che finte* (Venice: Francesco Storti, 1664), referred explicitly to the relation between truth and falsehood. Concerning seventeenth-century novels, see Albert N. Mancini, *Romanzi e romanzieri del Seicento* (Napoli: Societa editrice napoletana, 1981); and Marco Fantuzzi, *Meccanismi narrativi nel romanzo barocco* (Padua: Antenore, 1975).

58. This point is made also by Peter Burke, "Structural History in the Sixteenth and Seventeenth Centuries," *Storia della storiografia* 10 (1986): 71–72.

59. Bisaccioni, *Historia delle guerre civili,* 88, 91. Compare Alessandro Giraffi, *Le rivolutioni di Napoli* (Geneva: Filippo Alberto, 1648), Prima giornata; Giuseppe Donzelli, *Partenope liberata,* ed. Antonio Altamura (Naples, 1648; Naples: F. Fiorentino, 1970); Tommaso De Santis, *Storia del tumulto di Napoli* (Leyden, 1652; Trieste: Colombo Coen, 1858); and Agostino Nicolai, *Historia o vero narrazione giornale delle ultime rivolutioni della città e regno di Napoli* (Amsterdam, 1648; Amsterdam: Pluymer, 1660).

60. Bisaccioni, *Historia delle guerre civili,* 87: "Se non potete pagare, ite et

vendete l'onore delle mogli e delle figlie, e soddisfate." Compare Giraffi, *Le rivo-lutioni di Napoli,* Prima giornata; Donzelli, *Partenope liberata* (the only anti-Spanish account among these); De Santis, *Storia del tumulto;* and Nicolai, *Histo-ria o vero narrazione.* Bisaccioni's view also is at odds with the unpublished eyewitness reports, such as Giovanni Celoro Parascandolo, *Cronache inedite della rivoluzione di Masaniello* (Naples: Nuove edizioni, 1985); Francesco Cape-celatro, *Diario,* ed. Angelo Granito, 3 vols. (Naples: Stabilimento tipografico di G. Nobile, 1850–54); the reports of Vincenzo de' Medici to the grand duke of Tuscany, in "Documenti sulla storia economica e civile del regno," ed. Francesco Palermo, *Archivio storico italiano* 9 (1848): 348–53; "Sette lettere del card. Filo-marino al papa," ed. F. Palermo, ibid., 379–93; Ottaviano Sauli, "Relazione dei tumulti napoletani del 1647," ed. Luigi Correra, *Archivio storico per le provincie napoletane* 15 (1890): 355–87; and Andrea Rosso, "La rivoluzione di Masaniello visto dal residente veneto a Napoli," ed. Antonio Capograssi, *Archivio storico per le provincie napoletane,* n.s., 33 (1952): 167–235. Recent scholarship in-cludes Aurelio Musi, *La rivolta di Masaniello nella scena politica barocca* (Milan: Rizzoli, 1989); the long-term causes are examined in Rosario Villari, *The Revolt of Naples,* trans. James Newell with the assistance of John A. Marino, foreword by Peter Burke (Cambridge, U.K.: Polity Press, 1993) (original title, *Rivolta anti-spagnola a Napoli*).

61. Bisaccioni, *Historia delle guerre civili,* 95. De Santis, *Storia del tumulto,* 59, 65, has Maddaloni and Perrone fleeing into the Carmine after being accused of falsifying the document. Donzelli, *Partenope liberata,* 44–45, has Maddaloni delivered to Perrone when the privilege is discovered to be false.

62. Bisaccioni, *Historia delle guerre civili,* 97. Compare Nicolai, *Historia o vero narrazione,* 37. De Santis, *Storia del tumulto,* 57, suggests the crowd simply blew the powder up accidentally with their own lit torches.

63. Bisaccioni, *Historia delle guerre civili,* 104. De Santis, *Storia del tumulto,* 106; Nicolai, *Historia o vero narrazione,* 63.

64. Bisaccioni, *Historia delle guerre civili,* 105; compare Giraffi, *Le rivolu-tioni di Napoli,* end of Quinta giornata. De Santis, *Storia del tumulto,* 107, claims the viceroy changed his mind and decided not to offer any gifts to avoid feeding Masaniello's arrogance. Donzelli, *Partenope liberata,* 83, says Masaniello refused the first chain but was finally persuaded to take a second, cheaper one. He mentioned no title.

65. Girolamo Brusoni, *Historia dell'ultima guerra tra Veneziani e Turchi* (Bologna: Giovanni Recaldini, 1674), 1:101. Compare *Lettera di ragguaglio del combattimento e vittoria conseguita dall'armata della Serenissima Repubblica di Venezia sotto il comando dell'Ill.mo e Ecc.mo Sig. Zorzi Morosini nell'Archipel-ago* (Venice: Pinelli, 1662), 1.

66. Santacroce, *Frammenti istorici della guerra di Candia* (Bologna: A spese di G. B. e Giuseppe Corvo, Librai in Roma, 1647). He also published an *Esor-*

tazione a' principi cristiani a prender l'armi contra l'imperatore de' Turchi armato contra la Serenissima Repubblica Veneta (Venice: Valvasense, 1647), an appeal to the Christian princes on behalf of Venice.

67. Compare Kenneth Setton, *Venice, Austria, and the Turks in the Seventeenth Century* (Philadelphia: American Philosophical Society, 1992), 129; and *Avvisi di Ragusa: Documenti sull'impero turco nel sec. XVII e sulla guerra di Candia*, Orientalia Christiana analecta, no. 101, ed. Ivan Duòichev (Rome: Pontificum Institutum Orientalium Studiorum, 1935). Emmanuele Mormori claims that news about de La Vallette's preparations for a surprise attack leaked to the Turks, and they prepared so swiftly that prosecution of the design seemed imprudent (BNM, Codici italiani [Cod. ital.], VII, 101 [8382], fol. 23). Giovanni Comneno Papadopoli, *Memorie della guerra di Candia* (Syracuse University Library, Ranke ms. 77, fol. 50r) suggests that de La Vallette was a courageous captain, but his soldiers were untrained and his decisions were fully justified.

68. Santacroce, *Frammenti istorici della Guerra di Candia* (Bologna: Corvo, 1647), 257: "La varietà e l'ostinazione delle opinioni avea cominciato a germogliare nella precedenza, e autorità, discordie nella congiuntura presente, altrettanto perniciose quanto vane, e se bene per soddisfare alle comune pretendenze s'era scritto in Senato, e se ne aspettava più chiara dichiarazione, in ogni modo gli animi erano restati con qualche amarezza con molto danno del pubblico servizio." Compare Brusoni, *Historia dell'ultima guerra*, 1:63:

> Già buona pezza aveva cominciato a serpere tra i capi Veneti ostinazione di parere, per la pretensione di precedenza, e d'autorità, l'un sopra l'altro. Discordia sempre vana fra i capi d'un medesimo partito al cui servizio deono solamente indirizzare i propri affetti e riguardi, e in quelle contezze intempestiva e pericolosa affatto à pubblici interessi. E se bene per satisfare alle pretendenze dell'una e dell'altra parte se ne fosse scritto in senato, e se ne aspettasse la sua dichiarazione; non per tanto continuando negli animi qualche amarezza di disgusto, non potevano nelle consulte e nelle esecuzioni delle imprese far apparire che mascherato di partialità il zelo del pubblico servizio.

69. Brusoni, *Historia dell'ultima guerra*, 1:123; compare Virginio Dalla Spada, *Assedio e liberazione di Sebenico* (n.p., n.d. [1647]), 12. The battle is described in Setton, *Venice, Austria, and the Turks*, 149.

70. Brusoni, *Historia dell'ultima guerra*, 1:123:

> Aveva la Repubblica (come si disse nella passata campagna) condisceso alle supplicazioni della città di Sebenico per la fabbrica del forte di S. Giovanni, riconosciuto necessario, non che di grande vantaggio alla sua sicurezza, somministrandole il denaro per l'opera, e venne eretta in forma di stella secondo il disegno di Fra Antonio Leni Francescano Riformato, e ingegnere famoso, che per solo impulso di zelo cristiano vi si adoperò dal principio alla fine di queste occorrenze. Si attese pure ad assicurar la città con altre

linee, ridotti e contrascarpe; essendosi ancora prima disfatto il borgo di terra per levar ogni comodo al nemico d'alloggiarvi. È Sebenico tutto circondato d'asprezze, e tali che possono difendersi, e che mal difese, possono perdersi con la ruina della città e di tutta la provincia.

Compare Dalla Spada, *Assedio e liberazione*, 12:

Haveva la repubblica con sua inesplicabil humanità non ostante le diversità de' pareri contentato la città della costruzione d'esso forte di S. Giovanni posto alla sommità di quel monte, che le sovrasta, e che vale a gran vantaggio della sicurezza sua, e somministratole denaro per l'opera. Con questo s'haveva fatto il forte in forma di stella, con il disegno del Riformato ingegnere, che con il zelo di sua mera carità senz'altro fine, sempre vi si è adoprato, s'era atteso con altre linee, con altri ridotti e contrascarpe, ad assicurare la città, giacchè molto prima s'era anco distrutto il suo borgo da terra, per levarne ogni comodo al nemico; poichè le fortezze si fanno, dove la natura è stata scarsa, e dove prodiga, basta solo accompagnare le sue opere. Sebenico è circondato da asprezze, ma tali, che e valgon a difendersi e anco mal difese, possono perdersi e rovinare il tutto.

71. Brusoni, *Historia dell'ultima guerra*, 1:220: "Tenea ordine ancora dalla Porta, trovando il Capitano Generale in quel porto d'assediarlo per costringerlo con la fame ad una necessaria resa; e se l'avesse trovato fuori di combatterlo speditamente." Compare Giovanni Carlo Serpentino, *Lettera di ragguaglio della vittoria navale conseguita dall'armata della Serenissima Repubblica di Venezia sotto il comando del Procuratore Cap. Gen. da Mar Mocenigo contra Turchi nel Archipelago* (Venice: Pinelli, 1651), Aiiiv: "E se il Capitano Generale con l'armato si fosse trovato dentro del Porto, teneva commissione il Capitano Bassà d'assediarlo, per costringerlo con la fame ad una necessaria resa, e se l'incontrava fuori, combatterlo con tutto vigore per divertirlo dal soccorso della piazza."

72. Brusoni, *Historia dell'ultima guerra*, 1:220; compare Serpentino, *Lettera di ragguaglio della vittoria navale*, Aiiiv.

73. *Lettera di ragguaglio dell'impresa del Volo scritta da N.N. all'Ill.mo et Ecc.mo Sig. Cav. Michele Morosini* (Venice: Pinelli, 1655), Aiiv:

Si appicò subito Sua Eccellenza a riconoscere il sito della fortezza, che è posta nella parte più interna del golfo, che tiene il nome di Volo; discosta da Marina un tiro di moschetto, di forma quasi quadrata, circondata di muraglia bota di cannone, et adorna d'una bellissima fronte in Mare, difesa da due torrioni con una cittadella fortissima, munita e questa e quella da molti pezzi di cannone. Li habitanti di Volo, comandati da due Turchi, uno col titolo di Bassà, l'altro di Agà, veduta la nostra comparsa, benchè colti all'improvviso, si prepararono però intrepidi alla difesa e principiarono a scaricare il cannone con gran furia verso le galere, e per esser più liberi alla difesa fecero sortire le donne e i figlioli col bagaglio che le fu permesso dalle strettezze del tempo di raccogliere.

Compare Brusoni, *Historia dell'ultima guerra,* 1:249:

> Quivi riconosciuta la piazza ne intraprese immantinente l'attacco. Era la città discosta dalla marina a tiro di moschetto a forma quasi quadrata, con un recinto di due torrioni all'antica, oltre la cittadella, benissimo provveduta, come anche la città, d'artiglierie e ogni sorte d'armi; e di munizioni. Gli abitanti, benchè sovraccolti quasi improviso, non pertanto comandati da due Turchi, l'uno con titolo di Bassà, l'altro di Agà, intrapresero con grande ardire la difesa, scaricando il cannone a furia contro le galee. E per trovarsi più liberi e disinvolti sparsero fuori della città le donne e i fanciulli col bagaglio che in quella strettezza di tempo fù loro permesso di raccogliere.

74. Brusoni, *Historia dell'ultima guerra,* 1:249; compare *Lettera di ragguaglio dell'impresa del Volo scritta da N.N. all'Ill.mo et Ecc.mo Sig. Cav. Michele Morosini* (Venice: Pinelli, 1655), Aiiv.

75. Brusoni, *Historia dell'ultima guerra,* 1:274: "Continuando la Serenissima Repubblica l'anno 12 di guerra col più forte potentato del mondo nella costanza di difendere la fede e lo stato, benchè vuotati i tesori e sacrificato il sangue e le vite di tanti cittadini e sudditi, sempre la medesima d'infiammato pietosissimo zelo, unito conforme l'ordinario degli anni passati nel principio della campagna un valido corpo d'armata per impedire l'uscita dell'Ottomano da Castelli, avvanzossi e pervenne a quelle bocche a 23 maggio." Compare *Lettera di ragguaglio della vittoria navale conseguita a' Dardanelli dall'armata della Serenissima Repubblica di Venezia sotto il comando del già Ill.mo et Ecc.mo Sig. Lorenzo Marcello* (Venice: Pinelli, 1656), Av:

> Continuando la Serenissima Repubblica l'anno 12 di guerra col più forte potentato del mondo nella costanza di difendere la fede e lo stato, benchè vuotati i tesori e sacrificato il sangue e le vite di tanti cittadini e sudditi, sempre la medesima d'infiammato pietosissimo zelo, unito conforme l'ordinario degli anni passati nel principio della campagna il più valido corpo dell'armata per impedire l'uscita dell'Ottomano da Castelli, e formarsi in numero di 28 navi, 24 galee sottili, e 7 galeazze, con qualche altro legno minore si avvanzò con gran coraggio, a 23 maggio passato alle bocche.

76. Brusoni, *Historia dell'ultima guerra,* 2:198; compare *Relazione del combattimento glorioso seguito tra' galere della Serenissima Repubblica di Venezia e le galere del Bei . . . nelle acque di Fraschia* (Venice: Pinelli, 1668), Aiir.

77. Brusoni, *Historia dell'ultima guerra,* 2:312.

78. Ibid., 2:310.

79. Ibid., 1:234: "Acquistato il Turlulù voltarono i Veneti l'artiglieria contro S. Teodoro, da che spaventati quei difensori, spiegarono bandiera bianca per patteggiare la resa. Tentò bene il Bassà della Canea accorso alla spiaggia di Gogna d'inanimarli con molti tiri di cannone alla resistenza; ma in vano; perchè patteggiata la dedizione resero la piazza ai Veneti, salve le vite, e con sicurezza di condotta in Terraferma." Compare Andrea Valier, *Historia della guerra di Can-*

dia (Venice: Baglioni, 1679), 241: "Acquistato il posto subito fu indirizzato il cannone contro S. Teodoro. Onde vedendosi quel presidio bersagliato e di sotto e di sopra dalla fortezza presa, pose bandiera bianca e si rese. Nel principio dell'attacco il Bassà della Canea uscì dalla città conducendosi alla Platanea dirimpetto a quelle fortezze per animare i suoi alla difesa. Ma ad altro non servì la sua comparsa che ad essere spettatore della perdita delle piazze e di quei presidii."

80. Compare Valier, *Historia della guerra di Candia*, 241, with Brusoni, *Historia dell'ultima guerra*, 1:234. Valier's analysis of Turkish government is on pp. 352–54.

81. Valier, *Historia della guerra di Candia*, 1.

82. Vittorio Siri, *Il mercurio, ovvero Historia de' correnti tempi*, vol. 9 (Casale: Giorgio Del Monte, 1667), 642.

83. ASV, Segreteria di stato, Avvisi, busta 101, fol. 344, Venice, November 17, 1650.

84. Siri, *Il mercurio*, vol. 15 (Florence: Ippolito della Nave, 1682), 750.

85. Siri, *Il mercurio*, 9:623.

86. Siri, *Il mercurio*, vol. 5 (Casale: Giorgio Del Monte, 1655), pt. 1, 667. The next passages mentioned are at pp. 659, 666, 721, 723, 725–42, 763–804.

87. Siri, *Il mercurio*, vol. 7 (Casale: Giorgio Del Monte, 1667), 393. Also see vol. 8 (Casale: Giorgio Del Monte, 1667), 385. Compare the versions of these applications in MCV, ms. Dandolo C 975/70.

88. Siri, *Il mercurio*, vol. 12 (Paris: Sebastian Cramoisy, 1672), 959, 967.

89. Compare Gregorio Leti, *Le visioni politiche sopra gli interessi più reconditi di tutti i principi e repubbliche della Cristianità* ("Germania" [Geneva?], 1671), 10. Also see Setton, *Venice, Austria, and the Turks*, chap. 7; Papadopoli, *Memorie della guerra di Candia;* and Mormori, BNM, Cod. ital., VII, 101 (8382), fol. 23.

90. Siri, *Il Mercurio*, 15:813.

91. Peter Burke, "A Survey of the Popularity of Ancient Historians," *History and Theory* 5 (1966): 137, notes that the period 1550–99 yielded 510 recorded editions of ancient historians; in 1600–49 there were 451.

92. Luca Assarino, *Ragguagli di Cipro* (Bologna: Giacomo Monti and Carlo Zenero, 1642), n.p.

4 / Veritas Filia Temporis

1. For example, see Girolamo Brusoni, *Delle historie d'Italia, 1625–1678* (Turin: Zappata, 1680), 710; and Gregorio Leti, *Dialoghi politici, ovvero La politica che usano in questo tempo i principi e repubbliche italiane per conservare i loro stati e signorie* (Geneva: Chouet, 1666), 1:255. Many others are cited below.

2. Agostino Mascardi, *Dell'arte istorica* (Rome, 1636; Florence: Le Monnier, 1859), 2d treatise, chap. 2, p. 95.

3. These debates have been outlined by Richard H. Popkin in *The History of Skepticism from Erasmus to Spinoza* (Berkeley: University of California Press, 1979); Carlo Borghero, *Le certezze della storia: Cartesianismo, Pirronismo, e conoscenza storica* (Milan: Franco Angeli, 1983); not to mention, from a very different point of view, Alan Charles Kors, *Atheism in France, 1651–1729*, vol. 1, *The Orthodox Sources of Disbelief* (Princeton: Princeton University Press, 1990); and Sergio Zoli, *Europa libertina tra Controriforma e Illuminismo* (Bologna: Cappelli, 1989), updating René Pintard, *Le libertinage érudit dans la première moitié du XVIIe siècle*, 2 vols. (Paris: Boivin, 1943). But see Peter Burke, "Two Crises of Historical Consciousness," *Storia della Storiografia* 33 (1998): 3–16.

4. Paul Hazard, *La crise de conscience européene (1680–1715)*, 3 vols. (Paris: Boivin, 1935).

5. For the changes in social intercourse among the learned in this period, see Anne Goldgar, *Impolite Learning: Conduct and Community in the Republic of Letters, 1680–1750* (New Haven: Yale University Press, 1995).

6. Ariosto, *Orlando furioso,* ed. Santorre Debenedetti (Bari: Laterza, 1928), 32.32.

7. *La gazzetta de l'anno 1588,* ed. Enrico Stumpo (Florence: Giunti, 1988), where the passages in question, including those following, are at pp. 4, 22, 23, 37 (quote), 84 (quote), and 97 (quote).

8. Machiavelli, *Il principe,* ed. Luigi Russo (Florence: Le Monnier, 1931), chap. 18, para. 6.

9. Guicciardini, *Ricordi politici e civili,* ed. Roberto Palmarocchi (Bari: Laterza, 1933), no. 44.

10. Concerning Clapmar and his context, see Wilhelm Kühlmann, *Gelehrtenrepublic und Fürstenstaat: Entwicklung und Kritik des deutschen Späthumanismus in der Literatur des Barockzeitalters* (Tübingen: Max Niemeyer Verlag, 1982), 48. In general, see Richard Tuck, *Philosophy and Government, 1572–1651* (Cambridge: Cambridge University Press, 1993), chap. 2.

11. Giovanni Botero, *Della ragion di stato,* ed. Luigi Firpo (Turin: UTET, 1948), 113.

12. Ibid., 422–23.

13. Ammirato, *Della segretezza* (Venice: Giunti, 1598), 26. Aristotle's distinction, not quite so clear as Ammirato makes it out to be, is, of course, in *Metaphysics,* trans. Hugh Tredennick (New York: Putnam and Sons, 1933–35), vol. 1, 1.1.

14. The French context shared a similar confidence in historical methodology, according to the analysis of Donald R. Kelley in his introduction to *Foundations of Modern Historical Scholarship: Language, Law, and History in the French Renaissance* (New York: Columbia University Press, 1970). Compare Julian H. Franklin, *Jean Bodin and the Sixteenth-Century Revolution in the Method of Law and History* (New York: Columbia University Press, 1963), chap. 5; and George Huppert, *The Idea of Perfect History* (Urbana: University of Illinois

Press, 1970), 6–71. More recently, see Anthony Grafton, *Joseph Scaliger: A Study in the History of Classical Scholarship,* vol. 1, *Textual Criticism and Exegesis* (Oxford: Clarendon Press, 1983), chap. 3, and vol. 2, *Historical Chronology* (Oxford: Clarendon Press, 1993), pt. 4, chap. 11.

15. Concerning Casaubon's attack on Baronio, see Anthony Grafton, *Defenders of the Text: The Traditions of Scholarship in an Age of Science* (Cambridge: Harvard University Press, 1991), chap. 5. In addition, Eric Cochrane, *Historians and Historiography in the Italian Renaissance* (Chicago: University of Chicago Press, 1981), 372; and Giuliano Gliozzi, *Adamo e il nuovo mondo: La nascita dell'antropologia come ideologia coloniale, dalle genealogie bibliche alle teorie razziali (1500–1700)* (Florence: La Nuova Italia, 1977), address the cultural bases of judgments.

16. Giovanni Battista Leoni, *Delle considerazioni sopra l'istoria d'Italia di M. Francesco Guicciardini,* in appendix to Francesco Guicciardini's *Della istoria d'Italia* (Venice: Pasquali, 1738), 2:1.

17. Gian Michele Bruto, *Delle istorie fiorentine,* ed. Stanislao Gatteschi (Florence: Vincenzo Batelli, 1839), 1:xliii.

18. Cornelius Agrippa, *De incertitudine et vanitate scientiarum et artium* (1526), ed. Catherine M. Dunn (Northridge: California State University, 1974). Popkin's description of him is in *History of Skepticism,* 24.

19. Francesco Patrizi, *Della historia dieci dialoghi* (Venice: Andrea Arrivabene, 1560), 29r. Still useful, concerning the position of historical knowledge in Patrizi's philosophy, is Benjamin Brickman, "An Introduction to Francesco Patrizi's 'Nova de universis philosophia,'" Ph.D. diss., Columbia University, 1941. In addition, see Cesare Vasoli, *Francesco Patrizi da Cherso* (Rome: Bulzoni, 1989).

20. Patrizi, *Della historia,* 28v; also see 25v.

21. Ibid., 22r.

22. *L'autorità della storia profana,* ed. Albano Biondi (Turin: Giappichelli, 1973), 38. The treatise, originally entitled *De humanae historiae auctoritate,* was published posthumously as part of Cano's *De locis theologicis* (Salamanca: Matthias Gastius, 1563).

23. A helpful comparison might be made with the treatment of the English context in Barbara J. Shapiro, *Probability and Certainty in Seventeenth-Century England: A Study of the Relations between Natural Science, Religion, History, Law, and Literature* (Princeton: Princeton University Press, 1983); and B. J. Shapiro, "Early Modern Intellectual Life: Humanism, Religion, and Science in Seventeenth-Century England," *History of Science* 29 (1991): 45–71.

24. Bacon, *Novum organum,* ed. and trans. Peter Urbach and John Gibson (Chicago: Open Court, 1994), I.20.

25. Ibid., I.50, 1, 102.

26. Bacon's phrase is ibid., II.3. For the rest, an example among many, see the

introduction to *Filippo Buonarroti e la cultura antiquaria sotto gli ultimi Medici*, ed. Daniela Gallo (Florence: Cantini, 1986); and Giuseppe Olmi, *L'inventario del mondo: Catalogazione della natura e luoghi del sapere nella prima età moderna* (Bologna: Il Mulino, 1992). Compare Paula Findlen, *Possessing Nature: Museums, Collecting, and Scientific Culture in Early Modern Italy* (Berkeley: University of California Press, 1994), chap. 3, mainly devoted to patronage aspects and the idea of collecting. Panvinio and his world are the subject of Jean-Louis Ferrary, *Onofrio Panvinio et les antiquites romaines* (Rome: École française de Rome, 1996), although the background to this discussion is obviously Arnaldo Momigliano, "Ancient History and the Antiquarian," in *Studies in Historiography* (London: Weidenfeld and Nicholson, 1966), 1–39.

27. Note also the other participants in the debate, including Jacques-Auguste de Thou and Paolo Sarpi; see Peter Burke, "The Rhetoric and the Anti-Rhetoric of History in the Early Seventeenth Century," in *Anamorphosen der Rhetorik: Die Warheitsspiele der Renaissance,* ed. Gerhart Schröder, Barbara Cassin, Gisela Febel, and Michel Narcy (Munich: Wilhelm Fink Verlag, 1997), 71–79.

28. This is the argument of an entire work: see Campanella, *Del senso delle cose e della magia: Testo inedito italiano con le varianti dei codici e delle due edizioni latine,* ed. Antonio Bruers (Bari: Laterza, 1925).

29. Campanella, *Philosophiae rationalis partes quinque,* in *Tutte le opere,* ed. Luigi Firpo (Milan: Mondadori, 1954), 1223. He discusses the role of historiography also in *Metaphysica* (Turin: Bottega d'Erasmo, 1962, anastatic reprint of Paris, 1638, edition), bk. 5, chap. 2.

30. Concerning Campanella's philosophy, the most up-to-date statement is by John M. Headley, *Tommaso Campanella and the Transformation of the World* (Princeton: Princeton University Press, 1997), chap. 4. Still useful on the topic at hand are Bernardino M. Bonansea, *Tommaso Campanella: Renaissance Pioneer of Modern Thought* (Washington, D.C.: Catholic University of America Press, 1969), chap. 4; and Nicola Petruzzellis, "La metaphysique et l'historiographie de Campanella," *Organon* (Warsaw) 10 (1974): 209–22. Somewhat less useful is Giorgio Spini, "Historiography: The Art of History in the Italian Counter-Reformation," in Eric Cochrane, ed., *The Late Italian Renaissance, 1525–1630* (London: Macmillan, 1970), 114. Castelvetro's statement is in *Poeticae* (Bari: Laterza, 1978–79), 1:56.

31. Campanella, *Philosophiae rationalis,* 1225.

32. Tassoni, *Sentenze,* in *Pensieri e scritti preparatori,* ed. Pietro Puliatti (Modena: Panini, 1986), 5; and *Pensieri,* ibid., 5.41.565; 5.25.547. The passage from Sextus Empiricus is in *Against the Professors,* trans. R. G. Bury (Cambridge: Harvard University Press, 1987), 1.263, 149. Tassoni as a historian is analyzed by Pietro Puliatti, "Profilo storiografico del Tassoni," *Studi secenteschi* 27 (1986): 3–27.

33. Tassoni, *Pensieri,* 6.5, 576.

34. Ibid., 6.574.

35. Ibid., 6.576.

36. Lancellotti, *L'hoggidì*, vol. 2, *Gli ingegni non inferiori a' passati* (Venice: Guerrigli, 1636), 203. There is a useful chapter on Lancellotti in *La letteratura italiana: Storia e testi*, vol. 36, *Trattatisti e narratori del Seicento*, ed. Ezio Raimondi (Milan: Ricciardi, 1960). The idea that all historians err comes from an ancient source, the *Scriptores historiae Augustae*, Pesc. Nig., 1.1–2.

37. Lancellotti, *Farfalloni degli antichi historici* (Venice: Guerigli, 1659, published posthumously).

38. Lancellotti, *L'hoggidì*, 2:207.

39. The most up-to-date and comprehensive treatment is now Domenico Sella, *Italy in the Seventeenth Century* (New York: Longmans, 1997), chaps. 1–3. In addition, see Eric Cochrane, *Italy, 1530–1630* (New York: Longmans, 1988), chap. 9; Gigliola Pagano de Vitiis, *Mercanti inglesi nell'Italia del Seicento: Navi, traffici, egemonie* (Venice: Marsilio, 1990); Salvatore Ciriacono, *Acque e agricoltura: Venezia, l'Olanda, e la bonifica europea in età moderna* (Milan: Angeli, 1994), chap. 2; Peter Musgrave, *Land and Economy in Baroque Italy: Valpolicella, 1630–1797* (Leicester: Leicester University Press, 1992); Rita Mazzei, *Pisa Medicea: L'economia cittadina da Ferdinando I a Cosimo III* (Florence: Olschki, 1991); Paolo Malanima, "L'economia italiana nel Seicento: Un epoca di trasformazione economica," *Storia della società italiana*, ed. Giovanni Cherubini, vol. 11, *La controriforma e il Seicento* (Milan: Teti, 1989), 149–88; Antonio Calabria, *The Cost of Empire: The Finances of the Kingdom of Naples in the Time of Spanish Rule* (Cambridge: Cambridge University Press, 1991); and Luigi De Rosa, introduction to *Il Mezzogiorno agli inizi del Seicento* (Bari: Laterza, 1994), vii–lx.

40. The most insightful treatment of the problem is Rosario Villari, *Elogio della dissimulazione* (Bari: Laterza, 1987), chap. 1.

41. Accetto, *Della dissimulazione onesta*, ed. Salvatore S. Nigro (Naples, 1641; Genoa: Costa e Nolan, 1983), chap. 25.

42. Ibid., chap. 21, p. 22.

43. Gracián, *The Art of Worldly Wisdom*, trans. Joseph Jacobs (Boston: Shambhala Publications, 1993), maxim 130. Concerning this whole problem in early modern Europe, there is the exhaustive study by Perez Zagorin, *Ways of Lying: Dissimulation, Persecution, and Conformity in Early Modern Europe* (Cambridge: Harvard University Press, 1990).

44. Gracián, *The Art of Worldly Wisdom*, maxim 13.

45. Cited in Alberto Asor Rosa, *La cultura della Controriforma*, Letteratura italiana Laterza, no. 26 (Milan: Laterza, 1974), 104. A recent critical appraisal is in Maurizio Viroli, *From Politics to Reason of State: The Acquisition and Transformation of the Language of Politics, 1250–1600* (Cambridge: Cambridge University Press, 1992), 257–67, which now surpasses the previous treatment by Friedrich Meinecke, *Die Idee der Staatsräson in der neueren Geschichte* (Munich:

Oldenbourg, 1924), chap. 3. Still useful for biographical information is the entry by Luigi Firpo in *Dizionario biografico degli italiani* 11 (1969): 10–19.

46. Traiano Boccalini, *Ragguagli di Parnaso* (Bari: Laterza, 1910), vol. 1, ed. Giuseppe Rua, century 1, no. 29, p. 91.

47. Ibid., vol. 2, ed. Giuseppe Rua, century 2, no. 71.

48. Sarpi's recommendations are in *Scritti giurisdizionalistici,* ed. Giovanni Gambarin (Bari: Laterza, 1958), 213–20. Malvezzi's are in *Discorsi sopra Cornelio Tacito: Al serenissimo Duca Ferdinando II, granduca di Toscana* (Venice: Ginami, 1622), discourse 28.

49. Mascardi, *Dell'arte istorica,* 2d treatise, chap. 2, p. 94. Concerning Mascardi and his context, there is also Rodolfo De Mattei, "Storia e politica in Italia tra il Cinque e il Seicento," in *Storiografia e storia: Studi in onore di Eugenio Dupré Theseider,* 2 vols. (Rome: Bulzoni, 1974), 876–78.

50. Mascardi, *Dell'arte istorica,* 2d treatise, chap. 2, p. 92.

51. Ibid., 96.

52. Ibid., 1st treatise, chap. 2, pp. 34–35.

53. Ibid., 3d treatise, chap. 1, p. 160.

54. A preliminary bibliography for this literature is Sergio Bertelli, *Ribelli, libertini, ed ortodossi nella storiografia barocca* (Florence: Sansoni, 1973), chap. 8.

55. Enrico Jovane, *Il primo giornalismo torinese* (Turin: Di Modica, 1938), 61; Ugo Bellocchi, *Storia del giornalismo italiano* (Bologna: Edison, 1974–76), 3:39–43.

56. *Successi istorici della Serenissima Repubblica di Venezia in Levante* (Venice: Giovanni Parè, 1688), 8.

57. Walter Ong, *Orality and Literacy: The Technologizing of the Word* (London: Routledge, 1982), 132.

58. Cited in Daniel R. Woolf, *The Idea of History in Early Stuart England* (Toronto: University of Toronto Press, 1990), 248. On the subject, see also Royce Macgillivray, *Restoration Historians and the English Civil War* (The Hague: Nijhoff, 1974).

59. Samuel Butler's comments are in *Characters and Passages from Notebooks,* ed. A. R. Waller (Cambridge: Cambridge University Press, 1908), 375. For Thomas Hobbes's view of contemporary historians, see Fritz Levy, "The Background of Hobbes' *Behemoth,*" in *The Historical Imagination in Early Modern Britain: History, Rhetoric, and Fiction, 1500–1800,* ed. Donald R. Kelley and David Harris Sacks (Cambridge: Cambridge University Press, 1997), 226.

60. Capriata, *Dell'historie,* vol. 2 (Genoa: Farroni, 1649), Al lettore.

61. Assarino, *Delle guerre e dei successi d'Italia* (Turin: Zavatta, 1665), 1:1.

62. Bisaccioni, *Historia delle guerre civili di questi ultimi tempi* (Venice: Francesco Storti, 1653), 87.

63. Avogadro, *Mercurio veridico, ovvero Annali universali d'Europa* (Venice: Leni, 1648), 1.

64. Vittorio Siri, *Il mercurio, ovvero Historia de' correnti tempi,* vol. 6 (Casale: Giorgio Del Monte, 1655), frontispiece.

65. ASV, Miscellanea Armadio, 36, vol. 23 (ca. 1654), fol. 158.

66. The closest to a philosophical interpretation of these debates is Ugo Baldini, "La scuola galileiana," in *Storia d'Italia,* annali 3, *Scienza e tecnica nella cultura e nella società dal Rinascimento a oggi,* ed. Gianni Micheli (Turin: Einaudi, 1980), 383–468; in addition, confined to physics, there is Maurizio Torrini, *Dopo Galileo: Una polemica scientifica* (Florence: Olschki, 1979). Michael Segre, *In the Wake of Galileo* (New Brunswick: Rutgers University Press, 1991), somewhat misses the larger intellectual context. A useful survey is *La letteratura italiana: Storia e testi,* vol. 34, pt. 2, *Scienziati del Seicento,* ed. Maria Luisa Altieri Biagi and Bruno Basile (Milan: Ricciardi, 1980).

67. Gabriele Baroncini, "L'insegnamento della filosofia naturale nei collegi italiani dei Gesuiti, 1610–1670: Un esempio di nuovo aristotelismo," in *La "Ratio studiorum": Modelli culturali e pratiche educative dei Gesuiti in Italia tra cinque e Seicento,* ed. Gian Paolo Brizzi (Rome: Bulzoni, 1981), 163–216; Ugo Baldini, *Legem impone subactis: Studi su filosofia e scienza dei Gesuiti in Italia, 1540–1632* (Rome: Bulzoni, 1992).

68. The following is an interpretation of much information in Catherine Wilson, *The Invisible World: Early Modern Philosophy and the Invention of the Microscope* (Princeton: Princeton University Press, 1995). The Leeuwenhoek quote is from p. 224. A more positivist picture is traced by Marian Fournier, *The Fabric of Life: Microscopy in the Seventeenth Century* (Baltimore: Johns Hopkins University Press, 1996).

69. I will merely cite two classics: Giovanni Solinas, *Il microscopio e le metafisiche: Epigenesi e preesistenza da Cartesio a Kant* (Milan: Feltrinelli, 1967); and Arnold Thackray, *Atoms and Powers: An Essay on Newtonian Matter-Theory and the Development of Chemistry* (Cambridge: Harvard University Press, 1970).

70. Galileo's debate about this with Cesare Cremonini is examined in Luigi Olivieri, *Certezze e gerarchia del sapere* (Padua: Antenore, 1983), 136.

71. Conring's contribution is examined by Constantin Fasolt, "Conring on History," in *Supplementum Festivum: Studies in Honor of Paul Oskar Kristeller,* ed. James Hankins, John Monfasani, and F. Purnell Jr. (Binghamton, N.Y.: Medieval and Renaissance Texts and Studies, 1987). For Vico, see my conclusion.

72. This is my interpretation of the findings of Steven Shapin, *A Social History of Truth: Civility and Science in Seventeenth-Century England* (Chicago: University of Chicago Press, 1994). I keep in mind the caveats of Mordechai Feingold in *Isis* 87 (1996): 131–39 (book review).

73. The intellectual content of the debates related below is explored, in somewhat convoluted fashion, in Michele Rak, *La fine dei grammatici* (Rome: Bulzoni, 1973), passim. In addition, see Raffaele Ajello, "Cartesianismo e cultura

oltremontana al tempo dell'*Istoria civile,*" in *Pietro Giannone e il suo tempo,* ed. R. Ajello (Naples: Jovene, 1980), 1:181; and Maurizio Torrini, *Tommaso Cornelio e la ricostruzione della scienza* (Naples: Guida, 1977). From another point of view, see Joseph M. Levine, "Giambattista Vico and the Quarrel between the Ancients and the Moderns," *Journal of the History of Ideas* 52 (1991): 55–79.

74. Calabria, *The Cost of Empire,* chaps. 4–5; Giuseppe Galasso, *Napoli spagnolo dopo Masaniello,* 2 vols. (Florence: Sansoni, 1982), chaps. 4–7.

75. Giuseppe Ricuperati, "A proposito dell'accademia di Medina Coeli," *Rivista storica italiana* 84 (1972): 57–79; Maurizio Torrini, "L'Accademia degli Investiganti, Napoli, 1663–1670," *Quaderni storici* 16 (1981): 845–83.

76. The epistemology of Telesio and Bruno is usefully outlined in Leen Spruit, *Species Intelligibilis: From Perception to Knowledge* (Leyden: Brill, 1995), 2:198. Its later tradition and popularity in Naples is outlined by Maurizio Torrini, "Il problema del rapporto scienza-filosofia nel pensiero del primo Vico," *Physis* 20 (1978): 103–30.

77. On these aspects of Di Capua's work there is Michele Rak, "Una teoria dell'incertezza," *Filologia e letteratura* 15 (1969): 233–97. The following discussion is based on Di Capua, *Parere divisato in otto ragionamenti, ne' quali particolarmente narrandosi l'origine, e il progresso della medicina, chiaramente l'incertezza della stessa si manifesta* (Naples: Bulifon, 1681), 151 ff. A considerable portion of Di Capua's text is devoted to discrediting the ancient authorities.

78. Di Capua, *Parere divisato,* Ragionamento 2. On Boyle, see Shapin, *A Social History of Truth,* and Henry G. Van Leeuwen, *The Problem of Certainty in English Thought, 1630–1690* (The Hague: Nijhoff, 1963), 94–96.

79. Gian Vincenzo Gravina, *Discorso sopra l'Endimione* (1692), in *Scritti critici e teorici,* ed. Amedeo Quondam (Bari: Laterza, 1973), 52. The authoritative study of Gravina is A. Quondam, *Cultura e ideologia in Gian Vincenzo Gravina* (Milan: Mursia, 1968). The influence of Locke in Italy is discussed in Bruno Maiorca, "John Locke in Italia: Un secolo di bibliografia," *Rivista di filosofia* 67 (1976): 349–77.

80. Gian Vincenzo Gravina, *Delle antiche favole,* in *Scritti critici e teorici,* 44–48. The passage is analyzed in more detail in Rak, *La fine dei grammatici,* 268.

81. On Caloprese, see Silvio Suppa, *L'Accademia di Medinacoeli fra tradizione investigante e nuova scienza civile,* (Naples: Istituto italiano per gli studi storici, 1971), chaps. 1, 6. Passages from his *Lettura sopra la concione di Marfisa a Carlo Magno contenuta nel Furioso al canto 38* (Naples: Bulifon, 1691), esp. 64, are transcribed and analyzed in Rak, *La fine dei grammatici,* 154.

82. Pierre Gassendi, of course, offered a sense-oriented alternative. See Margaret Osler, *Divine Will and the Mechanical Philosophy: Gassendi and Descartes on Contingency and Necessity* (Cambridge: Cambridge University Press, 1994), 49.

83. A helpful antidote to much writing about Descartes's position is M. Glouberman, *Descartes: The Probable and the Certain* (Amsterdam: Rodopi, 1986).

An attempt, not entirely satisfactory, to synthesize the various elements in the Italian case is Claudio Manzoni, *I cartesiani italiani, 1660–1760* (Udine: Editrice "La nuova base," 1984), revising and updating the previous work of L. Berthé de Besaucèle, *Les cartésiens d'Italie* (Paris: Picard, 1920). Probably the first explicit précis of Descartes's position published in Italy was Matteo Giorgi's *Saggio della nuova dottrina di Renato Des-Cartes: Lettera all'Ill.mo Sig. Tommaso Fransone* (Genoa: Scionici, 1694).

84. Fardella's letter to Matteo Giorgi was published in the literary journal *Galleria di Minerva* 3 (1697): 43. The only monograph so far is Donatella Lauria, *Agostinismo e cartesianesimo in Michelangelo Fardella* (Catania: N. Giannotta, 1974); some of his writings have been collected in Michelangelo Fardella, *Pensieri scientifici e lettera antiscolastica,* ed. Salvatore Femiano, preface by Eugenio Garin (Napoli: Bibliopolis, 1986).

85. Fardella, letter, *Galleria di Minerva,* 3 (1697): 43.

86. Paolo Mattia Doria, *La vita civile: Distinta in tre parti, aggiuntovi un trattato della educazione del principe,* 2d ed. (Augusta, Italy: D. Hopper, 1710), 24:

Certa cosa è, che l'anima nel nostro nascere viene interamente nella materia sepolta; permodochè le pure sensazioni, che ella sente nel comparire in questo immenso teatro del mondo sensibile, sono le immagini delle cose esteriori, delle quali tutta ella si volge con la volontà, non dal raziocinio guidato, non essendo ancora capace; ond'è che le prime potenze, che l'anima esercita sono l'imaginazione, e la volontà; potenze certamente nell'anima, ma potenze, che solamente esercitano la loro facoltà nelle immagini, che da' corpi esteriori all'anima si suggeriscono. Egli è ben vero, però, che se ella a noi in un sì grande disvantaggio cagiona, quanto è quello di immergere la nostra anima prima ne' sensi, e nelle immagini, che nelle conoscenze pure; in ricompensa, ella ci somministra il modo di sprigionarsi da quelle, e di squarciare con la riflessione quel velo, che nell'ignoranza ci tiene miseramente inviluppati. Per prova di ciò veggiamo, che ella pone in tutte le umane menti quasi un ordinato progresso di geometria in quei raziocini medesimi, che gli uomini ne' loro consueti discorsi tentano di fare, e ne' quali, se l'ordine dalla natura prescritto ben seguir sapessero, potrebbero la conoscenza di quel vero, che hanno in loro stessi, perfettamente ischiarire.

Concerning Doria, the growing bibliography includes Vittorio Conti, *Paolo Mattia Doria: Dalla repubblica dei togati alla repubblica dei notabili* (Florence: Olschki, 1978). Doria's background and context is the subject of Enrico Nuzzo, *Verso la "Vita civile": Antropologia e politica nelle lezioni accademiche di Gregorio Caloprese e Paolo Mattia Doria* (Naples: Guida, 1984). That Doria can be considered a Cartesian only in the loosest sense of the term is apparent from Vincenzo Ferrone, "Seneca e Christo: La respubblica christiana di Paolo Mattia Doria," *Rivista storica italiana* 96 (1984): 47–52. Furthermore, note that Doria's political polemics were in a much more practical vein than his theoretical works.

Compare *Massime generali e particolari colle quali di tempo in tempo hanno gli Spagnoli governato il regno di Napoli,* ed. Vittorio Conti, intro. Giuseppe Galasso (Naples: Guida, 1973).

87. Doria, *La vita civile,* 15.

88. Ibid., 49.

89. John Wilmot, "A Satyr against Reason and Mankind," in *A Satire against Reason and Other Poems,* ed. Harry Levin (Norfolk, Conn.: New Directions, 1942), 5–11.

90. Gilbert Burnet, *Life and Death of the Earl of Rochester,* in *Lives, Characters, and An Address to Posterity* (London: J. Duncan, 1833), 210–11.

91. Lorenzo Magalotti, *Lettere familiari,* 2 vols. in 1, (Venice: Baglioni, 1762), vol. 1, letter 19. The letters, dated in the 1680s, are analyzed by Mario Praz, *Lettere sopra i buccheri con l'aggiunta di lettere contro l'ateismo* (Florence: Le Monnier, 1945), and Massimo Baldini, *Magalotti: Religione e scienza nel Seicento* (Brescia: La Scuola, 1984). Magalotti's career is analyzed in Eric Cochrane, *Florence in the Forgotten Centuries* (Chicago: University of Chicago Press, 1973), bk. 4.

92. Magalotti, *Lettere familiari,* vol. 1, letter 22.

93. Ibid., letter 13.

94. Ibid., vol. 2, letter 5.

95. Ibid., vol. 1, letter 10, p, 156. The following quotes are from this and the previous page.

96. Compare Susan Rosa, "Seventeenth-Century Catholic Polemic and the Rise of Cultural Rationalism: An Example from the Empire," *Journal of the History of Ideas* 57 (1996): 87–107.

97. Bayle's relation to Cartesianism is explored by Ciro Senofonte, *Pierre Bayle: Dal Calvinismo all'Illuminismo* (Naples: Edizioni scientifiche, 1978). The historical theory is outlined by Ruth Whelan in *The Anatomy of Superstition: A Study of the Historical Theory and Practice of Pierre Bayle* (Oxford: Voltaire Foundation, 1989). For everything else, the authority is still Elisabeth Labrousse, *Pierre Bayle,* 2 vols. (The Hague: Nijhoff, 1963–64).

98. Pierre Bayle, *Critique génerale de l'histoire du Calvinisme,* in his *Dictionnaire historique et critique* (Amsterdam: Brunel, 1740), 4:10, appendix.

99. Ibid., 4:13.

100. *Dictionnaire historique et critique,* s.v. "Pyrrho," also in *Historical and Critical Dictionary,* ed. Richard H. Popkin (New York: Bobbs-Merrill, 1965), 194–209.

101. Hardouin's form of argument is viewed in a new light by Bertram E. Schwarzbach, "Antidocumentalist Apologetics: Hardouin and Yeshayahu Leibowitz," *Révue de théologie et de philosophie* 115, 3d ser., no. 33 (1983): 373–90; in addition, see, with bibliography, Anthony Grafton, *Forgers and Critics* (Princeton: Princeton University Press, 1990), 72–73, on which see James

Hankins, "Forging Links with the Past," *Journal of the History of Ideas* 52 (1991): 509–18.

102. Concerning the earlier period, see Grafton, *Joseph Scaliger*, vol. 1, *Textual Criticism and Exigesis*. The transmission of historiographical methods from the North to the South is examined in Françoise Waquet, *Le modèle français et l'Italie savante: Conscience de soi et perception de l'autre dans la république des lettres, 1660–1750*, Collection de l'École française de Rome, no. 117 (Rome: École française de Rome, 1989), chap. 3.

103. In general, see Blandine Barret-Kriegel, *Les historiens et la monarchie* (Paris: Presses Universitaires Françaises, 1988), vol. 1, *Jean Mabillon,* and vol. 2, *La défaite de l'érudition*. In addition, see articles by Manfred Weitlauff and Karl Hausherger in *Historische Kritik in der Theologie,* ed. Georg Schwaiger (Göttingen: Vandenhoeck and Ruprecht, 1980). A recent contribution concerning Le Clerc's scholarly contribution is Maria Cristina Pitassi, *Entre croire et savoir: Le problème de la méthode critique chez Jean Le Clerc* (Leiden: Brill, 1987).

104. Jean Le Clerc, "La verité de la religion chrétienne," appended to his *De l'incredulité* (Amsterdam: H. Wetstein, 1696), read in the English translation published in London for John Churchill (1697), 124. Le Clerc's methodological reflections are in his *Ars critica,* 3 vols. (Amsterdam: George Gallet, 1697); Mabillon's are in *De re diplomatica* (Paris: L. Billaine, 1681); and Montfaucon's are in *Palaeographia graeca* (Paris: L. Guerin, 1708). Giambattista Vico's claim is in *The New Science,* trans. Thomas G. Bergin and Max Harold Fisch (Ithaca: Cornell University Press, 1968), para. 331.

105. On the English context, see Joseph Levine, *Humanism and History: The Origins of English Historiography* (Ithaca: Cornell University Press, 1987), chap. 6.

106. Arnaldo Momigliano, "Mabillon's Italian Disciples," in *Essays in Ancient and Modern Historiography* (London: Blackwell, 1977), 277–93, first published in *Terzo contributo alla storia degli studi classici* (Rome: Edizioni scientifiche, 1966), 135–52.

107. Benedetto Bacchini, *Istoria del monastero di S. Benedetto di Polirone* (Modena: Capponi, 1696), v. On the influence of Descartes in Bacchini's thought, there is Giuseppe Bedoni, "Origine e sviluppo del razionalismo cartesiano a Modena: Dal Michelangelo Fardella al Bacchini," in *Aspetti e problemi del Settecento modenese,* ed. Odoardo Rombaldi (Modena: Aedes Muratoriana, 1982), 2:241–58.

108. Bernard de Montfaucon, *L'antiquité expliquée et représentée en figures,* 15 vols. (Paris: F. Delaulne, 1719–24). On this work and the problem of interpretation of visual evidence in general, there is now the study of Francis Haskell, *History and Its Images: Art and the Intepretation of the Past* (New Haven: Yale University Press, 1993), especially chap. 5.

109. Francesco Bianchini, *La istoria universale provata con monumenti e fig-*

urata con simboli degli antichi (Rome: Antonio de' Rossi, 1697), 31: "Ogni professo d'historia confessa, che il punto più difficile, e più importante sia quello di rendere autorevole la relazione con i segni di verità che distinguono le narrazioni vere dalle favole de' romanzieri."

110. Ibid., 10: "Le figure dei fatti, ricavate da monumenti d'antichità oggidì conservate, mi sono sembrate simboli insieme e pruove dell'istoria . . . accomodati al genio della età nostra."

111. Francesco Bacchini, "Riflessioni a fogli concernenti la idea di una nuova accademia letteraria d'Italia pubblicati da Lamindo Pritanio," transcribed in Tommaso Sorbelli, "Benedetto Bacchini e la repubblica letteraria del Muratori," *Benedictina* 6 (1952–53): 95.

Conclusion

1. For further discussion of this trend, see Peter Burke, *The Fabrication of Louis XIV* (New Haven: Yale University Press, 1992), chap. 9. Also see Michel Foucault, *The Order of Things* (New York: Random House, 1970).

2. *The Autobiography of Giambattista Vico,* trans. Max Harold Fisch and Thomas Goddard Bergin (Ithaca: Cornell University Press, 1944), 132. Concerning Vico's early career, still useful is Fausto Nicolini, *La giovinezza di Giambattista Vico* (Bari: Laterza, 1932). Some interesting insights are in Harold Samuel Stone, *Vico's Cultural History: The Production and Transmission of Ideas in Naples, 1689–1750* (Leyden: Brill, 1997).

3. *Autobiography of Vico,* 137. Vico touched upon some of the themes below also in his inaugural lecture, *On the Study Methods of Our Time,* trans. Elio Gianturco (Ithaca: Cornell University Press, 1990), chap. 7, although obviously from a different point of view.

4. Amid the vast bibliography on Vico and his thought, his historiographical ideas are best analyzed by Ferdinand Fellmann, *Das Vico-Axiom: Der Mensch macht die Geschichte* (Freiburg: Alber, 1976); Leon Pompa, *Human Nature and Historical Knowledge* (Cambridge: Cambridge University Press, 1990), chap. 3; and Donald Phillip Verene, *Vico's Science of Imagination* (Ithaca: Cornell University Press, 1981). In the present connection, particularly useful is Joseph M. Levine, "Giambattista Vico and the Quarrel between the Ancients and the Moderns," *Journal of the History of Ideas* 52 (1991): 55–79.

5. Giambattista Vico, *The New Science,* trans. Thomas G. Bergin and Max Harold Fisch (Ithaca: Cornell University Press, 1968), para. 331.

6. Muratori's polemical work is analyzed in Sergio Bertelli, *Erudizione e storia in Ludovico Antonio Muratori* (Naples: Istituto italiano per gli studi storici, 1960), especially pp. 151–53. For imposture in eighteenth-century historiography, see Giuseppe Ricuperati, "Universal History: Storia di un progetto europeo. Impostori, storici e editori della 'Ancient Part,'" *Studi settecenteschi* 2 (1989): 7–90.

7. I refer once again to the first essay in William H. McNeill, *Mythistory and Other Essays* (Chicago: University of Chicago Press, 1986). Concerning just how much myth is necessary, there is also Marion Leathers Kuntz, "The Myth of Venice in the Thought of Guillaume Postel," *Supplementum Festivum: Studies in Honor of Paul Oskar Kristeller* (Binghamton, N.Y.: Center for Medieval and Early Renaissance Studies, 1987).

8. On Vico's isolation, compare Isaiah Berlin, *Vico and Herder* (New York: Viking, 1976), with the essays, especially by Mario Agrimi and Giovanni Santinello, in *Vico e Venezia*, ed. Cesare De Michelis and Gilberto Pizzamiglio (Florence: Olschki, 1982).

9. Concerning Vico's politics I prefer Giuseppe Giarrizzo, *Vico: La politica e la storia* (Naples: Guida, 1981), to Mark Lilla, *Giambattista Vico: The Making of an Anti-Modern* (Cambridge: Harvard University Press, 1994).

10. Vico, *The New Science*, para. 953. A broader discussion of the stage theory, one that omits the aspects connected with communication but which is nonetheless most useful, is in Leon Pompa, *Vico: A Study of the "New Science"* (Cambridge: Cambridge University Press, 1990), chaps. 9–12.

11. Vico, *The New Science*, para. 1102.

12. Ibid., para. 1105.

13. Ibid., para. 953.

14. The bibliography implied here is far too large to list except in very fragmentary fashion: John Brewer, *The Pleasures of the Imagination: English Culture in the Eighteenth Century* (New York: Farrar, Straus and Giroux, 1997), chap. 4; *Books and Their Readers in Eighteenth-Century England*, ed. Isabel Rivers (Leicester: Leicester University Press, 1982); Robert Darnton, *The Business of Enlightenment: A Publishing History of the "Encyclopédie"* (Cambridge: Harvard University Press, 1979); Robert Darton, *The Literary Underground of the Old Regime* (Cambridge: Harvard University Press, 1982); *Histoire de l'édition française*, ed. Henri-Jean Martin and Roger Chartier, vol. 2, *Le livre triomphant* (Paris: Promodis, 1983); Franco Venturi, *Settecento riformatore*, 5 vols. (Turin: Einaudi, 1969–90), especially vols. 3 (1979) and 4 (1984); Mario Infelise, *L'editoria veneziana del Settecento* (Milan: Angeli, 1989); Giuseppe Ricuperati, "Giornali e società nell'Italia dell'Ancien Régime," in *La stampa italiana dal cinquecento all'ottocento,* ed. Valerio Castronovo and Nicola Tranfaglia (Bari: Laterza, 1976), 67–372.

15. Quoted in *Illuministi italiani,* ed. Franco Venturi, vol. 5, *Riformatori napoletani* (Milan: Ricciardi, 1962), 748.

16. On this point, see Jürgen Habermas, *The Structural Transformation of the Public Sphere,* trans. Thomas Burger (Cambridge: MIT Press, 1989).

17. An interesting study of this problem in the old regime is Christopher Todd, *Political Bias, Censorship, and the Dissolution of the "Official" Press in Eighteenth-Century France* (Lampeter, Dyfed, Wales: Edwin Mellen Press, 1991).

18. A useful overview is Evan Charney, "Political Liberalism, Deliberative Democracy, and the Public Sphere," *American Political Science Review* 92 (1998): 97–111, detailing the Benhabib-Rawls debate. Compare Jürgen Habermas, *The Theory of Communicative Action,* trans. Thomas McCarthy, 2 vols. (Boston: Beacon Press, 1984–87).

Index

Index

Index

Index

Navailles, Philippe de Montault de Bénac, duke de, 94, 108
Neri, Achille, 165, 172, 175, 180
Newell, James, 186
Nicolai, Agostino, 185
Nicolini, Fausto, 201
Nigro, Salvatore S., 194
North, J. D., 164
Novati, Francesco, 172
Nussdorfer, Laurie, 159, 160, 166
Nuzzo, Enrico, 198

Olivares, Gaspar de Guzman, count of, and duke of San Lucar de Barromeda, 98
Olivieri, Luigi, 196
Olmi, Giuseppe, 193
Ong, Walter, 195
Orsini, Alessandro, 29
Osanna family, 67
Osbat, Luciano, 181
Osler, Margaret, 197
Ottoboni, Pietro. *See* Alexander VIII

Paganini, Gaudenzio, 18, 19
Paisey, David L., 168
Palermo, Francesco, 186
Pallavicino, Agostino, 66
Pallavicino, Ferrante, 48
Pallavicino, Sforza, 29, 100, 185
Palluzzi, Caterina, 57
Palmarocchi, Roberto, 191
Palmer, Paul A., 181
Panckoucke, Charles-Joseph, 153
Panvinio, Onofrio, 120
Paracelsus (Philippus Aureolus Theophrastus Bombastus von Hohnheim), 32
Parascandalo, Giovanni Celoro, 186
Parrino, Domenico Antonio, 67
Pascal, Blaise, 140
Pasquale, Carlo, 89, 91
Passano, Giovanni Battista, 185
Pastine, Onorato, 162, 169, 175
Pastor, Ludwig von, 159
Patrizi, Francesco, 3, 119, 127–28, 139, 192
Paul V (pope), 27, 29, 125
Pelizzari, Maria Rosaria, 172
Pelliccia, Guerrino, 160, 172

Peretti, Andrea Baroni, 28
Perrone, Domenico, 104
Persico, Giuseppe, 29
Petrucci Nardelli, Franca, 170
Petruzzellis, Nicola, 193
Phelps, John, 72
Philip III (king of Spain), 55
Philip IV (king of Spain), 97, 98
Piccolomini family, 39
Pigna, Giambattista, 88
Pinelli, Giovanni Pietro, 62, 107
Pintard, René, 163, 191
Pirovano, Filippo, 40
Pitassi, Maria Cristina, 200
Pitteri, Francesco, 70
Pius V (pope), 27
Pizzamiglio, Gilberto, 202
Poli, Giovanni, 32, 55
Poliziano, Angelo, 144
Pompa, Leon, 201, 202
Popkin, Richard H., 1, 155, 191, 192, 199
Porcia, Gregorio, 63
Pory, John, 53
Pozza, Neri, 175
Preto, Paolo, 184
Proto-Giurleo, Ulisse, 175
Pulci, Alessio, 62
Puliatti, Pietro, 193
Purnell, F., Jr., 196

Quondam, Amedeo, 167, 197
Quorli, Giovanni, 12, 43, 71

Raabe, Paul, 168
Racine, Jean, 90
Radziejowscy, Hieronym, 75
Raimondi, Ezio, 194
Rak, Michele, 196, 197
Ranalli, Ferdinando, 182
Ranum, Orest, 4, 156, 182
Raymond, Joad, 3, 156
Regii, Vincenzo, 40
Renaudot, Théophraste, 54, 73, 76
Rhodes, Denis E., 175
Ricci, Corrado, 161
Ricciotti, Giuseppe, 179
Ricuperati, Giuseppe, 156, 197, 201, 202
Ridolfi, Nicolò, 30

Index

Library of Congress Cataloging-in-Publication Data

Dooley, Brendan Maurice, 1953–
The social history of skepticism : experience and doubt in
early modern culture / Brendan Dooley.
p.   cm — (The Johns Hopkins University studies in historical and
political science : 117th ser., 2)
Includes bibliographical references and index.
ISBN 0-8018-6142-X (alk. paper)
1. Journalism—History.   2. Journalism—Italy—History.   3. Press and
politics—History.   4. Press and politics—Italy—History.   5. Skepticism—
History.   6. Historiography—Political aspects.
I. Title. II. Series.
PN4801.D66   1999
070.9—dc21   99-11406

CIP